Intimate Behaviour

Desmond Morris was born in Wiltshire in 1928. After gaining a degree in zoology from Birmingham University, he obtained his D.Phil. from the University of Oxford. He became curator of mammals at London Zoo in 1959, a post he held for eight years.

He was already the author of some fifty scientific papers and seven books before completing *The Naked Ape* in 1967, which was to sell over 10 million copies throughout the world and be translated into almost every known language.

Desmond Morris has made many television programmes and films on human and animal behaviour, his friendly and accessible approach making him popular with both adults and children, and he is now one of the best-known presenters of natural history programmes.

He is also an accomplished artist and his books include *The Biology of Art*, *The Art of Ancient Cyprus* and *The Secret Surrealist*, as well as his familiar series of *Manwatching*, *Bodywatching*, *Animalwatching* and *Babywatching*. His new study of the meaning of gestures, *Bodytalk: A World Guide to Gestures*, is published by Jonathan Cape.

BY DESMOND MORRIS

The Biology Of Art
The Mammals
Men And Snakes (co-author)
Men And Apes (co-author)
Men And Pandas (co-author)
Zootime
Primate Ethology (editor)
The Naked Ape
The Human Zoo
Intimate Behaviour
Patterns Of Reproductive Behaviour
Manwatching
Gestures (co-author)
Animal Days
The Soccer Tribe
Inrock
The Book Of Ages
The Art Of Ancient Cyprus
Bodywatching
The Illustrated Naked Ape
Dogwatching
Catwatching
The Secret Surrealist
Catlore
The Animals Roadshow
The Human Nestbuilders
Horsewatching
The Animal Contract
Animalwatching
Babywatching
Christmas Watching
The Naked Ape Trilogy
The Human Animal
The Illustrated Catwatching
Bodytalk

Desmond Morris

INTIMATE
BEHAVIOUR

V
VINTAGE

Published by Vintage 1994

2 4 6 8 10 9 7 5 3 1

First published in Great Britain by
Jonathan Cape Ltd, 1971

Vintage
Random House, 20 Vauxhall Bridge Road, London SW1V 2SA

Random House Australia (Pty) Limited
20 Alfred Street, Milsons Point, Sydney
New South Wales 2061, Australia

Random House New Zealand Limited
18 Poland Road, Glenfield,
Auckland 10, New Zealand

Random House South Africa (Pty) Limited
PO Box 337, Bergvlei, South Africa

Random House UK Limited Reg. No. 954009

A CIP catalogue record for this book
is available from the British Library

ISBN 0 09 948221 5

Printed and bound in Great Britain by
Cox & Wyman, Reading, Berkshire

CONTENTS

Acknowledgments   vi

Introduction   vii

1 The Roots of Intimacy   1

2 Invitations to Sexual Intimacy   17

3 Sexual Intimacy   44

4 Social Intimacy   67

5 Specialized Intimacy   98

6 Substitutes for Intimcacy   118

7 Object Intimacy   134

8 Self-Intimacy   149

9 Return to Intimacy   160

Chapter References   172

Bibliography   175

ACKNOWLEDGMENTS

Although in the past no books have been devoted specifically to the subject of *Intimate Behaviour*, I have been greatly helped by a large number of papers and volumes on associated topics and on special aspects of the problem. These I gratefully acknowledge, and details concerning them can be found in the bibliography on pages 175–78. As I have been writing for a general audience, I have not included specific references to these works in the text, but a chapter-by-chapter guide is given on pages 172–4.

In addition, I would like to express my debt to my scientific colleagues and, above all, to my personal intimates, from whom I have learned so much. In particular, I would like to thank my wife Ramona, my publisher Tom Maschler and my assistant Trisha Pike. Without their help these pages could not have been written.

INTRODUCTION

To be intimate means to be close, and I must make it clear at the outset that I am treating this literally. In my terms, then, the act of intimacy occurs whenever two individuals come into bodily contact. It is the nature of this contact, whether it be a handshake or a copulation, a pat on the back or a slap in the face, a manicure or a surgical operation, that this book is about. Something special happens when two people touch one another physically, and it is this something that I have set out to study.

My method has been that of the zoologist trained in ethology, that is, in the observation and analysis of animal behaviour. I have limited myself, in this case, to the human animal, and have given myself the task of observing what people do – not what people say, or even what they say they do, but what they actually do.

The method is simple enough – merely to use one's eyes – but the task is not as easy as it sounds. The reason is that, despite the self-discipline, words persist in filtering through and preconceived ideas repeatedly get in the way. It is hard for an adult human being to look at a piece of human behaviour as if he were seeing it for the very first time, but that is what the ethologist must attempt to do if he is to bring new understanding to the subject. The more familiar and commonplace the behaviour, of course, the worse the problem becomes; in addition, the more intimate the behaviour, the more emotionally charged it becomes, not only for the performers, but also for the observer.

Perhaps this is why, despite their importance and interest, so few studies have been made of commonplace human intimacies. It is far more comfortable to study something as remote from human involvement as, say, the territorial scent-marking behaviour of the giant panda, or the food-burying behaviour of the green acouchi, than it is to tackle scientifically and objectively something as 'well known' as the human embrace, the mother's kiss or the lover's caress. But in a social environment that is ever more crowded and impersonal, it is becoming increasingly important to reconsider the value of close personal relationships, before we are driven to ask the forlorn question, 'Whatever happened to love?' Biologists are often wary of using this word 'love', as if it reflected no more than some kind of culturally inspired romanticism. But love is a biological fact. The subjective, emotional rewards and agonies associated with it may be deep and mysterious, and difficult to deal with scientifically, but the outward signs of love – the actions of loving – are readily observable, and there is no reason why they should not be examined like any other type of behaviour.

It has sometimes been said that to explain love is to explain it away, but this is quite unjustified. In a way, it is an insult to love, implying that, like an ageing, cosmetic-caked face, it cannot stand scrutiny under a bright light. But there is nothing illusory about the powerful process of the formation of strong bonds of attachment between one individual and another. This is something we share with thousands of other animal species – in our parent-offspring relationships, our sexual relationships and our closest friendships.

Our intimate encounters involve verbal, visual and even olfactory elements, but, above all, loving means touching and body contact. We often talk about the way we talk, and we frequently try to see the way we see, but for some reason we have rarely touched on the way we touch. Perhaps touch is so basic – it has been called the mother of senses – that we tend to take it for granted. Unhappily, and almost without our noticing it, we have gradually become less and less touchful, more and more distant, and physical untouchability has been accompanied by emotional remoteness. It is as if the modern urbanite has put on a suit of emotional armour and, with a velvet hand inside an iron glove, is beginning to feel trapped and alienated from the feelings of even his nearest companions.

It is time to take a closer look at this situation. In doing so, I shall endeavour to keep my opinions to myself, and to describe human behaviour as seen through the objective eyes of a zoologist. The facts, I trust, will speak for themselves, and will speak loudly enough for the reader to form his own conclusions.

THE ROOTS OF INTIMACY

As AN ADULT human being, you can communicate with me in a variety of ways. I can read what you write, listen to the words you speak, hear your laughter and your cries, look at the expressions on your face, watch the actions you perform, smell the scent you wear and feel your embrace. In ordinary speech we might refer to these interactions as 'making contact', or 'keeping in touch', and yet only the last one on the list involves bodily contact. All the others operate at a distance. The use of words like 'contact' and 'touch' to cover such activities as writing, vocalization and visual signalling is, when considered objectively, strange and rather revealing. It is as if we are automatically accepting that bodily contact is the most basic form of communication.

There are further examples of this. For instance, we often refer to 'gripping experiences', 'touching scenes' or 'hurt feelings', and we talk of a speaker who 'holds his audience'. In none of these cases is there an actual physical grip, touch, feel or hold, but this does not seem to matter. The use of physical-contact metaphors provides a satisfying way of expressing the various emotions involved in the different contexts.

The explanation is simple enough. In early childhood, before we could speak or write, body contact was a dominant theme. Direct physical interaction with the mother was all-important and it left its mark. Still earlier, inside the womb, before we could see or smell, leave alone speak or write, it was an even more powerful element in our lives. If we are to understand the many curious and often strongly inhibited ways in which we make physical contact with one another as adults, then we must start by returning to our earliest beginnings, when we were no more than embryos inside our mothers' bodies. It is the intimacies of the womb, which we hardly ever consider, that will help us to understand the intimacies of childhood, which we tend to ignore because we take them so much for granted, and it is the intimacies of childhood, re-examined and seen afresh, that will help us to explain the intimacies of adult life, which so often confuse, puzzle and even embarrass us.

The very first impressions we receive as living beings must be sensations of intimate body contact, as we float snugly inside the protective wall of the maternal uterus. The major input to the developing nervous system at this stage therefore takes the form of varying sensations of touch, pressure and movement. The entire skin surface of the unborn child is bathed in the warm uterine liquid of the mother. As the child grows and its swelling body presses harder against the mother's tissues, the soft embrace of the enveloping bag of the womb becomes gradually stronger, hugging tighter with each passing week. In addition, throughout this period the growing baby is subjected to the varying pressure of the rhythmic breathing of the maternal lungs, and to a gentle, regular swaying motion whenever the mother walks.

Towards the end of pregnancy, in the last three months before birth, the baby is also capable of hearing. There is still nothing to see, taste or smell, but things that go bump in the night of the womb can be clearly detected. If a loud, sharp noise is made near to the mother's belly, it startles the baby inside and makes it jump. The movement can easily be recorded by sensitive instruments and may even be strong enough for the mother to feel it herself. This means that during this period before birth the baby is undoubtedly capable of hearing the steady thump of the maternal heartbeat, 72 times every minute. It will become imprinted as the major sound-signal of life in the womb.

These, then, are our first real experiences of life – floating in a warm fluid, curling inside a total embrace, swaying to the undulations of the moving body and hearing the beat of the pulsing heart. Our prolonged exposure to these sensations in the absence of other, competing stimuli leaves a lasting impression on our brains, an impression that spells security, comfort and passivity.

This intra-uterine bliss is then rudely and rapidly shattered by what must be one of the most traumatic experiences in our entire lives – the act of being born. The uterus, in a matter of hours, is transformed from a cosy nest into a straining, squeezing sac of muscle, the largest and most powerful muscle in the whole human body, athlete's arms included. The lazy embrace that became a snug hug now becomes a crushing constriction. The newly delivered baby displays, not a happy, welcoming grin, but the strained, tightly contorted facial expressions of a desperate torture victim. Its cries, which are such sweet music to the anxiously waiting parents, are in reality nothing short of the wild screams of blind panic, as it is exposed to the sudden loss of intimate body contact.

At the moment of birth the baby appears floppy, like soft, wet rubber, but almost at once it makes a gasping action and takes its first breath. Then, five to six seconds later, it starts to cry. Its head, legs and arms begin to move about with increasing intensity and for the next thirty minutes it continues to protest in irregular outbursts of limb-thrashing, grasping, grimacing and screaming, after which it usually subsides exhausted into a long sleep.*

The drama is over for the moment, but when the baby reawakens it is going to need a great deal of maternal care, contact and intimacy to compensate it for the lost comforts of the womb. These post-uterine substitutes are provided by the mother, or those who are helping her, in a number of ways. The most obvious one is the replacement of the embrace of the womb by the embrace of the mother's arms. The ideal maternal embrace enfolds the baby, bringing as much of its body surface into contact with the mother as is possible without restricting breathing. There is a great difference between embracing the baby and merely holding it. An awkward adult who holds the infant with a minimum of contact will soon discover how dramatically this reduces the comforting value of the action. The maternal chest, arms and hands must do their best to re-create the total engulfment of the lost womb.

Sometimes the embrace alone is not enough. Other womb-like elements have to be added. Without knowing quite why, the mother starts to rock her child gently from side to side. This has a strong soothing effect, but if it fails she may get up and start slowly walking back and forth with the baby cradled in her arms. From time to time she may joggle it up and down briefly. All these intimacies have a comforting influence on a restless or crying child, and they do so, it seems, because of the way they copy certain of the rhythms experienced earlier by the unborn baby. The most obvious guess is that they succeed by re-creating the gentle swaying motions felt inside the womb whenever the mother walked about during her pregnancy. But there is a catch to this. The speed is wrong. The rate of rocking is considerably slower than the rate of normal walking. Furthermore, 'walking the baby' is also done at a pace that is much slower than an average walk of the ordinary kind.

Experiments were carried out recently to ascertain the ideal rocking speed for a cradle. At very low or very high speeds the movements had little or no soothing effect, but when the mechanically operated cradle was set at between sixty and seventy rocks per minute there was a striking change, the babies under observation immediately becoming much calmer and crying much less. Although mothers vary somewhat in the speed at which they rock their babies when they hold them in their arms, the typical maternal rocking rate is much the same as that in the experiments, and the pace when 'walking the baby' is also in that

* New birthing techniques that leave the naked newborn in close, gentle contact with its mother's body for some time after delivery have been shown to reduce dramatically the struggling and screaming described here.

region. An average walking rate under ordinary circumstances, however, usually exceeds a hundred paces per minute.

It seems, therefore, that although these comforting actions may well soothe by virtue of the way they copy the swaying motions felt inside the womb, the speed at which they are carried out requires some other explanation. There are two rhythmic experiences available to the unborn child, apart from the mother's walking: the steady rise and fall of her chest as she breathes, and the steady thump of her heartbeat. The breathing rate is much too slow to be considered, being roughly between ten and fourteen respirations per minute, but the heartbeat speed, at 72 beats per minute, looks like the ideal candidate. It appears as if this rhythm, whether heard or felt, is the vital comforter, reminding the baby vividly of the lost paradise of the womb.

There are two other pieces of evidence that support this view. First, the recorded heartbeat sound, if played experimentally to babies at the correct speed, also has a calming effect, even without any rocking or swaying movement. If the same sound is played faster, at over a hundred beats per minute – that is, at the speed of normal walking – it immediately ceases to have any calming effect. Second, as I reported in *The Naked Ape*, careful observations have revealed that the vast majority of mothers hold their babies in such a way that their infants' heads are pressed to the left breast, close to the maternal heart. Even though these mothers are unaware of what they are doing, they are nevertheless successfully placing their babies' ears as close as possible to the source of the heartbeat sound. This applies to both right-handed and left-handed mothers, so that the heartbeat explanation appears to be the only one that fits.

Clearly this is susceptible to commercial exploitation by anyone who takes the trouble to manufacture a cradle that can be mechanically rocked at heartbeat speed, or that is equipped with a small machine that plays a non-stop amplified recording of the normal heartbeat sound. A de luxe model incorporating both devices would no doubt be even more effective, and many a harassed mother could simply switch on and relax as it automatically and relentlessly calmed her baby to sleep, just as her washing machine so efficiently deals with the baby's dirty clothing.

Inevitably it is only a matter of time before such machines do appear on the market, and undoubtedly they will do a great deal to assist the busy mother of modern times, but there is an inherent danger in their use if it becomes excessive. It is true that mechanical calming is better than no calming, both for the mother's nerves and for the baby's well-being, and where demands on the mother's time are so heavy that she has no other choice, then mechanical calming will certainly be advantageous. But old-fashioned maternal calming is always going to be better than its mechanical replacement. There are two reasons for this. First, the mother does more than the machine could ever do. Her comforting actions are more complex and contain special features that we have yet to discuss. Second, the intimate interaction between mother and child that occurs whenever she comforts it by carrying, embracing and rocking it provides the important foundation for the strong bond of attachment that will soon grow between them. True, during its first months after birth the baby will respond positively to any friendly adult. It accepts any intimacies from any individual who offers them, regardless of who they are. After a year has passed, however, the child will have learned its own mother and will have started to reject intimacies from strangers. This change is known to occur around the fifth month in most babies, but it does not happen overnight and there is great variability from child to child. It is therefore difficult to predict with certainty the exact moment at which the infant will begin to respond selectively to its own mother. It is a critical time, because the strength and quality of the later bond of attachment will depend on the richness and intensity of the body-contact behaviour that occurs between mother and infant at just this threshold phase.

Obviously, excessive use of mechanical mothers during this vital stage could be dangerous. Some mothers imagine that it is the provision of food and other similar rewards that make the baby become attached to them, but this is not so. Observations of deprived children and careful experiments with monkeys have shown conclusively that it is instead the tender intimacies with the soft body of the mother which are vital in producing the essential bond of attachment that will be so important for successful social behaviour in later life. It is virtually impossible to give too much body-loving and contact during these critical early months, and the mother who ignores this fact will suffer for it later, as will her child. It is difficult to comprehend the warped tradition which says that it is better to leave a small baby to cry so that it does not 'get the better of you', which is encountered all too often in our civilized cultures.

To counterbalance this statement, however, it must be added that when the child is older, the situation changes. It then becomes possible for the mother to be over-protective and to hold her child back just when it should be striking out and becoming more independent. The worst twist that can happen is for a mother to be under-protective, strict and disciplinary with a tiny infant, and *then* over-protective and clinging with an older child. This completely reverses the natural order of bond development, and sadly it is a sequence that is frequently observed today. If an older child, or adolescent, 'rebels', this twisted pattern of rearing is very likely to be found lurking in the background.

Unfortunately, by the time this happens it is a little late in the day to correct the early damage that has been done.

The natural sequence I have described here – love first, freedom later – is basic not only to man, but also to all the other higher primates. Monkey mothers and ape mothers keep up the body-contact intimacies non-stop from the moment of birth for many weeks. They are greatly aided, of course, by the fact that baby monkeys and apes are strong enough to cling to them for long periods of time without assistance. In the great apes, such as the gorilla, the babies may take a few days to get started as active clingers, but after that, despite their weight, they manage it with remarkable tenacity. The smaller monkeys cling from the moment of birth, and I have even seen one half-born baby clutching tightly with its hands to the body of its mother during delivery, while the rear part of it was still inside the womb.

The human baby is much less athletic. Its arms are weaker and its short-toed feet are clingless. It therefore poses a much greater problem for the human mother. Throughout the early months it is she who must perform all the physical actions that serve to keep her and her baby in bodily contact. Only a few fragments of the infant's ancestral clinging pattern remain, rudimentary reminders of its ancient, evolutionary past, and even these are of no practical use today. They last for little more than two months after birth and are known as the grasp reflex and the Moro reflex.

The grasp reflex arrives early, the sixth-month-old foetus already having a strong grip. At birth, stimulation of the palm results in a tight clasping of the hand, and the grasp is strong enough for an adult to lift the whole weight of the baby's body in this way. Unlike the young monkey, however, this clinging cannot be sustained for any length of time.

The Moro reflex can be demonstrated by sharply and swiftly lowering the baby through a short distance – as if it were being dropped – while supporting it under its back. The infant's arms quickly fling outwards, with the hands opening and the fingers spreading wide. Then the arms come together again, as if groping for an embrace to steady itself. Here we can see clearly the ghost of the ancestral primate clinging action that is employed so effectively by every healthy young monkey. Recent studies have shown this even more clearly. If the baby feels itself dropping down while at the same time its hands are held and allowed to grasp, its reaction is not first to fling its arms wide before making the embracing action, but simply to go straight into the tight clinging response. This is precisely what a startled young monkey would do if it were grasping lightly on to the fur of its resting mother, who then suddenly leapt up in alarm. The infant monkey would instantly tighten its grip in this way, ready to be carried off rapidly by the mother to safety. The human baby, until it is eight weeks old, still has enough of the monkey left in it to show us a remnant of this response.

From the human mother's point of view, however, these 'monkey' reactions are of no more than academic interest. They may intrigue zoologists, but they do nothing in practical terms to lighten the parental burden. How, then, can she deal with the situation? There are several alternatives. In most so-called primitive cultures, the baby is almost constantly in touch with the mother's body during its early months. When the mother is resting, the baby is held all the time, either by herself or by someone else. When she sleeps, it shares her bed. When she works or moves about, it is carried strapped firmly to her body. In this way she manages to provide the almost non-stop contact typical of other primates. But modern mothers cannot always go to such lengths.

An alternative is to swathe the unheld baby in a sheath of clothes. If the mother cannot offer the baby the snug embrace of her arms or close contact with her body, day and night, hour after hour, she can at least provide it with the snug embrace of a wrapping of smooth, soft clothing, as an aid to replacing the lost engulfment of the womb. We usually think of clothing the baby merely as an act of keeping it warm, but there is more to it than this. The embrace of the material, as it wraps around and makes contact with the body surface of the infant, is equally important. Whether this wrapping should be loose or firm, however, remains a hotly debated point. Cultures vary considerably in their attitude towards the ideal tightness of this post-natal cloth-womb.

In the Western world today, tight swaddling is generally frowned upon, and the baby, even when new-born, is wrapped only lightly, so that it can move its body and limbs freely if it feels so inclined. Experts have expressed the fear that 'it might cramp the child's spirit' to wrap it more firmly. The vast majority of Western readers would instantly agree with this comment, but it does bear looking at more closely. The ancient Greeks and Romans swaddled their babies, yet even the most fanatical anti-swaddler would have to admit that there were quite a few uncramped spirits among their number. British babies, up to the end of the eighteenth century, were swaddled, and many Russian, Yugoslav, Mexican, Lapp, Japanese and American Indian babies are still swaddled at the present day. Recently the matter was examined scientifically, with both swaddled and unswaddled babies checked for discomfort by sets of sensitive instruments. The conclusions were that swaddling did in fact make the babies less fretful, as was shown by reduced heartbeat rate, breathing rate and crying frequency. Sleep, on the other hand, was increased. Presumably this is because the tight wrapping is more reminiscent of the tight womb-hug experienced by the advanced foetus during the final weeks of its gestation.

If this appears to be entirely in favour of the swaddlers, it should nevertheless be remembered that even the bulkiest, most belly-swelling foetus is never so tightly hugged by the womb that it cannot manage occasional kicks and struggles. Any mother who has felt these movements inside her will be aware that she is not 'swaddling' her unborn infant to the point of total immobility. A moderately close swaddling after birth is therefore probably more natural than the really tight binding that is applied in some cultures. Furthermore, swaddlers tend to prolong unnecessarily the close wrapping of their infants, well beyond the point where it is advisable. It may be helpful during the earliest weeks, but if it is extended over a period of months it may start to interfere with the healthy growing processes of muscular and postural development. Just as the foetus has to leave the real womb, so the new-born must soon leave the cloth-womb, if it is not to become 'overdue' at its next stage of maturation. We normally speak of babies being premature or overdue only in relation to the moment of their birth, but it is useful to apply this same concept to the later stages of childhood development as well. At each phase, from infancy to adolescence, there are relevant forms of intimacy, of bodily contact and caring, that should occur between parent and child if the offspring is to pass through the various stages successfully. If the intimacy offered by the parent at any particular stage is either too advanced or too retarded for that particular stage, then trouble may ensue later.

Up to this point we have been looking at some of the ways in which the mother helps her baby to relive some of its womb-time intimacies, but it would be wrong to give the impression that comforts during the early post-birth phase are no more than prolongations of foetal comforts. Such extensions provide only one part of the picture. Other interactions are taking place at the same time. The baby stage has its own, new forms of comfort to be added. They include fondling, kissing and stroking by the mother, and the cleaning of the baby's body surface with gentle, tactile manipulations such as rubbing, wiping and other mild frictions. Also, there is more to the embrace than merely embracing. In addition to offering the overall enveloping pressure of her arms, the mother frequently does something else. She pats the baby rhythmically with one of her hands. This patting action is restricted largely to one region of the baby's body, namely the back. It is delivered at a characteristic speed, and with a characteristic strength, neither too weak nor too strong. To call it a 'burping' action is misleading. It is a much more widespread and basic response of the mother's, and is not limited to that one specific form of infantile discomfort. Whenever the baby seems to need a little extra comforting, the mother embellishes her simple embrace by the addition of back-patting. Frequently she adds swaying or rocking movements at the same time, and often coos or croons softly with her mouth held near to the baby's head. The importance of these early comforting actions is considerable, for, as we shall see later, they reappear in many forms, sometimes obvious, sometimes heavily disguised, in the various intimacies of adult human life. They are so automatic to the mother that they are seldom thought about or discussed, with the result that the transformed roles they play in later life are usually overlooked.

In origin, the patting action is what students of animal behaviour refer to as an intention movement. This can best be illustrated by giving an animal example. When a bird is about to fly, it bobs its head as part of the action of taking off. During evolution this head-bobbing may become exaggerated as a signal to other birds that it is about to depart. It may perform vigorous, repeated head-bobs for some time before actually taking off, giving its companions the warning message that it is about to leave and enabling them to be ready to accompany it. In other words, it signals its intention to fly, and the head-bobbing is referred to as an intention movement. Patting by human mothers appears to have evolved as a special contact signal in a similar way, being a repeated intention movement of tight clinging. Each pat of the mother's hand says, 'See, this is how I will cling tightly to you to protect you from danger, so relax, there is nothing to worry about.' Each pat repeats the signal and helps to soothe the baby. But there is more to it than this. Again, the example of the bird can help. If the bird is mildly alarmed, but not sufficiently to fly away, it can alert its companions simply by giving a few mild head-bobs, but without actually taking off. In other words, the intention-movement signal can be given by itself, without being carried through into the full action of flight. This is what has happened with the human patting action. The hand pats the back, then stops, then pats again, then stops again. It is not carried through into the full danger-protection clinging action. So the message from the mother to the baby reads not only 'Don't worry, I will cling to you like this if danger threatens,' but also 'Don't worry, there is no danger, or I would be clinging to you tighter than this.' The repeated patting is therefore doubly soothing.

The signal of the softly cooing or humming voice soothes in another way. Again, an animal illustration may help. When certain fish are in an aggressive mood, they indicate this by lowering the head-end of the body and raising the tail-end. If the same fish are signalling that they are definitely not aggressive, they do the exact opposite, that is, they raise the head and lower the tail. The soft cooing of the mother works on this same antithesis principle. Loud, harsh sounds are alarm signals for our species, as they are for many others. Screams, shouts, snarls and roars are widespread mammalian messages of pain, danger, fear and aggression. By employing tonal qualities which are the antithesis of these sounds, the human mother can, as it were, signal the opposite of these messages, namely, that all is well. She may use verbal messages in her cooing and crooning, but the words are, of course, of little importance. It is the soft, sweet, smooth tonal qualities of the cooing that transmit the vital, comforting signal to the infant.

Another important new, post-womb pattern of intimacy is the presentation of the nipple (or bottle-teat) for sucking by the baby. Its mouth experiences the intrusion of a soft, warm, rubbery shape from which it can squeeze a sweet, warm liquid. Its mouth senses the warmth, its tongue tastes the sweetness, and its lips feel the softness. Another very basic comfort – a primary intimacy – has been added to its life. Again, it is one that will reappear in many disguises later, in adult contexts.

These, then, are the most important intimacies of the baby phase of the human species. The mother embraces her offspring, carries, rocks, pats, fondles, kisses, strokes, cleans and suckles it, and coos, hums and croons to it. The baby's only really positive contact action at this early stage is to suck, but it does have two vital signals that act as invitations to intimacy and encourage the mother to perform her close-contact actions. These signals are crying and smiling. Crying initiates contact and smiling helps to maintain it. Crying says 'come here' and smiling says 'please stay'.

The act of crying is sometimes misunderstood. Because it is used when the baby is hungry, uncomfortable or in pain, it is assumed that these are the only messages it carries. If a baby cries, a mother often automatically concludes that one of these three problems must exist, but this is not necessarily the case. The message says only 'come here'; it does not say why. If a baby is well fed, comfortable and in no pain, it may still cry, simply to initiate intimate contact with the mother. If the mother feeds it, makes sure there is no discomfort, and then puts it down again, it may immediately restart its crying signal. All this means, in a healthy baby, is that it has not had its quota of intimate bodily contact, and it will go on protesting until it gets it. In the early months the demand is high, and the baby is fortunate in having a powerful attraction-signal in its happy smile, to reward the mother for her labours.

Amongst primates, the smile of the human baby is unique. Monkey and ape babies do not have it. They simply do not need it, because they are strong enough to cling on to their mother's fur and stay close to her in this way by virtue of their own actions. The human baby cannot do this and somehow has to make itself more appealing to the mother. The smile has been evolution's answer to the problem.

Crying and smiling are both backed up by secondary signals. Human crying starts out in a monkey-like way. When a baby monkey cries, it produces a series of rhythmic screaming sounds, but sheds no tears. During the first few weeks after birth, the human baby cries in the same tearless way, but after this initial period, weeping is added to the vocal signal. Later, in adult life, the weeping can occur separately, by itself, as a silent signal, but for the infant it is essentially a combined act. For some reason, man's uniqueness as a weeping primate has seldom been commented on, but clearly it must have some specific significance for our species. Primarily it is, of course, a visual signal and is enhanced by the hairlessness of our cheeks, on which tears can glisten and trickle so conspicuously. But another clue comes from the mother's response, which is usually to 'dry the eyes' of her infant. This entails a gentle wiping away of the tears from the skin of the face – a soothing act of intimate body contact. Perhaps this is an important secondary function of the dramatically increased secretion of the lachrymal glands that so often floods the face of the young human animal.

If this seems far-fetched, it is worth remembering that the human mother, as in many other species, has a strong basic urge to clean the body of her offspring. When it wets itself with urine, she dries it, and it is almost as if copious tears have evolved as a kind of 'substitute urine' serving to stimulate a similar intimate response at times of emotional distress. Unlike urine, tears do not help to remove waste products from the body. At low levels of secretion they clean and protect the eyes, but during full weeping their only function appears to be that of transmitting social signals, and they then justify a purely behavioural interpretation. As with smiling, the encouragement of intimacy seems to be their main business.

Smiling is supported by the secondary signals of babbling and reaching. The infant grins, gurgles and stretches out its arms towards its mother in an intention movement of clinging to her, inviting her to pick it up. The mother's response is to reciprocate. She smiles back, 'babbles' to the baby, and reaches out her own arms to touch it or lift it. Like weeping, the smiling complex does not appear until about the second month after birth. In fact, the first month could well be called the 'monkey phase', the specifically human signals appearing only after these first few weeks have passed.

As the baby moves on into its third and fourth months, new patterns of body contact begin to appear. The early 'monkey' actions of the grasp reflex and the Moro reflex disappear and are replaced by more sophisticated forms of *directed* grasping and clinging. In the case of the primitive grasp reflex, the baby's hand automatically took hold of any object pressed into it, but now the new, selective grasping becomes a positive action in which the infant co-ordinates its eyes and its hands, reaching out for and grabbing a particular object that catches its attention. Frequently this is part of the mother's body, especially her hair. Directed grasping of this kind is usually perfected by the fifth month of life.

In a similar way, the automatic, undirected clinging movements of the Moro reflex make way for orientated hugging in which the baby clings specifically to the mother's body, adjusting its movements to her position. Directed clinging is normally established by the sixth month.

Leaving the baby stage behind and passing on to the later period of childhood, it becomes obvious that there is a steady decline in the extent of primary bodily intimacy. The need for security, which extensive body contact with the parent has satisfied so well, meets a growing competitor, namely the need for independent action, for discovering the world, for exploring the environment. Clearly this cannot be done from the encompassing circle of the mother's arms. The infant must strike out. Primary intimacy must suffer. But the world is still a frightening place, and some form of indirect, remote-control intimacy is needed to maintain the sense of security and safety while independence is asserting itself. Tactile communication has to give way to increasingly sensitive visual communication. The baby has to replace the confining, hampering security of the embrace and the cuddle with the less restricting device of exchanged facial expressions. The shared hug makes way for the shared smile, the shared laugh, and all the other subtle facial postures of which the human being is capable. The smiling face, which earlier was an invitation to an embrace, now replaces it. The smile, in effect, becomes itself a symbolic embrace, operating at a distance. This enables the infant to function more freely and yet, at a glance, to re-establish emotional 'contact' with the mother.

The next great phase of development arrives when the child begins to speak. In the third year of life, with the acquisition of a basic vocabulary, verbal 'contact' is added to the visual. Now the child and its mother can express their 'feelings' towards one another in words.

As this phase progresses, the early, primary intimacies of direct body contact are inevitably restricted still further. It becomes babyish to be cuddled. The strongly growing need for exploration, independence and separate, individual identity increasingly dampens down the urge to be held and fondled. If parents over-express these primary body contacts at this stage, the child does not feel protected, but mauled. Being held now becomes being held back, and the parents have to adjust to the new situation.

For all this, body contact does not disappear completely. In times of pain, shock, fear or panic, the embrace will still be welcomed or sought, and even at less dramatic moments some contact will still occur. There are considerable changes, however, in the form which it takes. The all-embracing hugs shrink to small fragments of their former selves. The semi-embrace, the arm around the shoulder, the pat on the head and the hand-clasp begin to appear.

The irony of this phase of later childhood is that, with all the stresses that exploration brings, there is still a great inner need for the comfort of bodily contact and intimacy. This need is not so much reduced as suppressed. Tactile intimacy spells infancy and has to be relegated to the past, but the environment still demands it. The conflict that results from this situation is resolved by the introduction of new forms of contact that provide the required bodily intimacy without giving the impression of being babyish.

The first sign of these disguised intimacies appears early and takes us almost back to the baby stage. It starts in the second half of the first year of life and has to do with the use of what have been called 'transitional objects'. These are, in effect, inanimate mother-substitutes. There are three common ones: a favourite sucking-bottle, a soft toy and a piece of soft material, usually a shawl or a particular piece of bedding. In the early baby phase they were experienced by the infant as part of the intimate contacts it had with its mother. They were not preferred to the mother then, of course, but were nevertheless strongly associated with her bodily presence. In her absence they become substitutes for her, and many children will refuse to go to sleep without their comforting proximity. The shawl or the soft toy has to be in the cot at bedtime, or there is trouble. And the demands are quite specific – it has to be *the* toy or *the* shawl. Similar but unfamiliar ones will not do.

At this stage the objects are employed only when the mother herself is not available, which is why they become so important at bedtime, when contact with the mother is being broken. But then, as the child grows, a change takes place. Now, as the infant becomes more independent of the mother, the favourite objects become more, rather than less, important as comforters. Some mothers misinterpret this and imagine that the infant is feeling unnaturally insecure for some reason. If the child becomes desperate for contact with its 'Teddy', or 'shawly' or 'cuddly' – these objects always seem to acquire a special nickname – the mother may look upon it as a backward step. In fact, it is just the reverse. What the child is doing, in effect, is saying, 'I want body contact with my mother, but that would be too babyish. I am too independent for that now. Instead I will make contact with this object, which will make me feel secure without throwing me back into my mother's arms.' As one authority has put it, the transitional object 'is reminiscent of the pleasurable aspects of mother, is a substitute for mother, but is also a defense against re-envelopment by mother'.

As the infant grows older and the years pass, the comforter may persist with remarkable tenacity, surviving in some cases even into middle childhood. In rare cases it may last into adulthood. We are all familiar with the nubile girl sprawled on her bed clutching her giant Teddy bear. I say 'rare cases', but that requires qualification. It is certainly rare for us to retain an obsession for precisely the same transitional object that we employed in infancy. For most of us the nature of the act would become too transparent. Instead, we find substitutes for the substitutes – sophisticated adult substitutes for the childish mother-body substitutes. When the baby-shawl becomes transformed into a fur coat we treat it with more respect.

Another form of disguised intimacy in the growing child is found embedded in the development of rough-and-tumble play. If it is baby-ish to embrace and cuddle but the need is still there, then the problem can be solved by embracing the parent in such a way that the body contact involved does not look like an embrace. The loving hug becomes a mock-aggressive bear-hug. The embrace becomes a wres-tling-match. In play-fighting with the parent, the child can once again relive the close intimacy of babyhood whilst hiding behind the mask of aggressive adulthood.

This device is so successful that mock body-fighting with the parent can be seen even in later adolescence. Still later, between adults, it is usually restricted to a friendly punch on the arm or thump on the back. Admittedly, the play-fighting of childhood involves more than merely disguised intimacy. There is a great deal of body-testing as well as body-touching, of exploring new physical possibilities as well as reliv-ing old ones. But the old ones are certainly there and they are import-ant – much more so than is usually recognized.

With the arrival of puberty, a new problem asserts itself. Bodily contact with the parent is now further curtailed. Fathers find that their daughters suddenly become less playful. Sons become body-shy with their mothers. In the post-baby phase, the need for independent action began to express itself, but now, at puberty, the need intensifies and introduces a powerful new demand: privacy.

If the baby's message was 'hold me tight', and the child's was 'put me down', that of the adolescent is 'leave me alone'. One psychoanalyst has described the way in which, at puberty, 'The young person tends to isolate himself; from this time on, he will live with the members of his family as though with strangers.' This statement makes its point, of course, by over-emphasis. Adolescents do not go around kissing strangers, but they do continue to kiss their parents. True, the actions have now become more formalized – the smacking kiss has become a peck on the cheek – but brief intimacies do still take place. As with adults, however, they are at this stage largely limited to greetings, farewells, celebrations and disasters. In fact, the adolescent is already adult – sometimes super-adult – as far as his or her family intimacies are concerned. With unconscious ingenuity, loving parents overcome this problem in a variety of ways. A typical example is the 'clothing-adjustment' pattern. If they cannot perform a direct loving touch, they can nevertheless make body contact by disguising it as 'let me straighten your tie' or 'let me brush your coat'. If the reply is 'stop fussing, mother' or 'I can do it myself', then this means that the adolescent has, equally unconsciously, seen through the trick.

When post-adolescence arrives and the young adult moves outside the family, then – from the point of view of body intimacy – it is as if a second birth has been experienced, the womb of the family being abandoned as was the womb of the mother two decades before. The primary sequence of changing intimacies – 'hold me tight/put me down/leave me alone' – now goes back to the beginning again. The young lovers, like the baby, say 'hold me tight'. Occasionally they will even call one another 'baby' as they say it. For the first time since babyhood, intimacies are once again extensive. As before, the body-contact signals begin to weave their magic and a powerful bond of attachment starts to form. To emphasize the strength of this attach-ment, the message 'hold me tight' becomes amplified by the words 'and never let me go'. Once the pair-formation is completed, however, and the lovers have set themselves up as a new two-piece family unit, the second babyhood phase is over. The new intimacy sequence moves relentlessly on, copying the first, primary one. The second babyhood gives way to the second childhood. (This is the true second childhood, and is not to be confused with the senility phase, which appears much later and has sometimes been mistakenly referred to as the second childhood.)

Now the enveloping intimacies of courtship begin to weaken. In extreme cases, one or both members of the new pair start to feel trapped, their independence of action threatened. It is normal enough, but it feels unnatural and so they decide it was all a mistake and split up. The 'put me down' of the second childhood is replaced by the 'leave me alone' of the second puberty, and the primary family separ-ation of adolescence becomes the secondary family separation of divorce. But if divorce creates a second adolescence, then what is this neo-adolescent doing alone, without a lover? So, after the divorce, each of the ex-pair members finds a new lover, goes through the second babyhood stage once more, remarries and, with a crash, is back at the second childhood. To their astonishment, the process has repeated itself.

This description may be a cynical over-simplification, but it helps to make the point. For the lucky ones, and even today there are many of them, the second adolescence never comes. They accept the conversion of the second babyhood into the second childhood. Augmented with the new intimacies of sex and the shared intimacies of parenthood, the pair-bond survives.

In later life the loss of the parental factor is softened by the arrival of new intimacies with the grandchildren, until eventually the third and final babyhood appears on the scene with the approach of senility and the helplessness of old age. This third run-through of the intimacy sequence is short-lived. There is no third childhood, at least in earthly terms. We end as babies, snugly tucked in our coffins, which are softly padded and draped – just like the cradles of our first babyhood. From the rock of the cradle we have passed on to the rock of ages.

For many, it is difficult to contemplate the third great intimacy-sequence ending there. They refuse to accept that the third babyhood does not continue into a third childhood, to be found in heaven. There the condition is ideal and permanent, and there is no fear of being over-mothered, for God the Father has no wife.

In tracing these patterns of intimacy from the womb to the tomb, I have dwelt at greater length on the early phases of life, passing more swiftly over the later stages of adulthood. With the roots of intimacy exposed in this way, we can now look more closely at adult behaviour in the chapters that follow.

2

INVITATIONS TO SEXUAL INTIMACY

E VERY HUMAN BODY is constantly sending out signals to its
social companions. Some of these signals invite intimate contact
and others repel it. Unless we are accidentally thrown against someone's body, we never touch one another until we have first carefully
read the signs. Our brains, however, are so beautifully tuned in to the
delicate business of assessing these invitation signals that we can often
sum up a social situation in a split second. If we unexpectedly spot a
loved one amongst a crowd of strangers, we can be embracing them
within a few moments of setting eyes on them. This does not imply
carelessness; it simply means that the computers inside our skulls are
brilliant at making rapid, almost instantaneous calculations concerning the appearance and mood of all the many individuals we encounter
during our waking hours. The hundreds of separate signals coming
from the details of their shape, size, colour, sound, smell, posture,
movement and expression, crowd at lightning speed into our specialized sense organs, the social computer whirrs into action, and out
comes the answer, to touch or not to touch.

As babies, our small size and our helplessness act as powerful stimuli
encouraging adults to reach out and make friendly contact with us. The
flat face, the large eyes, the clumsy movements, the short limbs and the
generally rounded contours, all contribute to our touch-appeal. Add to
this the broad smile and the alarm signal of crying and screaming, and
the human infant is clearly a massive invitation to intimacy.

If, as adults, we send out similar signals of helplessness or pain, as, for
instance, when we are sick or the victims of an accident, we provoke a
pseudo-parental response of much the same kind. Also, when we are
performing the first tentative body contact, in the form of shaking
hands, we nearly always accompany it with a smiling facial expression.

These are the basic invitations to intimacy; but, with sexual maturity,
the human animal moves into a whole new sphere of contact signals –
the signals of sex appeal – which serve to encourage a male and female
to start touching one another with more than mere friendliness in mind.

Some of the sex signals are universal and apply to all adult human
beings; others are cultural variations on these biological themes. Some
concern our adult appearances as males and females, and others have

to do with our adult behaviour – our postures, gestures and actions. The simplest way to survey them is to make a tour of the human body, pausing briefly at each of the main points of interest in turn.

The crotch. Since we are dealing with sexual signals, it is logical to start with the primary genital region, and work our way outwards. The crotch is the major taboo zone, and this is not merely because it is the site of the external reproductive organs. Packed into this one small area of the body are all the main taboo subjects: urination, defecation, copulation, fellation, ejaculation, masturbation and menstruation. With this array of activities it is little wonder that it has always been the most concealed area of the human body. To expose it directly to view as a visual invitation to intimacy is much too strong a sexual signal to be employed as a preliminary device, before a relationship has progressed through the earlier stages of body contact. Ironically, by the time that a relationship has reached the more advanced phase of genital intimacy, it is usually too late for visual displaying, so that the first experience of the partner's genitals is normally tactile. The act of looking directly at the genitals of the opposite sex therefore plays a comparatively small role in modern human courtship. There is, nevertheless, considerable interest in this region of the body, and if direct exposure of the genitals is not possible, alternatives can still be found.

The first is to employ articles of clothing which underline the nature of the organs hidden beneath them. For the female this means wearing trousers, shorts or bathing costumes which are one size too small for comfort, but which, by their tightness, cut into the genital cleft and thereby reveal its shape to the attentive male eye. This is an exclusively modern development, but the male equivalent has a longer history. For a period of nearly two hundred years (from roughly 1408 to 1575) many European male genitals were indirectly displayed in all their glory by the wearing of a codpiece. This began life in a modest way as a front flap which formed a small pouch at the fork of the extremely tight trousers, or hose, worn by the males of the day. The hose were, in fact, so tight that they had little choice. 'Cod' is an old word for scrotum, hence the name 'codpiece'. As the years passed, it grew dramatically in size until it became a blatant phallus-piece, rather than a mere scrotum-piece, and gave the impression that the wearer was the possessor of a permanently erect penis. To emphasize the point further, it was often differently coloured from the surrounding material, and even decorated with gold and jewels. Eventually the codpiece went so far that it began to become something of a joke, so that when Rabelais described the one worn by his hero, he was able to comment that 'For the codpiece sixteen yards of material was required. The shape was that of a triumphal arch, most elegant and secured by two gold rings fastened to enamel buttons, each the size of an orange and set with heavy emeralds. The codpiece protruded forward as much as three feet.'

Today such extravagant penile displays are missing from the world of fashion, but an echo can still be found, for the young male of the 1960s and 1970s has once again started to wear his 'hose' too tight. Like the modern female, he squeezes himself into closely fitting jeans and bathing costumes, in which he is forced to change the resting position of his penis. Unlike the older males, who still fill the generation gap between their legs with a loosely hanging penis beneath their slacker slacks, the younger male of today walks with his penis in the upright position. Held firmly in its vertical posture by the snugly clinging material, it presents a mild but distinctly visible genital bulge to the interested female eye. In this way the young male's costume once again permits him to display a pseudo-erection and, as with the earlier codpiece, this has surprisingly happened without any undue criticism from puritan quarters. It remains to be seen whether the codpiece itself will make a come-back in the years ahead, and how far the trend will have to go before this male embellishment once again becomes so sexually obtrusive that it falls into disrepute.

Other modern costume-genital displays are of a frankly exotic nature and not in wide use. They include female bathing costumes and panties trimmed with fur in the pubic area, or with lace-up fronts which imitate the shape of the genitals. Another form of indirect genital display that has, without comment, survived the passage of time is the Scotsman's sporran, a symbolic genital pouch worn in the scrotal region and frequently covered with symbolic pubic hair.

A less direct way of transmitting visual genital signals is to use some other part of the body as a 'genital-echo', or copy. This enables a primary sexual message to be transmitted, whilst keeping the real· genitals completely obscured. There are several ways in which this is done and to understand them we must look again at the anatomy of the female sex organs. For purposes of symbolism, they consist of an orifice – the vagina – and paired flaps of skin – the minor and major labia. If these are covered up, then any other body organs or details that resemble them in some way are likely to become employed as 'genital-echoes', for signalling purposes.

As orifice-substitutes, candidates available are the navel, the mouth, the nostrils and the ears. All have mild taboos associated with them. It is impolite to pick the nose or clean the ear with a finger in a public place. This contrasts with a cleaning action such as wiping the forehead, or rubbing the eyes, which we permit without comment. The mouth is frequently covered for some reason, if not with a veil, at least when we are yawning, gasping or giggling. The navel is even more taboo, having frequently been air-brushed out of photographs completely in past decades, to protect our eyes from its suggestive shape. Of these four types of 'aperture', only the mouth and the navel appear to have been specifically employed as genital-orifice substitutes.

The mouth is by far the most important of these, and transmits a great deal of pseudo-genital signalling during amorous encounters. I suggested in *The Naked Ape* that the unique development of everted lips in our species may well be part of this story, their fleshy pink surfaces having developed as a labial mimic at the biological, rather than the purely cultural, level. Like the true labia, they become redder and more swollen with sexual arousal, and like them they surround a centrally placed orifice. Since the earliest historical times, the lip signals of the female have been heightened by the application of artificial colouring. Lipstick is today a major cosmetic industry and, although the colours vary from fad to fad, they always return before long to something in the pink-red range, thereby copying the flushing of the labia during the advanced stages of sexual arousal. This is not, of course, a conscious imitation of the genital signals; it is merely 'sexy' or 'attractive', with no further questions asked.

The lips of the adult female are typically slightly larger and fleshier than those of the male, which is what one would expect if they are playing a symbolic role, and this size difference has sometimes been exaggerated by spreading the lipstick over a wider area than the lips themselves. This also mimics the enlargement they undergo when sexually engorged with blood.

Many authors and poets have seen the lips and mouth as a powerfully erotic region of the body, with the male tongue inserting itself, penis-like, into the female mouth during deep kissing. It has also been suggested that the structure of the lips of a particular female reflects the structure of the (as yet unseen) genitals below. A woman with fleshy lips is supposed to be the possessor of fleshy labia; one with tight, thin lips to have tight, thin genitals. Where this is in fact the case, it does not, of course, reflect the precision of the body-mimicry, but merely the overall somatotype of the female in question.

The navel has excited far less comment than the mouth, but some curious things have been happening to it in recent years which reveal that it does have a distinct role to play as a genital-echo. Not only was it painted out of early photographs, but its exposure was also expressly forbidden by the original 'Hollywood Code', so that harem dancing-girls in pre-war films were always obliged to appear with ornamental navel-covers of some kind. No real explanation was ever given for this taboo, except for the lame excuse that the exposure of the navel might start children asking what it was for and thereby precipitate an awkward 'facts of life' interlude for the parent. In adult contexts, however, this is clearly nonsensical, and the true reason was obviously that the navel is strongly reminiscent of a 'secret orifice'. Since harem girls are likely, at the drop of a veil, to start wriggling their abdomens about in an Eastern belly-dance, with the result that this pseudo-orifice starts gaping, stretching and writhing in a sexually inviting manner, Hollywood decided that this indelicate piece of anatomy would have to be masked. Ironically, as we started to move into the second half of the twentieth century and the grip of the Hollywood Code was beginning to relax in the West, the Arab world, with its new-found republican spirit, set about reversing the trend. Egyptian belly-dancers were officially informed that it was improper and undignified to expose the navel during their 'traditional folklore' performances. In future, their new government insisted, the midriff would be suitably covered by some kind of light cloth. And so, as the European and American navels fought their way back, in the cinemas and on the beaches, the blind orifices of North Africa retreated into a new obscurity.

Since their reappearance, the naked navels of the Western world have undergone a curious modification. They have started to change shape. In pictorial representations, the old-fashioned circular aperture is tending to give way to a more elongated, vertical slit. Investigating this odd phenomenon, I discovered that contemporary models and actresses are six times more likely to display a vertical navel than a circular one, when compared with the artist's models of yesterday. A brief survey of two hundred paintings and sculptures showing female nudes, and selected at random from the whole range of art history, revealed a proportion of 92 per cent of round navels to 8 per cent of vertical ones. A similar analysis of pictures of modern photographic models and film actresses shows a striking change: now the proportion of vertical ones has risen to 46 per cent. This is only partly due to the fact that the girls have become generally much slimmer, for although it is true that a fat, sagging female cannot offer the contemplator of navels a vertical slit, it is equally true that a skinny female need not do so either. Modigliani's slender girls display navels that are quite as round as those of Renoir's plump models. Furthermore, two young girls of the 1970s with similar figures can easily display the two distinct navel shapes.

How this change has come about, and whether it has been unconsciously arrived at or knowingly encouraged by modern photographers, is not entirely clear. It appears to have something to do with a subtle alteration in the trunk posture of the displaying model, possibly partly connected with an exaggerated intake of breath. The ultimate significance of the new navel shape is, however, reasonably certain. The classical round navel, in its symbolic orifice role, is rather too reminiscent of the anus. By becoming a more oval, vertical slit, it automatically assumes a much more genital shape, and its quality as a sexual symbol is immensely increased. This, apparently, is what has been happening since the Western navel came out into the open and began to operate more overtly as an erotic signalling device.

The buttocks. Leaving the crotch and its substitute echoes and passing round to the back of the pelvic region, we come to the paired, fleshy hemispheres of the buttocks. These are more pronounced in the female than the male and are a uniquely human feature, being absent in other species of primates. If a human female were to bend down and present her buttocks visually to a male, as if she were adopting the typical primate invitation-to-copulation posture, her genitals would be seen framed by the two hemispheres of smooth flesh. This association makes them an important sexual signal for our species, and one that probably has a very ancient biological origin. It is our equivalent of the 'sexual swellings' of other species. The difference is that, in our case, the condition is permanent. In other species the swellings rise and fall with the menstrual cycle, reaching their maximum size when the female is sexually receptive, around the time of ovulation. Naturally, as the human female is sexually receptive at virtually all times, her sexual 'swellings' remain permanently 'inflated'. As our early ancestors became more upright in their standing posture, the genitals came to be displayed more from the front than the rear, but the buttocks still retained their sexual significance. Even though copulation itself became an increasingly frontal affair, the female could still send out sexual signals by emphasizing her rump in some way. Today, if a girl slightly increases the undulations of her buttocks when she walks, it acts as a powerful erotic signal to the male. If she adopts a posture in which they are 'accidentally' protruded a little more than usual, this has the same effect. Sometimes, as in the famous 'bottoms up' cancan dance posture, the full version of the ancient primate rump-presentation display is still to be seen, and jokes about the man who wants to slap or caress the bottom of the girl who has innocently bent down to pick up a dropped object are commonplace.

From earlier days, there are two buttock phenomena that deserve comment. The first is the natural condition known as 'steatopygia', and the second is the artificial device of the bustle. Literally, steatopygia means fat-rumped, and refers to a remarkably pronounced protuberance of the buttocks found amongst certain human cultures, notably the Bushmen of Southern Africa. It has been suggested that this is a case of fat-storage similar to that of the camel's hump, but since it is much more exaggerated in females than males, it seems more likely that it is a specialization of the sexual signals that emanate from this region of the body. It looks as if the

Bushman females went further in the development of this signal than other races. It is even possible that this condition was typical of most of our early ancestors, but that later on it was reduced in favour of a more athletically adaptable compromise in the shape of the less ambitious female buttocks we see around us today. Certainly the Bushmen were once much more common than they are now, and owned much of Africa before the later Negro expansion.

It is also curious that so many prehistoric female figurines, from Europe and elsewhere, frequently show a similar condition, with huge protruding buttocks which are completely out of proportion with the general obesity of the bodies depicted. There are only two explanations. Either prehistoric women were endowed with huge rumps, sending out massive sexual signals to their males, or the prehistoric sculptors were so obsessed with the erotic nature of buttocks that, like many cartoonists of the present day, they permitted themselves a considerable degree of artistic licence. Either way, the prehistoric buttocks reigned supreme. Then, strangely, in region after region, as the art forms advanced, the big-buttocked females began to disappear. In the prehistoric art of every locality where they occur, they are always the earliest figures to be found. Then they are gone, and more slender females move in to take their place. Unless fat-rumped females really were common in earlier days and then gradually died out, the reason for this widespread change in prehistoric art remains a mystery. The male interest in female buttocks survived, but with a few exceptions they now became reduced to the natural proportions we observe on the cinema screens of the twentieth century. The dancing girls depicted on the murals of ancient Egypt could easily find work in a modern night-club and, had Venus de Milo lived, she would have had a hip measurement of no more than 38 inches.

The exceptions to this rule are intriguing, since, in a sense, they demonstrate a throw-back to prehistoric times and show man's revived interest in gross exaggeration of the female rump region. Here we move from the fleshy phenomenon of steatopygia to the artificial device of the bustle. The effect is the same in both cases – namely, a vast enlargement of the buttock region – but with the bustle this was done by inserting thick padding, or some kind of framework, beneath the female costume. In origin it was a sort of crinoline-in-retreat. The habit of padding the hips all round the pelvic region occurred frequently in European fashions, and all that was needed to permit a new rump-display to appear on the scene was to remove the padding at the front and sides of the body. This made the creation of the bustle a 'reduction' rather than an exaggeration and permitted its introduction into high fashion to take place without undue comment. Having arrived negatively in this way, it managed to avoid its obvious sexual implications. The hooped and padded bustle of the 1870s vanished after a few years, but returned in triumph in an even more exaggerated form in the 1880s. Now it became a great shelf sticking out at the back, kept in place by wire netting and steel springs, and created an impression that even a tired Bushman would have responded to. By the 1890s, however, this too was gone, and the increasingly athletic female of the twentieth century has never wished to reinstate it. Instead, the enlarged buttocks of modern times have been confined to rarely used 'bottom-falsies', to provocative 'come-hither' posturing and to the drawing-boards of the cartoonists.

The legs. Moving downwards from the pelvic region, the female legs have also been the subject of considerable male interest as sexual signalling devices. Anatomically, the outsides of the female thighs have a greater fat deposit than in the male, and at certain periods a plump leg has therefore been an erotic one. At other times, the mere exposure of leg flesh has been sufficient to transmit sexual signals. Needless to say, the higher the exposure goes, the more stimulating it becomes, for the simple reason that it then approaches more closely the primary genital zone. Artificial aids to the legs have included 'calf-falsies', to be worn under opaque stockings, but these have been as rarely used as 'bottom-falsies'. High-heeled shoes have been much more commonly adopted, the tilt of the foot supposedly enhancing the leg contour and also increasing the apparent length of the legs, which relates to the fact that elongation of the limbs is a characteristic of adolescent maturing. 'Legginess' equals sexual maturity, and therefore sexiness.

The feet themselves have often been squeezed into shoes which are much too tight for them, a tendency that results from the fact that the foot of the adult female is slightly smaller than that of the adult male. It therefore follows that to increase this difference a little will make the female foot more feminine, as a sexual signal to the male. The petite foot has often been praised by male admirers, and many a female has suffered tortures to obtain it. Byron's words sum up the traditional masculine attitude, when he writes of 'feet so small and sylph-like, suggesting the more perfect symmetry of the fair forms which terminate so well'. This view of the female foot is reflected in the perennial story of Cinderella − a tale that can be traced back at least two thousand years − where her ugly sisters have feet too big to fit into the tiny glass slipper. Only the beautiful heroine has small enough feet to win the heart of the Prince.

In China the trend towards small female feet was once taken to horrifying lengths, young girls often having to undergo such tight binding that they suffered serious deformity. The bound foot, or 'golden lily', which looked so attractive in its tiny decorated shoe, had more the appearance of a deformed pig's trotter when it was viewed unshod. So important was this painful practice that a girl's commercial value was measured by the smallness of her feet, her shoes being displayed to establish her worth during the bartering over bride-price. The modern woman whose 'feet are killing her' is merely echoing in a mild way this ancient phenomenon. The official reason given to explain the custom of the 'golden lilies' was that it showed that the female in question did not need to work – because she was so crippled that she could not. But her husband did not need to work either, yet his feet remained un-crushed, so that the exaggerated sex-difference element provides a more basic explanation. This rule applies in many other cases as well. A particular distortion, or exaggeration, is officially performed for reasons of 'high fashion' or status, but the deeper explanation is that the modification in question in some way emphasizes a female (or male) biological characteristic. The artificial tightening of the female waist is another case in point.

In addition to their anatomy, the posture of the legs is capable of transmitting sexual signals. In many cultures, girls are told that it is improper to stand or sit with the legs wide apart. To do this is to 'open' the genitals, and even if they are not visible, the message remains fundamentally the same. With the advent of female trousers and the disappearance of strict codes of etiquette, the legs-apart posture has become much more common in recent years, and is used with increasing frequency by model girls in advertisements. What was once a too-powerful signal has now become merely challenging; what was shocking is now no more than tantalizing. But nevertheless, a girl in a skirt still obeys the old rules. To expose the opened crotch, clad only in panties, remains too strong an invitation signal in most cases.

The traditionally 'polite girl' therefore keeps her legs together, but there is a danger, also, if she goes too far in this direction and presses them too tightly against one another. If she does this, or crosses them so vigorously that her thighs are squeezed together, she begins to 'protest too much' and thereby makes a new kind of sexual comment. As with all puritan statements, she reveals that she has sex very much on her mind. In fact, the girl who tries to protect her genitals unduly draws almost as much attention to them as the one who exposes them to view. Similarly, if a skirt rides up slightly when a girl sits down and exposes more leg than she intended, she only enhances the sexuality of the situation by making attempts to tug it down again. The only non-sexual signal is the one that avoids both extremes.

For the male, the opening of the legs carries much the same signal as with the female, because here, too, it says 'I am exposing my genitals to you.' Sitting with the legs wide apart is the gesture of a dominant, confident male (unless, of course, he is so fat that he cannot get them together).

The belly. Moving up above the genital region now, we come to the belly, which has two characteristic shapes: flat and 'pot'. Lovers tend to be flat-bellied, while pot-bellies are most commonly seen in starving children and overfed men. The adult female is less likely to become pot-bellied than the adult male, even if she becomes equally over-weight. This is because, as a female, her tissues are hungrier for fat in the thigh and hip region than around the belly. If a male and female go far enough, of course, they will both end up with much the same spheroid shape, but at milder levels of overeating the difference in fat-distribution is marked. Many comparatively skinny men manage to develop moderate-sized pot-bellies in middle and old age. What is the explanation for this?

Sometimes a visual joke says more than the artist intended or even understood. A cartoon of a pot-bellied, middle-aged man standing on a beach shows him being approached by a beautiful young girl in a bikini. As she comes near, he spots her and starts to contract his sagging stomach, so that when she is abreast of him his chest is swollen out and his belly held tightly in. As she passes by, the stomach slowly begins to sag again until, as she disappears in the distance, it is completely back to its gross, original shape. This joke was clearly intended to reflect a conscious control of the man's body contour – and his sexual image – but what it also depicts is something that happens unconsciously and semi-permanently, as part of the male human sexual display. For sexual excitement, or prolonged sexual interest, has the automatic effect of tightening up the stomach muscles. Regardless of individual variations, this is revealed in the general difference in the body contour of young males and old males. Young males are more sexually potent than older ones, and their general body shape goes in more as it goes down. They have the typical masculine display shape of our species, with broadened shoulders, expanded chests, and narrow hips. The flat belly is part of this general body-tapering. The older male tends towards sagging, rounded shoulders, flattened chest, and heavier hips. The swollen belly again is part of this now *inverted* tapering of the body contour. With this shape, the older male says plainly, 'I am past the pair-formation stage.'

In modern times, older males, who have made youthfulness and sexual potency into high-status cults, struggle desperately to stem the tide of this almost inevitable contour inversion. They diet ruthlessly, they indulge in physical training, they sometimes even wear tight corsets, and they consciously hold in their loosening stomach muscles as best they can. It would, of course, be much simpler if they could keep on falling in love over and over again. Belly-wise, they would find that an affair is as good as a diet and a corset combined, and that the physical exercise comes built-in. Under the influence of their passionate emotions, their stomach muscles would automatically contract and stay contracted, for by the act of falling in love they would be genuinely and biologically returning to a youthful condition, and their body would do its best to match their mood. Many men do, of course, take steps in this direction from time to time, but unless the process is a more or less continuous one, irreversible contour inversion will have started to take its toll, and their body success will be limited. Needless to say, such steps also play havoc with the older male's true biological role, which is by now that of the parental head of an established family unit.

The situation has not always been like this. Long ago, before the miracles of modern medicine stretched out our lives to such an unnatural extent, most older males soon vanished beneath the turf. To judge by our primate body weight and various other features of our life cycle, the natural life-span for man is probably somewhere between forty and fifty years, no more. Beyond that everything is a bonus. Also, in previous historical periods, a dominant, ageing male has often maintained his status more by his social power than by his youthfulness. An attractive young female has frequently been bought rather than wooed. A fat lord, or a fat master of the harem, cared little about his gross shape or the anti-sexual signals he transmitted. In the harem, this situation gave birth to the phenomenon of belly-dancing. Originally this consisted of the performance of pelvic thrusts by the female on the podgy, incapacitated form of her lord and master. Unable to make the thrusting movements himself, he had to be serviced by trained girls who would be able to take over the masculine role in the encounter, inserting his immobile penis into their vaginas, and then undulating and jolting their pelvises to stimulate it to a climax, in what amounted to little more than an act of fertile masturbation. The clever and varied movements developed by such females to arouse their fat, dominant males formed the basis of the famous Eastern belly-dance and, as a visual preliminary, this became more and more elaborate, until it grew into the display we see so often today in night-clubs and cabarets.

For the modern male, sexual conquests with no thought given to the masculine invitation signals are largely limited to brief visits to prostitutes. For his long-term relationships, he now has to rely much more heavily on his personal sexual appeal. In this respect he has returned to a much more natural situation for the human species, but at the same time his life-span has been artificially elongated. It is this situation that has led to the new concern about 'youthfulness and vigour' for the male who, as he leaves his twenties behind, inevitably starts to feel the decline of his sexual powers. Coasting to a natural death at forty, this would not have posed such a problem, leaving just enough time to rear the offspring and be off. But now, with something more like half a century confronting the post-parental male, the problem has become acute, and we have all the diet books, health farms and other paraphernalia of contemporary life to prove it.

The waist. Here we return again to the sexual-signalling world of the female. The waist is narrower in the female than the male, or appears to be so because of her widened, childbearing hips and her swollen, rounded breasts. Narrowness of waist has therefore become an important female sexual signal, available for artificial exaggerations of the type we have met before. The signal can be made more powerful directly or indirectly, either by tightening the waist or by enlarging the bust and hips. The maximum signal can be transmitted by doing both at once. Busts can be magnified by holding or pushing them up with tight clothing, by padding them out, or by cosmetic surgery. The hips can be enlarged by padding or by the wearing of stiff clothing that curves out from the body. The waist itself can be reduced by tight lacing or the wearing of a belt.

Female waist corsets have a long and sometimes unhappy history. In previous eras they have occasionally become so severe that they have damaged the rib and lung development of young girls and interfered with their healthy respiration. In late Victorian times, an attractive girl was one whose waist measurement in inches was the same as her age at her last birthday. To achieve this goal many young ladies were forced to sleep in their tightly laced corsets, as well as wear them throughout the day. In historical periods when the crinoline was fashionable, the restrictions on the waist could be eased considerably, because, of course, any waist looked small by comparison with the enormous apparent hip width provided by the huge skirts.

Twentieth-century waists have suffered much less from the artificial compressions of the corset, and frequently have been completely free of them, relying instead on the 'compressions' of a rigid diet. The average British woman of today has a waist measurement of $27\frac{3}{4}$ inches. The model girl Twiggy, the typical *Playboy* 'playmate' and the average Miss World all have a 24-inch waist. Modern female athletes, making more masculine demands on their bodies, tend towards a 29-inch waist.

These figures acquire more meaning when they are related to the bust and hip measurements, thereby revealing the 'waist indentation' factor that transmits the essential female contour signal. Twiggy ($30\frac{1}{2}$–24–33) and Miss World (36–24–36) now part company, the latter sending out a much more powerful waist signal.

There is a further waist factor that requires comment. Indentation comes from both above and below, and one can be greater than the other. Miss World is perfectly balanced – from both bust to waist and hip to waist, she indents by 12 inches. The average British female, however ($37-27\frac{1}{4}-39$), goes in more from hip to waist than she does from bust to waist. The fact that her hips are two inches larger than her bust gives her what is called a 2-inch 'drop'. This is common in the average female of other Western countries as well. In Italy it is also 2 inches; in Germany and Switzerland it is $2\frac{3}{8}$ inches; in Sweden and France, $3\frac{1}{8}$ inches.

These figures show a marked and significant difference from the *Playboy* 'playmate', a typical example being 37–24–35: in other words, a 2-inch 'rise', rather than a 'drop'. That she is referred to as being 'big-bosomed' is therefore not merely a reflection of her breast size. Her bust measurement is exactly the same as that of the average British female. Her apparent 'bustiness' is more the result of the fact that, although her bust measurement is no bigger, both her waist and hip measurements are roughly four inches smaller, giving her a top-heavy contour which magnetically draws attention to her breasts. To find such an unusual female is not easy. Since, for the purposes of the magazine, the girl is to be photographed with her breasts naked, the problem is a strictly biological one – artificial aids cannot help her. To consider this more fully, we can now leave the waist behind and concentrate more specifically on the chest region.

The breasts. The adult female of the human species is unique amongst primates in possessing a pair of swollen, hemispherical mammary glands. These remain protuberant and swollen even when she is not producing milk and are clearly more than a mere feeding device. I have suggested that, in their shape, they can better be thought of as another mimic of a primary sexual zone; in other words, as biologically developed copies of the hemispherical buttocks. This gives the female a powerful sexual signal when she is standing vertically, in the uniquely human posture, and facing a male.

There are two other echoes of the basic buttock shape, but they are less powerful than the breast signals. One is the smooth, rounded shoulder of the female, which, if it is 'only just' exposed by the pulling down of a blouse or sweater, presents a suitably curved hemisphere of flesh. This is a common erotic device in periods of low-cut dresses. The other echo is found in the smooth, rounded knees of the female, which, when the legs are bent and pressed together, present another pair of feminine hemispheres to the eyes of the male. Again, knees have frequently been referred to in an erotic context. As with the shoulders, they make their greatest impact when they are 'only just' exposed by the skirt. If the whole leg is visible, some of their impact is lost because they then become merely the rounded ends of the thighs, rather than a pair of hemispheres in their own right. But these are much milder buttock-echoes, and it is with the breasts that the major impact is achieved.

It is important to distinguish here between the childhood reaction to the female breast and the adult sexual one. Most men see their interest in the female bosom as purely sexual. By contrast, some scientific theorists have viewed it as purely infantile. Both views are one-eyed, because both factors are operating. The male lover who kisses the nipple of his female's breast may well be harking back to the pleasures of infancy, rather than kissing a pseudo-buttock, but the amorous male who ogles or fondles a female's breasts may well be responding primarily to their hemispherical buttock shape, rather than reliving the feeling of his mother's breast with his infantile hand. To the tiny hand of an infant, the mother's breast is too vast an object to be cupped or clasped in the palm, but to the adult hand it presents a rounded surface remarkably reminiscent of the buttock hemisphere. Visually the same is true, a pair of breasts offering an image that is much closer to that of a pair of buttocks than to the looming shape seen at close quarters by a baby being suckled.

This sexual significance of the female breasts is therefore of primary importance to our species, and although this is not the whole story, it plays a major role in society's perennial preoccupation with the feminine bosom. For the early English Puritans it meant flattening the breasts completely with a tight bodice. In seventeenth-century Spain, the measures taken were even more severe, young ladies having lead plates pressed into their swelling bosoms in an attempt to prevent their development. Such steps do not, of course, indicate a lack of interest in the female breast, which could only be demonstrated by completely ignoring it. Rather, they show acceptance of the fact that sexual signals do come from this region and, for cultural reasons, have to be stopped.

A much more widespread and frequent tendency has been for the breasts to be emphasized in some way. This emphasis has nearly always been to make them not so much larger as more upstanding. In other words, the tendency has been to improve their hemispherical, pseudo-buttock appearance. They are pushed up by tight dresses, so that they bulge above them, or they are pushed together to make the cleavage between them more like that between the real buttocks, or they are clasped in stretched brassières so that they protrude forward instead of sagging down. At some points in history, even greater attention has been paid to the problem, an ancient Indian love manual advising that 'Continuous treatment with antimony and rice water will cause the breasts of a young girl to become large and prominent so that they will steal the heart of the connoisseur as a robber steals gold.'

In a few primitive cultures, however, sagging or drooping breasts do find favour, and young girls are encouraged to pull at them regularly in order to hasten their downward turn. Also, nearer home, the small-breasted, or even flat-chested, female has her ardent followers, and these exceptions to the general rule require explanation. The social anthropologist would probably merely put them down to 'cultural variations' and leave the matter there. Every culture and every period has its own special standards of beauty, he would say, and virtually anything goes, providing it becomes the accepted fashion for a particular tribe or society. There is no basic biological theme with variations, but merely a wide range of equally valid alternatives, and each one must be looked at on its own merits. But to take such a view is to beg the fundamental issue of why the adult male and female human animals have evolved so many different body details, differences which are typical for our species as a whole. The typical female *does* have swollen breasts which are lacking in the male, she *does* display them regardless of the presence or absence of milk production for her offspring, and other species of primate *do* lack this prominent visual feature. They do therefore present a basic biological theme for *Homo sapiens*, variations from which must be viewed as unusual and requiring special explanation, rather than simply as equally valid cultural alternatives that require none, except to say that they are 'differing tribal customs'.

To understand the exceptions, it helps to look at the 'life cycle' of a typical female breast. In the child it starts out as no more than a nipple on a flat chest. Then, at puberty, it swells into a breast-bud. At this stage the swelling points straight forward. As it grows and becomes heavier, its weight begins to pull it down, its underside becoming slightly more curved than its upper surface. The nipples, however, still project straight out in front. This is the condition of the older teenage girl. Then, as she moves into her twenties and the breast continues to swell, it slowly begins to turn downwards until, in middle age, a full-breasted female shows a marked sag if she does not employ some artificial booster device. There are, then, three basic stages: small for the immature girl, pointed and protuberant for the young adult, and drooping for the older adult.

Viewed in this light, the cultural variations begin to make more sense. If, for some reason, immature girls are thought of as sexually appealing, then small breasts will be favoured. If older women are preferred, then drooping breasts will be in fashion. For the vast majority, the intermediate stage will be preferred, since it represents the true phase of first sexual activity in the human female. Under-developed females will imitate the pointed, protuberant condition by padding their small bosoms, the older ones who wish to give the impression of being in the first bloom of sexual life will imitate it by adding an artificial up:hrust.

In cases where pseudo-immature girls are preferred, there are several possible explanations. For the male living in a sexually repressed, puritan culture, flattening the female breast helps to damp down the strong sexual signal. For the male who has a strong inclination to play the 'father' role to a 'daughter' bride, the little-girl look of small breasts will be appealing. For the latent homosexual, small breasts give a more boyish look, which will be strongly attractive. Going to the other extreme, in societies where the maternal role of the female has become culturally much more important than the sexual one, the sagging breasts of the older female will be more appealing, even in younger girls. The latter must then 'age' their breasts by pulling at them to make them hang down.

For the majority of human beings, however, the maximum breast-appeal will come at the point where the hemispheres have reached their fullest protrusion *before* becoming so large that they begin to droop downwards. This explains the dilemma of the *Playboy* photographer, for as one breast quality (increased size) grows, the other (non-droop) diminishes. To take a picture of a super-breast, he has to search for a rare girl who has retained the firmness of her young breast past the point where it has already swollen to a full adult size. It is interesting that this limits him to a narrow age range in the late teens. Clearly this is the most vital point in the life cycle for this type of sexual signalling, and is the phase which older females are attempting to imitate and artificially prolong with their various breast-supporting techniques.

The super-breast effect is indirectly enhanced by selecting girls with modest-sized waists and hips. Here we come back to the question of the more general change in female body contour that occurs with age. Tests have shown that the average adult female puts on three pounds in weight every five years. The small proportion of this that goes on the breasts is what continues to pull them down as the years pass. The hips and thighs get an unfair share of this increase, giving the middle-aged female her characteristic 'hippy' (in the old sense) appearance. This is what accounts for the 'drop' mentioned earlier – the slightly larger size of hip than bust measurement. In some parts of the world, especially the Mediterranean region, this change can occur with startling rapidity as girls pass through their twenties. At one moment they are slim and slender and then, almost overnight, they start swelling out in the pelvic region, to assume the typical 'maternal' shape of the older woman. In other regions the change is more gradual, but the basic trend is the same. Not until very old age is there a reversal, when the body starts to shrink again.

To many Western women who wish to stay young-looking, this natural biological tendency of the species presents a severe challenge and demands the constant agonies of diet control. It is not merely that they are fighting gluttony, they are fighting nature as well. They must not merely eat 'normally', they must deliberately undereat, if they are to retain their girlish figures. The situation has not always been as extreme as it is today. In the past, a plumply rounded adult female figure has been perfectly acceptable sexually. There is nothing unfeminine about ample curves. They do, however, signal the maternal rather than the virginal phase, and the modern woman, under the influence of the contemporary youth-cult, wishes to remain a flesh-virgin, even while she copulates and bears children.

That the plump curves of the adult female are essentially linked to the maternal, rather than the courting, phase of life, is borne out by the fact that for every seven pounds a married woman with a child puts on, an unmarried woman only gains two pounds. The moral of this is that if a female wishes to remain girl-shaped, she should retain girl-status. Being unmarried, regardless of age, means that, biologically speaking, she is still displaying to a potential mate and therefore tends to stay the shape that has evolved to fit such a context. Once she becomes married, she begins to slip into the more 'comfortable' maternal shape, and her body contour starts to signal this new condition.

Although this trend is viewed by most modern women as merely a nuisance, it is too basic to be an accident. In biological terms it must have some value. One reason often given for it is that the plump, broad-hipped woman is a better child-bearer, but there seems to be little evidence to support this, especially as most of the added pelvic width consists not of a broader spacing of the bones that surround the birth-passage, but of heavy layers of fat. (The average human female body contains 28 per cent fat, the average male only 15 per cent.) There is another, more sexual explanation that seems to make better sense. The slender-girl shape is the one men enjoy visually – stare at, touch lightly, kiss, and fall in love with. The fuller, more womanly shape is the one they spend years copulating with. Perhaps, then, what happens is that the ideal visual shape changes to become the ideal tactile body, the 'dancing gazelle' becoming a cushion of 'pneumatic bliss'. Such a change would certainly explain the difference between the bony fashion model, who is to be seen but not touched, and the full-bodied female, who is to be embraced and hugged, and has already completed her biological task of attracting and becoming bonded with an adult male.

I am dealing here, of course, with extremes. In the case of the average female, the girlish body is not so bony as to be unpleasant to copulate with, and the womanly body is not so full as to be uneasy on the eye. The change is only a minor one, and both stages are successful in both a visual and a tactile sense. What has gone wrong is that modern society has swallowed the romantic myth that young lovers stay dreamily in love for ever, year in and year out, with the maximum intensity of the pair-formation stage lasting permanently, even after the pair has become fully bonded. Instead of accepting that the state of being crazily 'in love' must inevitably mature into a condition of deep but less violent 'loving', the married couple struggle to maintain the breathless ardour of their first contacts, and the physical contours that went with them. When, as must happen, they sense the initial intensity slackening, they imagine that something must have gone wrong and feel let down. In retrospect, those early Hollywood movies may have a lot to answer for.

Body skin. For both sexes and in all cultures, a smooth, clean, disease-free skin has a major sexual significance. Wrinkles, dirt and skin diseases are always anti-erotic. (The deliberately scarred or tattooed skin that occurs in some cultures is a different matter and adds to rather than detracts from the owner's sex appeal.)

In addition, the female body and limb skin is less hairy than that of the male, so that she not only attempts to increase its smoothness by the use of oils, lotions and massage, but also depilates it in a variety of ways, to exaggerate the sexual difference. Depilation has been used in many cultures and for thousands of years. It was practised, not only by certain 'primitive' tribes, but also in particular by the ancient Greeks, where women went so far as to remove much of the pubic hair as well, this being done either by tugging the hairs out manually – 'myrtle bunches pulled out by the hand', to quote one classical author – or by singeing them off with a burning lamp or hot ashes.

In modern times, females have depilated themselves with electric or safety razors and, more recently, by chemical means. Beauty experts claim that 80 per cent of women in Britain are the possessors of 'unwanted' body hair, which, although far more sparse and light than the male equivalent, nevertheless makes them feel a shade too masculine for comfort. In addition to shaving and the application of hair-dissolving creams, lotions and aerosol sprays, the beauty advisers recommend several other alternatives, such as waxing, rubbing, plucking and electrolysis. Waxing involves heating a special wax until it can be applied to the skin as a soft mould which then hardens. Once it is firm, it is stripped away, pulling the small body hairs with it. This is essentially the same device as that used from early times by Arab women, except that in their case they used a thick syrup of equal parts of water and sugar, with lemon juice added. This was poured on to the offending skin and allowed to harden, then ripped off in a similar way.

At first sight it is surprising that modern males, so many of whom daily endure a long struggle to depilate their stubble-strewn faces, have never risked experimenting with anything beyond the traditional razor shave. At second sight, however, a hidden factor emerges. This is not cowardice, or lack of initiative, but the result of a paradoxical desire to appear bearded even when beardless. Shaving always leaves a masculine blue sheen to the lower face, a tell-tale ghost of the beard that was. If, with some new technique, the adult male beard could be banished for ever, so would that virile blue sheen, and the treated face would begin to look too feminine to please its owner. Instead, by the time he dies, the average clean-shaven man will have spent well over two thousand hours scraping and rubbing at his face – a high price to pay for so contradictory a signal.

During the intense phases of pre-copulatory and copulatory activity, the whole of the body-skin surface of both the male and the female undergoes considerable change in textural quality. It glows with heat and, at the point of orgasm, there may be profuse sweating. In erotically posed photographs, models are sometimes shown displaying these conditions as visual signals. The skin may be oiled or greased to make it shine, or sprayed with water to give the impression of profuse sweating. In such cases the water is not meant to be consciously thought of as sweat, the water is plainly water and the model can often be seen to be rising from a pool or a bath to prove it. It would be too direct a comment to make the skin look obviously sweaty. Instead, the dampened surface makes its impact by unconscious association. The same is true of the habit of using a high level of red in printing colour pictures. This gives the girl's skin an erotic, flushed appearance, as though she is sexually overheated, and is a commonly used device in many magazines. Editorial requests to 'have the red brought up' do not, however, go so far that the viewer becomes consciously aware of what is being done.

Products have recently been marketed to produce an erotic skin glow artificially on a more private basis. Lovers can now cover themselves with various strange substances that make them look (and feel) as though they are in an advanced arousal condition before they have even begun to perform pre-copulatory contacts. For example, 'Love Foam' comes in aerosol cans. When it is sprayed on it looks rather like shaving cream, but when rubbed into the skin, according to the manufacturers, it makes the body 'take on a magical glow'. For even more exotic tastes, there is a substance which goes by the colourful name of 'Orgy Butter'. Called 'The Luxury Lubricant', it is advertised as 'A bold, red warm body rub ... Gives a slippery, sensual effect. Works into the skin with rubbing, providing an after-glow.' Here, quite clearly, are the vital arousal signals – red/slippery/glow – once again mimicking the vaso-dilation and sweating of the real arousal state of the human body skin.

The shoulders. The rounded female shoulder has already been mentioned, but the larger male shoulder also deserves a comment. Width of shoulders becomes an important secondary sexual characteristic that starts to develop at puberty. The shoulders of the male adolescent widen out more extensively than those of the female, and by the time the young adult stage is reached the male is decidedly more broadshouldered than his female companion. Like the other contour differences, this one has also been exaggerated artificially in various ways. Throughout history, male clothing has repeatedly involved an extra padding of the shoulder region, making it appear even larger as a masculine signal. The extreme situation is reached with the military epaulet, which not only makes the shoulders appear wider but also makes them much more angular. In this way they provide a double contrast with the narrower and more rounded shoulders of the female, and completely lose their hemispherical visual quality.

The jaw. There are several important sexual differences in the head region, and the first of these concerns the jaw and chin. The average human male has a slightly heavier jaw and chin region than the average female. For some reason this fact is seldom commented on, and yet it remains the one certain give-away clue in the case of an otherwise perfectly disguised male transvestite or female impersonator. Such men can pad out their body contours, depilate all visible areas of skin, cover their faces in heavy make-up, have wax injections to give themselves artificial breasts, and generally present such an alluring female appearance that occasionally a sailor in a foreign port has found himself, rather late in the transaction, involved with a 'female' prostitute who is not all that 'she' at first seemed to be. But even the very best of transvestites can do nothing about his jaw and chin, short of major surgery. Unless, by chance, he happens to be an abnormally small-jawed male, he will always present a tell-tale, heavy-jowled appearance to a discerning eye.

In some races, especially in the Far East, the extra heaviness of the male jaw and chin is less pronounced, and it is significant that in these same races there is typically a much less marked beard growth. It seems as if there is a connection between these two features. Jutting the jaw forward, by either sex, is an aggressive act – an intention movement of thrusting forward into the attack. It is the opposite of the submissive lowering of the head that occurs during a meek bowing action. The male, by having a more powerful jaw, is, so to speak, performing a permanent assertive jut. That this is important as a masculine trait is borne out by the fact that males who have receding chins are sometimes sneered at as 'chinless wonders', implying that they lack the normal male assertiveness.

Since one of the most obvious masculine characteristics of our species is the possession of a beard, it seems highly probable that this evolved in company with the more jutting jaw, the heavier bony structure providing a better base for the hairs, and the two features together producing a maximum virile jut. The peculiar chin of our species is important here. Unlike other primates, we have an outward protuberance of bone in the chin region, a protuberance which anatomists have now decided has no internal mechanical function. In the past, many theories have been put forward to explain this unique human feature, relating it to special properties of the jaw muscles and the tongue, but all of these arguments have recently been demolished. Instead, our chin jut is now accepted as primarily a signal feature and, as such, it must be seen as one that underlies the assertive jutting of the male beard.

The cheeks. Moving up the face and avoiding the mouth, which was dealt with earlier, we come to the cheeks. Here the most important signal is the blush, a reddening of the skin caused by vaso-congestion. This always starts in the cheek region, where it is most obvious, and may then spread to cover the whole of the face, the neck and, in some cases, the upper part of the trunk. Blushing is more common in females than males, and in young females than older ones. Accompanying the reddening there is a turgidity of the skin which takes on a surface glow that is visible even in a Negro blush. Blushing occurs in all human races and even in the deaf/blind, so that it appears to be a basic biological characteristic of the species. Darwin devoted a whole chapter to the subject of blushing and concluded that it reflected shyness, shame, or modesty, and indicated 'self-attention to personal appearance'. Its sexual significance is illustrated by the fact that the records show that girls who blushed freely when being offered for sale in ancient slave-markets for use in harems fetched higher prices than those that did not. As an invitation to intimacy, whether desired or not, the blush seems to have been a powerful signal.

The eyes. The most important of human sense organs, these not only see all the various signals we have been examining, but also transmit some on their own account. We all make and break eye contacts repeatedly during face-to-face encounters, looking at people to check their changing moods and then looking away to avoid the threat of staring at them. Between lovers, however, the stare can become more prolonged without being disconcerting or aggressive. Lovers 'gaze deeply into one another's eyes' for a particular reason. Under the influence of strong emotions of a pleasant kind, our pupils dilate to an unusual degree, the small dark spot in the centre of the eye becoming a great black disc. Unconsciously, this transmits a powerful signal to the loved one, indicating the intensity of the love felt by the dilator. This fact has only recently been studied scientifically, but it has been known for centuries, Italian beauties of earlier days having placed drops of belladonna into their eyes in order to create the effect artificially. In modern times a similar device has been used by advertisers, who, using black ink instead of belladonna, have touched up photographs of model girls, enlarging their pupils to make them more appealing.

Another change that takes place in the eyes when emotions run high is a slight increase in tear production. In an intensely loving condition this does not usually go to the extreme of producing tears that actually start to run from the eye, but merely gives the eye surface an increased glistening quality. These are the shining eyes of love, and combine with the pupil dilation to leave no doubt about the condition of the signaller.

Eye movements of various kinds also invite intimacy. Apart from the well-known wink, the rolling of the eyes is also reported to be a direct invitation to copulation in certain cultures. A demure dropping of the eyes also transmits its message in the female, while a slight narrowing of them can indicate interest on the part of a male. When making a first encounter, the holding of a glance slightly longer than is usual can also make an impact, acting as a hint, so to speak, of the deep gazing that may develop later.

A wide-eyed, or magnified, stare is sometimes employed by a female inviting intimacy, and associated with this is the feminine device of fluttering the eyelashes or batting the eyelids. The word 'bat' used in this connection is a modification of 'bate', which means a beating of wings, and, in our culture at least, is a decidedly non-masculine action, so much so that it is sometimes used by a male when he is mockingly imitating a female gesture. Perhaps because eyelash movements of this kind are so essentially feminine, a great deal of lash exaggeration is practised by females at the present time. This began with the use of mascara, to make the eyelashes look heavier and more conspicuous, then moved on to eyelash curlers, and finally, in the 1960s, culminated with the development of sets of long artificial lashes which were added to the real ones. Today, one company alone offers no less than fifteen different styles of artificial eyelashes, including 'Wispy-tipped Starry Lashes' that 'open up eyes' and 'Raggedy Lashes' that 'enlarge small eyes'. These are fixed to the upper eyelids, as are such exotic concoctions as 'Cluster-lashes', 'Natural-fluff Lashes' and 'Super-sweepers'. For the lower eyelid, there are 'Winged Under-lashes' to 'widen, brighten eyes'. As in so many other parts of the body, when the female has something that sends out an important feminine signal, she makes the most of it. This new trend to exaggerate the eyelash region would certainly provide a feast for an amorous male Trobriander, who, as an important part of his love-making, regularly bites off the lashes of his loved one. Luckily for the latter, eyelashes grow remarkably quickly, each one only lasting for three to five months even in the unbitten condition.

The eyebrows. Above the eyes the human animal possesses two unique patches of hair at the bottom of an otherwise hairless forehead. The eyebrows were once thought to operate as devices for stopping the sweat running down into the eyes, but their basic function is that of signalling changing moods. They are raised in fear and surprise and lowered in anger, knitted together in anxiety and cocked in a questioning glance. At the moment of a friendly acknowledgment they are flicked quickly once up and down.

The eyebrows of the female are less thick and bushy than those of the male, so, once again, they are available for exaggeration to make a female condition more feminine. They have frequently been plucked to make them thinner, and in the 1930s they were reduced to a mere pencil line. Even this extreme was exceeded in earlier days, however, Japanese brides once going so far as to shave them off altogether at the time of their marriage.

The sexual nature of this comparatively trivial modification to the female appearance is well illustrated by the fact that, in 1933, a girl who applied for a post as a nurse in a London hospital was warned by the matron that, amongst other things, she would not be permitted to continue plucking her eyebrows. A complaint was made, her case was taken up, and the London County Council was urged to give the matron an official rebuke, but the request was refused. The hospital patients were therefore spared the undue stimulation of a sensuously plucked eyebrow, and unmodified female shapes continued to glide through the long white corridors.

The face. Before leaving the facial region, it is worth taking a last glance at it as a whole, rather than as a set of smaller details. It is, without any doubt, the most expressive region of the entire human body, capable of transmitting incredibly varied and subtle emotional messages by means of its complex expressions. By contracting and relaxing the special muscles, particularly those around the mouth and eyes, we can signal everything from joy and surprise to sadness and anger. As a device for inviting intimacy, this is of major importance. A face that is soft and smiling, or alert and excited, attracts us strongly. One that is forlorn and helpless, or in agony, may also stimulate us to approach and console. A tense, hard or grumpy face has the opposite effect. This is common enough knowledge, but there is an interesting long-term effect that operates on the human face, and which deserves brief comment.

Where facial expressions are concerned, we can speak of an 'on-face' and an 'off-face'. The on-face is the one we use during social encounters. We speak of 'putting on a happy face', or 'putting a good face on it', and we try to avoid 'losing face' in public. If we want to appear friendly, we adopt a soft, smiling expression. Alternatively, we set our faces into a grim or pompous look to cope with more serious occasions. When we are alone and unseen, however, we let our faces go off-duty. When this happens they arrange themselves into the posture typical of our overall long-term mood. The basically anxiety-ridden man, who tried his best to look happy at the party, now tenses up his solitary face, revealing his true emotional condition, but revealing it, of course, to no one but himself. (Unless he catches sight of himself in a mirror, even he may not be aware of it.) The basically happy and contented man, who tried his best to look sad and serious at the funeral, now relaxes his solitary face, with his lips softened and the furrows in his brow smoothed out.

Most of us change our long-term moods from time to time, so that our facial muscles do not experience prolonged exposure to one particular off-face condition. We may feel depressed in the morning but happy again by the evening, and in our solitary moments our facial postures will vary accordingly. For individuals who live in a state of more or less permanent private anxiety, depression or anger, the situation is different. For them, there is a danger that their off-faces will become completely set. In such instances, the facial musculature seems to become moulded in one basic expression. The crease lines on the forehead, around the mouth and at the side of the nose become almost permanent.

Such people find it hard to switch to the appropriate on-face during social encounters. The anxious person still looks anxious even when smiling a greeting. The grumpy man still looks grumpy even when laughing at a joke. The set of the muscles somehow survives and the on-face becomes superimposed on the off-face, rather than replacing it. In this way, facial expressions can tell us something about a person's past as well as his present emotional condition.

It is not clear how long these off-face wrinkles will last after there has been a fundamental change in a way of life. If someone who has been anxious and worried all his life suddenly achieves a contented condition, the wrinkles will not vanish overnight. If the person in question is elderly when this welcome change occurs, they may never fade. Certainly, in all such cases there will be a period of time when the old set-face will be lingering on despite the fact that its message is no longer relevant, but I know of no studies in which the length of this period has been measured.

These comments also apply, incidentally, to the general body posture of the human being. There are slumped bodies and alert bodies, stiffly tense bodies and softly lithe ones. Again, we are capable of changing our body-muscle tensions to match our social moods and occasions, but, as with the face, a prolonged, extreme condition can give us a set posture that is difficult to shake off even when we want to. Rounded shoulders can develop into a permanent hunch that even winning a million cannot straighten out, and a tense stiff-legged walk can become a companion for life.

The hair. Finally we reach man's crowning glory, his densely packed mop of roughly 100,000 head-hairs. In some races these are woolly or frizzy, in others they hang down long and straight, or flow in the wind. They grow at a rate of nearly five inches a year, and each one lasts up to six years before it falls out and is replaced. This means that the average uncut head of straight hair would reach down to the hips, and must have given an unbarbered, primitive human being an extraordinary appearance, when compared with any other species of primate. While our body hair became stunted and almost invisible at a distance, our head hair ran amok.

Apart from the fact that older males, but not older females, tend to become bald in many cases, there is no sex difference in the head hair. Biologically, both men and women are long-haired, and this characteristic has developed as a species recognition signal, rather than a sexual one. Culturally, however, it has frequently been modified as a gender signal. Sometimes men have worn longer hair than women, but usually the reverse has been the case. In recent centuries, masculine hair has been cropped basically as an anti-parasite device, aggressive army sergeants referring to long male hairs as 'louse-ladders'. Women have nearly always maintained a moderate hair length; it is the men who have fluctuated wildly from one extreme to the other. In the past this has sometimes led to the wearing of huge, drooping male wigs, a practice still seen today in the case of British judges. In general, however, the longer locks of recent times have become so firmly associated with the female sex that for a man to wear his hair in anything remotely approaching its natural length has been quite wrongly viewed as essentially feminine. During the last decade this situation has changed dramatically amongst young males, and hair length seems once again to be re-establishing itself in its truly non-sexual role. It is perhaps ironic that, although it is modern hygiene that has made this so much less of a parasite risk, it is the anti-hygiene hippie movement that has taken the lead.

Cleaning, grooming, washing and oiling the hair has always been an important accompaniment to its cultural use as a sexual signal. Ancient urbanites, like their modern counterparts, were prepared to go to great lengths to obtain the desired effect. The oldest known hair tonic consisted of 'Paws of a dog, one part; kernels of dates, one part; hoof of a donkey, one part. Cook thoroughly with oil and anoint.' Today, glistening, gleaming, swishing hair remains almost every girl's ideal and, as the advertisers repeatedly tell us, hair that is 'dull and lifeless' ruins its owner's chances of inviting intimacy.

In this grand tour of the signalling human body the different parts have been taken one by one, but there is still the whole person to be considered. The isolated parts are displayed not singly but all at once, in a general combination and in a specific context. It is the tremendously varied way in which they can combine with one another, and the great range of contexts in which they can be presented, that makes social interaction so complex and so fascinating. Every time we enter a room, or walk down a street, we are transmitting a mass of signals, some purely biological and others culturally modified, and we are always unconsciously aware of this fact and adjusting them in a hundred subtle ways as we move through our many kinds of social encounter. Nearly always we are striving to send out a balanced set of signals, some attracting intimacy, others repelling it. Just occasionally we go much further in one direction or the other, either displaying our invitations blatantly, or presenting ourselves in a hostile, rejecting manner to those around us.

Throughout this chapter, in surveying the various visual invitations to sexual intimacy, I have tended to dwell on extremes. I have selected the most vivid examples in order to underline the points I have been making. Codpieces, corsets and epaulets may seem remote from the ordinary signals of sex appeal used by the average adult of today, but they nevertheless help to draw our attention to the less exaggerated devices – the tight trousers, the belts and the padded shoulders – that are more widely and less obviously employed. Similarly, belly-dancing may be no more than an exotic form of entertainment, but again its inclusion in this survey helps us to appreciate the less extreme dance movements used nightly by hundreds of thousands of ordinary girls at parties and discotheques.

Whether, as adults, we go to great lengths to improve and display our visual signals of sex appeal, or whether we treat the whole business in a more off-hand manner, whether we resort to artificial aids (and there are few of us who do not employ *some*), or whether we scorn them and prefer a more 'natural' approach, we are all of us constantly transmitting a complex set of visual signals to our companions. Many of these signals inevitably have to do with our adult sexual qualities, and even when we are totally unaware of what we are doing, we never stop 'reading the signs'. In this way we prepare ourselves for a major social step – the step that leads us to initiate the first tentative contact with a potential sexual partner and carries us over a vital threshold into the whole complex world of sexual intimacy itself.

3

SEXUAL INTIMACY

IN DISCOVERING HIS personal identity, the growing child must reject the soft embrace of his mother's arms. At last, as a young adult, he stands alone. As a baby, his trust in his mother was unlimited, his intimacy total. Now, in maturity, both his relationships with other adults and his intimacies with them are severely limited. Like them, he keeps his distance. Blind trust is replaced by alert manœuvring, dependency by interdependency. The gentle intimacies of infancy that gave way to the joyful games of childhood have become the tough social transactions of adulthood.

There is no denying the excitement. There are things to explore, goals to achieve and status to be raised. But where did all the loving go? Loving was an act of giving, giving oneself without question to another person, but adult relationships are not like that . . .

Up to this point my words could apply as much to a growing monkey as to a growing human. The pattern is the same. But now comes a difference. If the monkey is a male, it will never again, as an adult, know the total intimacy of a loving bond. Until the day it dies, it will continue to exist in the loveless world of rivalries and partnerships, of competition and co-operation. If it is a female, it will eventually regain the loving condition, as a mother with an infant of its own, but like the male it will know no such bond with another adult monkey. Close friendships, yes; partnerships, yes; brief sexual encounters, yes; but total intimacy, no.

For the adult human, however, there is such a possibility. He is capable of forming a powerful and lasting bond of attachment for a member of the opposite sex that is much more than a mere partnership. To say that 'marriage is a partnership', as is so often done, is to insult it, and to completely misunderstand the true nature of a bond of love. A mother and her baby are not 'partners'. The baby does not trust the mother because she feeds and protects him; he loves her because she is who she is, not because of what she does. In a partnership one merely exchanges favours; the partner does not give for the sake of giving. But between a pair of adult human lovers there develops a relationship like that between mother and child. A total trust develops and, with it, a total bodily intimacy. There is no 'give and take' in true loving, only

44

giving. The fact that it is 'two-way giving' obscures this, but the 'two-way receiving' that inevitably results from it is not a condition of the giving, as it is in a partnership; it is simply a pleasing adjunct to it.

For the cautious, calculating adult, the entry into such a relationship appears a hazardous affair. The resistance to 'letting go' and trusting is enormous. It breaks all the rules of bargaining and dealing that he is so used to in all his other adult relationships. Without some help from the lower centres of his brain, his higher centres would never permit it. But in our species that help is forthcoming and, often against all reason, we fall in love. For some, the natural process is suppressed, and if they do enter into a state of marriage or its equivalent, they do so as if it were a business transaction: you rear child, I earn money. This 'baby-buying', or 'status-buying', has sadly become commonplace in our crowded human zoos, but it is fraught with dangers. The mated pair are held together, not by internal bonds of attachment, but by the external pressures of social convention. This means that the couple's natural potential for falling in love still lies waiting inside their brains and can leap into action without warning at any time, to create a true bond somewhere outside their official one.

For the lucky ones this sequence does not take place. As young adults, they find themselves falling in love uncontrollably and forming a true bond of attachment. The process is a gradual one, although it does not always appear to be. 'Love at first sight' is a popular concept. It is, however, usually a retrospective judgment. What occurs is not 'total trust at first sight', but 'powerful attraction at first sight'. The progress from first attraction to final trust is nearly always a long and complex sequence of gradually increasing intimacies, and it is this sequence that we must now examine.

To do so, the simplest method is to take a pair of 'typical lovers', as seen in our Western culture, and follow them through the process of pair-formation from first glimpse to ultimate copulation. In doing this we must always remember that there is in reality no such thing as the 'typical lover', any more than there is the 'average citizen' or 'man in the street'. But it helps if we start out by trying to imagine one, and then, afterwards, consider the variations.

All animal courtship patterns are organized in a typical sequence, and the course taken by a human love affair is no exception. For convenience we can divide the human sequence up into twelve stages, and see what happens as each threshold is successfully passed. The twelve (obviously over-simplified) stages are these.

1. *Eye to body*. The most common form of social 'contact' is to look at people from a distance. In a fraction of a second it is possible to sum up the physical qualities of another adult, labelling them and grading

45

them mentally in the process. The eyes feed the brain with immediate information concerning the sex, size, shape, age, colouring, status and mood of the other person. Simultaneously a grading takes place on a scale from extreme attractiveness to extreme repulsiveness. If the signs indicate that the individual in view is an attractive member of the opposite sex, then we are ready to move on to the next phase in the sequence.

2. *Eye to eye*. While we view others, they view us. From time to time this means that our eyes meet, and when this happens the usual reaction is to look away quickly and break the eye 'contact'. This will not happen, of course, if we have recognized one another as previous acquaintances. In such cases, the moment of recognition leads instantly to mutual greeting signals, such as sudden smiling, raising of the eyebrows, changes in body posture, movements of the arms and eventually vocalizations. If, on the other hand, we have locked eyes with a stranger, then the rapid looking away is the typical reaction, as if to avoid the temporary invasion of privacy. If one of the two strangers does continue to stare after eye contact has been made, the other may become acutely embarrassed and even angry. If it is possible to move away to avoid the staring eyes, this will soon be done, even though there was no element of aggression in the facial expressions or gestures accompanying the stare. This is because to perform prolonged staring is in itself an act of aggression between unfamiliar adults. The result is that two strangers normally watch one another in turn, rather than simultaneously. If, then, one finds the other attractive, he or she may add a slight smile to the next meeting of glances. If the response is returned, so is the smile, and further, more intimate contact may ensue. If the response is not returned, a blank look in reply to a friendly smile will usually stop any further development.

3. *Voice to voice*. Assuming there is no third party to make introductions, the next stage involves vocal contact between the male and female strangers. Invariably the initial comments will concern trivia. It is rare at this stage to make any direct reference to the true mood of the speakers. This small-talk permits the reception of a further set of signals, this time to the ear instead of the eye. Dialect, tone of voice, accent, mode of verbal thinking and use of vocabulary permit a whole new range of units of information to be fed into the brain. Maintaining this communication at the level of irrelevant small-talk enables either side to retreat from further involvement, should the new signals prove unattractive despite the promise of the earlier, visual signals.

4. *Hand to hand*. The previous three stages can all occur in seconds, or they may take months, with one potential partner silently admiring the other from a distance, not daring to make vocal contact. This new

stage, the hand to hand, may also take place quickly, in the form of the introduction handshake, or it is likely to be delayed for some considerable time. If the formalized, non-sexual handshake does not come into operation, then the first actual body contact to occur is likely to be disguised as an act of 'supporting aid', 'body protection' or 'directional guidance'. This is usually performed by the male towards the female and consists of holding her arm or hand to help her cross a street, or climb over an obstruction. If she is about to walk into an obstacle or danger spot, then the hand of the male can quickly take the opportunity to reach out swiftly and take her arm to alter her course or check her movement. If she slips or trips, a supporting action with the hands may also facilitate the first body contact. Again, the use of acts which are irrelevant to the true mood of the encounter is important. If the body of the girl has been touched by the man in the act of assisting her in some way, either partner can still withdraw from further involvement without loss of face. The girl can thank the man for his help and leave him, without being forced into a position where she has to deliver a direct rebuff. Both parties may be well aware that a behaviour sequence is just beginning, and that it is one that may lead eventually to greater intimacies, but neither as yet does anything which openly states this fact, so that there is still time for one to back out without hurting the other's feelings. Only when the growing relationship has been openly declared will the action of hand-holding or arm-holding become prolonged in duration. It then ceases to be a 'supportive' or 'guiding' act and becomes an undisguised intimacy.

5. *Arm to shoulder*. Up to this point the bodies have not come into close contact. When they do so, another important threshold has been passed. Whether sitting, standing or walking, physical contact down the side of the body indicates a great advance in the relationship from its earlier hesitant touchings. The earliest method employed is the shoulder embrace, usually with the man's arm placed around the girl's shoulders to draw the two partners together. This is the simplest introduction to trunk contact because it is already used in other contexts between mere friends as an act of non-sexual companionship. It is therefore the smallest next step to take, and the least likely to meet rebuff. Walking together in this posture can be given the air of slight ambiguity, half way between close friendship and love.

6. *Arm to waist*. A slight advance on the last stage occurs with the wrapping of the arm around the waist. This is something the man will not have done to other men, no matter how friendly, so that it becomes more of a direct statement of amorous intimacy. Furthermore, his hand will now be in much closer proximity to the genital region of the female.

7. *Mouth to mouth*. Kissing on the mouth, combined with the full frontal embrace, is a major step forward. For the first time there is a strong chance of physiological arousal, if the action is prolonged or repeated. The female may experience genital secretions and the male's penis may start to become erect.

8. *Hand to head*. As an extension of the last stage, the hands begin to caress the partner's head. Fingers stroke the face, neck and hair. Hands clasp the nape and the side of the head.

9. *Hand to body*. In the post-kissing phase, the hands begin to explore the partner's body, squeezing, fondling and stroking. The major advance here is the manipulation by the male of the female's breasts. Further physiological arousal occurs with these acts and reaches such a pitch that, for many young females, this is a point at which a temporary halt is called. Further developments mean increasing difficulty in breaking off the pattern without continuing to completion, and if the bond of attachment has not reached a sufficient level of mutual trust, more advanced sexual intimacies are postponed.

10. *Mouth to breast*. Here the threshold is passed in which the interactions become strictly private. For most couples this will also have applied to the last stage, especially where breast manipulations are concerned, but advanced kissing and body-fondling does occur frequently in public places under certain circumstances. Such actions may cause reactions of disapproval in other members of the public, but it is rare in most countries for serious steps to be taken against the embracing couple. With the advance to breast-kissing, however, the situation is entirely different, if only because it involves the exposure of the female breast. Mouth-to-breast contacts are the last of the pre-genital intimacies and are the prelude to actions which are concerned not merely with arousal, but with arousal to climax.

11. *Hand to genitals*. If the manual exploration of the partner's body continues, it inevitably arrives at the genital region. After tentative caressing of the partner's genitals, the actions soon develop into gentle, rhythmic rubbing that simulates the rhythm of pelvic thrusting. The male repeatedly strokes the labia or clitoris of the female and may insert his finger or fingers into the vagina, imitating the action of the penis. Manual stimulation of this kind can soon lead to orgasm for either sex, and is a common form of culmination in advanced pre-copulatory encounters between lovers.

12. *Genitals to genitals*. Finally, the stage of full copulation is reached and, if the female is a virgin, the first irreversible act of the entire sequence occurs with the rupture of the hymen. There is also, for the first time, the possibility of another irreversible act, namely that of fertilization. This irreversibility puts this concluding act in the se-

quence on to an entirely new plane. Each stage will have served to tighten the bond of attachment a little more, but, in a biological sense, this final copulatory action is clearly related to a phase where the earlier intimacies will already have done their job of cementing the bond, so that the pair will want to stay together after the sex drive has been reduced by the consummation of orgasm. If this bonding has failed, the female is liable to find herself pregnant in the absence of a stable family unit.

These then are twelve typical stages in the pair-formation process of a young male and female. To some extent they are, of course, culturally determined, but to a much greater extent they are determined by the anatomy and sexual physiology common to all members of our species. The variations imposed by cultural traditions and conventions, and by the personal peculiarities of certain unusual individuals, will alter this major sequence in a number of ways, and these can now be considered against the background of the typical sequence through which we have just passed.

The variations take three main forms: a reduction of the sequence, an alteration in the order of the acts and an elaboration of the pattern.

The most extreme form of reduction is forcible mating, or rape. Here the first stage runs as quickly as is physically possible to the last stage, with all the intervening phases condensed to the absolute minimum. After eye-to-body contact has been made by the male, he simply attacks the female, omitting all arousal stages, and goes as rapidly to genital-to-genital contact as her resistance will allow. The non-genital body contacts are limited purely to those necessary to overpower her and strip her genital region of clothing.

Viewed objectively, rape in the human species lacks two important ingredients: pair-formation and sexual arousal. The rapist male, by omitting all the intermediate stages of the sexual sequence, clearly does not allow a bond of attachment to grow between himself and the female in question. This is obvious enough, but it is relevant in biological terms, because our species does require this personal attachment to develop, as a means of safeguarding the successful rearing of the offspring that may result from the copulation. There are other species, with little or no parental responsibilities, where, in theory, rape would create no problems. That it is rare is due, amongst other things, to the physical difficulty of achieving the goal of rape. A man without a pair of grasping hands and verbalized threats would find it virtually impossible, and this is a dual advantage which other species lack. Even where animal rape does seem to occur, appearances can be deceptive. For example, carnivores can, and most carnivore species do, grab their females by the scruff of the neck with their jaws during the act of mating, as if to prevent their mates from escaping, but there is still the problem of successfully inserting the penis into the vagina of a writhing female form. If the female is unresponsive, the male stands little chance. The truth is that the superficially savage act of neck-gripping in male carnivores is a rather specialized movement. Although it looks like the act of a rapist male, it is in fact the carnivore equivalent of a gentle parental embrace in our own species. The bite is strongly inhibited, so that the teeth do not harm the female. This is the pattern of behaviour a parent carnivore employs towards its young when carrying them from place to place. The male is, in effect, treating the female like a cub or a kitten, and if she is sexually responsive to him, she reacts like one, going limp in his jaws as she once did when being protectively transported by her mother in early life.

For the human male animal, rape is comparatively easy. If physical force is not enough, he can add threats of death or injury. Alternatively he can contrive to render the female unconscious or semi-unconscious, or can enlist the aid of other males to hold her still. If the absence of the female's sexual arousal makes penis insertion difficult or painful, he can always resort to the use of some alternative form of lubrication to replace the missing natural secretions.

For the female in question these proceedings are, to say the least, both unsatisfying and unsatisfactory, and, to say the most, may result in severe trauma and psychological damage. Only in cases of rape where the partners are already known to one another and where the female has a strong masochistic streak is there any chance at all of an emotional attachment developing as a result of this violent reduction of the normal sexual sequence of our species.

I have gone into this question of rape at some length because it bears a close relationship to another form of sexual reduction which is much more widespread and important in our culture. To contrast it with the violent rape we have been discussing, we might call it 'economic rape'. Unlike the violent kind, it occurs, not in derelict building-sites or damp hedgerows, but in decorously draped boudoirs and cosy bedrooms. It is the loveless mating act of the marriage of economic convenience, the act of couples who marry and copulate with only the barest hint of a true bond of attachment.

In past centuries, the parentally controlled status marriage was commonplace. Today it is becoming increasingly rare, but the psychological scar it left on the children it spawned is more lasting. As growing, developing witnesses to this loveless relationship, the offspring of the match were themselves in danger of becoming sexually crippled, so that they were incapable of expressing the full amatory sequence typical of our species. Their sexual anatomy was in perfect working order; their physiological arousal mechanisms were operating efficiently; but their ability to relate these biological features to a deep and lasting bond of attachment will have been stunted by the atmosphere in which they matured. They, in turn, will find it difficult to make successful pair-bonds, but social pressures will encourage them to try, and once again the next generation of children will suffer. Such a reverberation is difficult to eliminate, and the untold damage caused by past cultural interferences with the natural human process of falling deeply in love is still with us today, even though the parentally controlled marriage is fading into history.

The pattern of 'economic rape' is not, of course, as extreme as that of violent rape, in the way in which it condenses the full twelve-stage sequence. Superficially it may appear very similar to the full pattern, with the partners 'going through the motions' of the different stages, one by one, until copulation is reached. But if we examine the actions in detail we find that they are all reduced in intensity, duration and frequency.

Take first the classic case of the young couple who are pushed together to satisfy the economic or status relationship of their two families. In earlier centuries, their pre-marital courtship might typically involve no more than a few abbreviated embraces and kisses, following prolonged verbal exchanges. Then, with little knowledge of one another's bodies or sexual emotions, they are thrust together into a marriage bed. The bride is advised that nasty but necessary things will have to be done to her by her bridegroom in order to ensure the future population of the nation, and that while this is going on, she is to 'lie still and think of England'. The male is given rudimentary instruction concerning female anatomy and told to be gentle with his bride because she will bleed when he penetrates her. With this information the young couple perform their sexual duties as simply and quickly as possible, with a minimum of pleasure and a minimum of pair-bonding. For the female, there is rarely if ever an orgasm. For the male, there is an unresponsive object in his bed, which happens to be his wife, but which sexually is little more than an object, the vagina of which he uses like a hand to masturbate his penis. In their public, social lives the young couple will, naturally, be provided with a set of rules enabling them to simulate a loving relationship. Each of the public intimacies, severely restricted in the form it can take, is precisely described and defined by the books of polite etiquette, so that it will become almost impossible to tell the true loving couple from the false. Almost, but not quite, and for the children it will be painfully easy, for they have not yet had their heads crammed with detailed rules of conduct, and they will intuitively detect the degree of lovingness or lovelessness in their parents' relationship. And so the damage will go on.

If this description seems bizarre today, in the latter half of the twentieth century, then this is not because such marriages no longer occur, but rather because they are less blatantly organized than they once were. A much greater show of loving is put on nowadays to mask such relationships, but a show it remains nevertheless. Parents are less involved than they were, which also disguises the pattern. Now it is one or both members of the pair who set out themselves to construct an economically based marriage. Behind her wedding veil the bride's lips are moving, but she is not overcome with emotion; she is busy calculating her alimony rating. The man at her side with a faraway expression on his face is not lost in a romantic dream, he is working out the impact his socially efficient bride will have on his business colleagues. Admittedly, the brides no longer lie still and think of wherever-it-is on their wedding nights. Instead, they check their orgasm frequencies against the national average for their age group, educational level, and racial and urban background. If they fall below the required level, they employ a firm of private investigators to find out where the husband is relocating the additional 1.7 orgasms per week that they should be getting. Meanwhile the husbands are trying to estimate how many early evening drinks they can consume before running the risk of alcoholically impairing their ability to achieve an insertable erection later that night. All too often it is these that are the sweet mysteries of life in modern urbania.

In looking at reductions in the sexual sequence, we have progressed from rape, to the parentally controlled marriage of the past, to the so-called 'bitch/bastard' marriage of modern times. The obsession with orgasm frequency in the last of these is an important new development that appears to lead us away from the reduction and compression of the full sexual sequence that we were discussing. Indeed, it looks like a swing in the other direction, towards elaboration rather than reduction. But the matter is not quite so simple. Basically, what has happened in the new 'sexual freedom' is that the later stages have been given much greater emphasis. The elaboration of the sequence has all been concentrated at one end of it – the copulatory end. The earlier courtship patterns, so important for pair-formation, instead of being elaborated, have been reduced and simplified. It is worth trying to discover the way this has come about.

In earlier centuries, the courtship stages were prolonged in time, but severely restricted in intensity. Insistence on obeying formal rules of procedure, down to the last detail, reduced their emotional impact. Then, after marriage, the later pre-copulatory and copulatory patterns were strongly curtailed by ignorance and anti-erotic propaganda. The males solved this problem with brothels and mistresses. The females, by and large, did not solve it. In the first half of the present century the situation changed. Parental control was loosened and serious attempts were made at sexual education, with the publication of books on 'married love'. The result was that young couples were much freer to search for a partner that suited them and to indulge in less formalized courtship activities. The phenomenon of the chaperone vanished. The rules of conduct for body contact were relaxed, so that virtually all stages of the sexual intimacy sequence were permitted, excluding only the final, genital ones. These pre-marital activities were, however, still expected to cover a considerable period of time. Eventually, when marriage did take place, the couple were able to take to their mating bed with a much greater knowledge of one another's bodies and emotional personalities. Efficient contraception had appeared on the scene, combining with the new sexual knowledge to make marital pleasures less restricted and more satisfying.

During this phase there was a tendency for young couples, before marriage, to indulge in prolonged 'petting sessions'. The idea that they were now allowed to go so far, but no further, seemed good in theory, but was difficult in practice. The reason is obvious enough. Unlike the young couples of earlier days, they were now permitted to go past the first stages of courtship – the ones which helped to form a bond of attachment, but which did not produce strong physiological arousal of the sex organs – and on into the stages which were really concerned with pre-copulatory stimulation. The half-way mark between the two is the act of the mouth-to-mouth kiss. Simply performed this is a pleasant bonding act, but energetically repeated it is also the starting point of pre-copulatory arousal.

This led to a new type of crisis for the young lovers. Prolonged petting resulted in prolonged erections for the males and prolonged sexual secretions for the females. One of three things then happened: they broke off the sequence in accordance with 'official ruling' and remained intensely frustrated, or they continued by non-copulatory means to achieve mutual orgasm, or they broke the rules and copulated. If they used the second method and masturbated or fondled one another to orgasm, and if they continued to do this over a long pre-marital period, there was always the danger that this pattern of climax would begin to assume too great a significance in their sexual relationship, making for difficulties when, eventually, they were able to complete the act of copulation after marriage. If they chose the third alternative and broke the rules, there was the problem of guilt and secrecy. Nevertheless, despite these difficulties, the prolonged pre-marital phase was strongly conducive to the formation of a power-ful bond of attachment, so that it had a great deal to commend it over the previous situation, when the couple were severely restricted in their actions.

Moving on now to more recent times, a new change has occurred. Although official attitudes may still be the same, they are less strictly enforced. With further improvements in contraception, virginity has lost its significance for many young girls. The non-copulation rule that was once reluctantly broken is now commonly ignored. Virginity, far from being prized, has almost become a stigma, an indication of some kind of sexual inadequacy. Pre-marital copulation is an accepted pattern by the young lovers, if not by their parents. The result of this development, which is more widespread than some people like to admit, is that the lovers no longer experience the intense 'petting frustrations' of their predecessors, nor are they in danger of becoming fixated on masturbatory activities. Instead, their courtship grows naturally, and without undue postponement, into the full twelve-stage sexual sequence.

Assuming the existence of adequate venereal hygiene and efficient, readily available contraception, what, if any, is the danger of this new situation? The answer, as some have seen it, is the 'tyranny of the orgasm', the need created by the social pressures of the new permissive convention to achieve maximum copulatory performance. This is seen as a threat to the person who truly falls in love, but who is incapable of sufficiently impressive orgasmic achievements.

There is something curiously short-sighted about this criticism. Earlier I did mention the obsession with orgasm frequency, but that was in connection with the loveless marriage, the modern equivalent of the economic or status marriage. There, as I pointed out, the female may feel she has failed if her sexual athleticism is below standard, because she is concerned, even in matters of sex, with the business of status. But if two young people are in love today, they will laugh at the desperate athleticism of the copulating non-lovers. For them, as for true lovers at all points in history, a fleeting touch on the cheek from the one they adore will be worth more than six hours in thirty-seven positions with someone they do not. This has always been so, but for these new lovers there is the added advantage that, circumstances permitting, they are no longer restricted to a mere cheek touch. They can do anything they wish with one another's bodies, as much *or* as little as they wish. If the powerful bond of attachment has formed, then it will be the quality of the sexual behaviour that counts, not its mere quantity. For them, the new conventions simply permit, they do not insist, as some critics seem to think.

Another point which the critics seem to miss is that when a couple have started to fall in love, they will not want to omit the earlier stages of the sexual sequence. They will not give up holding hands merely because they are permitted to copulate. Furthermore, they are not the ones who will be likely to have much trouble in quite naturally enjoying maximum orgasmic pleasure when they reach the final stages of the sequence. The emotional intensity of their personal relationship will ensure this, and they will happily reach climax after climax without having to resort to the contorted wrestlers' postures of the ubiquitous modern sex manuals.

Perhaps the greatest danger that the permissive young lovers face today is an economic one, for they still inhabit a complex, economically structured society, and it was no accident that economics came to figure so largely in the marriages of yesterday. Previously this aspect was safeguarded by all the rigid restrictions placed on early sexual behaviour. Sexual intimacy suffered, but social status was ensured and organized. Now the social status of the young pair has become a problem, as sexual intimacy blossoms. How can a pair of seventeen-year-old lovers, who are fully sexually mature, who have developed a powerful bond of attachment, and who are enjoying a full sexual life, set up home in our modern economy? Either they have to wait in a kind of social limbo, or they have to 'drop out' of the accepted social pattern. The choice is not an easy one, and the problem has yet to be solved.

We arrived at this discussion by considering the ways in which the sexual sequence becomes reduced from its full expression. We must now leave the young lovers, fully expressing it, but enduring considerable social problems in so doing, and return to the reductions once more. What of the sexually active non-lover? We have dealt with the rapist and the sexually inhibited marriage partners who reduced their copulatory stages to a child-spawning minimum, but what about the loveless sexual athletes of today? How do they reduce the sexual sequence of the typical lovers? For them, the later genital stages are not expressed as the culmination of a pattern, but as a replacement for it. In earlier times this was precisely what occurred when a man visited a prostitute. There was no holding of hands, no cuddling or murmuring of sweet nothings, merely a quick business transaction and then straight to direct genital contact. What we might call 'commercial rape'. In previous generations this was often a young man's first introduction to copulation, but today such professional services are hardly necessary. Instead they are replaced by what is referred to as 'sleeping around'. In such cases there is frequently a massive reduction in the early stages of the sequence, just as there was with the visit to the prostitute. The situation is summed up by the girl in the cartoon who says 'Boys simply don't want to kiss any more', as she returns late at night to her room in an obvious post-copulatory condition, exhausted and with her clothes dishevelled, but with her make-up still neatly intact.

The result of this type of reduction is to provide the maximum of copulatory activity with the minimum of pair-bond development. As a status device this may permit repeated ego-boosting, but as a source of intense pleasure it degrades sexual activity to the level of something like urinating. It is not surprising, therefore, that for the 'permissive', non-loving copulator some elaboration of the consummatory act becomes desirable. If it has lost its emotional intensity along with its powerful bond of personal attachment, then it must be given some increased physical intensity as a compensation. This is where the illustrated sexual manuals come on the scene, and it is worth analysing some of them to see what they recommend.

A sample taken at random from the large number now on sale included a combined total of several hundred photographs, each showing a young naked couple in the act of 'making love'. Of these illustrations, no more than 4 per cent showed any of the first eight stages in my twelve-stage sequence described earlier. By contrast, 82 per cent showed full copulation, each book including between thirty and fifty posture variations. This means that the vast majority of all the various sexual intimacies were illustrated as the final stage of genital/genital contact, and clearly demonstrates the great emphasis placed on this concluding element of the sequence. Whereas previous censorship limited the illustration of amorous activities to the earlier stages, the removal of this censorship, instead of enriching the situation, has simply had the effect of shifting concentration from one end of the scale to the other. The implied message is that the act of copulation should be made as complex and varied as possible, and forget about the rest. Many of the postures shown are obviously uncomfortable, if not actually painful to maintain for any length of time, except possibly for trained circus acrobats. Their inclusion can only reflect a desperate search for copulatory novelty as a means to obtaining further arousal. The emphasis is no longer on loving, but on sexual athletics.

There is, of course, nothing harmful about these patterns as amusing and playful additions to sexual behaviour, but if obsession with them replaces and excludes the personal emotional aspects of the interaction between the male and female involved, then their ultimate effect is to decrease the true value of the relationship. They may elaborate one element of the sexual sequence, but overall they reduce it.

Young lovers who *need* these copulation variations, rather than merely play with them in an exploratory fashion from time to time, are perhaps not young lovers at all. At a later point, when they have passed right through the intense pair-formation stage of their lives, and have arrived at the more mellow pair-maintenance phase, they may well find that some embellishments and novel additions to their sexual activities will provide a valuable way to re-heighten intensity, but if as young lovers they are truly in love it is surprising if this will be necessary.

Needless to say, this does not mean that any of these sexual intimacies, no matter how contrived or unusual, should be condemned or suppressed. Providing they are performed voluntarily in private by adults and cause no physical harm, there is no biological reason why they should be outlawed or attacked by society. In certain countries this is still, however, the case. One example concerns oral/genital contacts, which I omitted from my earlier twelve-stage list. The reason why they were not included is because they do not represent a clear-cut stage in the progress from first encounter between the lovers to final copulation. In the vast majority of cases they appear only after the first copulations have occurred, as a further embellishment of the genital intimacies. Later, when copulation has become a regular feature of a relationship, they are frequently included as a standard pre-copulatory pattern, and evidence from ancient art and history indicates that they have long been so employed.

Modern American surveys indicate that today oral/genital contacts are used by about half of all married couples as part of their pre-copulatory activities. The application of the male mouth to the female genitals was recorded in 54 per cent of cases, that of female mouth to male genitals in 49 per cent. Although this is well below the figures for the other pre-copulatory patterns in my twelve-stage list (mouth to mouth, hand to breast, mouth to breast, and hand to genitals all occur in over 90 per cent of cases), an average of roughly 50 per cent of the population for mouth-to-genital contact can hardly justify calling this activity 'abnormal'. Yet despite this, and despite the fact that it occurs widely in other mammalian species, it is often regarded as an 'unnatural' intimacy. It is condemned by the Judaeo-Christian religious codes, even between married partners, and in many places it is not only considered immoral but is also illegal. It is surprising to find that, right into the second half of the twentieth century, this has been the case in almost all the states in the United States of America. To be more specific, in only Kentucky and South Carolina can an American married couple privately engage in any kind of oral/genital contact without breaking the law. This means that in recent times 50 per cent of all other Americans have, technically speaking, been sexual law-breakers at some time in their married lives. In the states where it is outlawed, the act is rated as a felony everywhere except in New York, where it is classified as a mere 'misdemeanor'. In the states of Illinois, Wisconsin, Mississippi and Ohio, the law has applied a curious kind of sexual inequality, the act being legal when the husband makes oral contact with his wife's genitals, but a felony when she performs a similar intimacy with him.

These strange legal restrictions have seldom been applied in practice and have been rendered nonsensical in recent years, during which open sale and advertisement of flavoured vaginal douches has been permitted in America, but they do appear from time to time in divorce cases, where oral/genital acts have been cited as factors contributing to 'mental cruelty' in marriage. It has also been pointed out that, in theory, these laws could lead to instances of blackmail. Biologically, as I have already pointed out, there is no case against mouth-to-genital contacts. On the contrary, if they heighten the emotional intensity of pre-copulatory activities, they will merely serve to tighten the bonds of attachment between the mated pair and thereby strengthen the married condition which is so vigorously protected in so many other ways by the Church and the laws of the land.

If we examine the exact form which this type of intimacy takes in the human species, it is possible to detect a difference between man and the other mammals that employ mouth-to-genital contacts. Usually, in other species, the action begins as sniffing and nuzzling and then extends into licking. Rhythmic friction is less common. The significance of the act lies in the acquisition of detailed information concerning the state of the partner's genitals. Unlike man, other mammalian species only come into full sexual condition at certain times of the year, or at certain restricted phases of the menstrual cycle, and it is important for the partner, especially the male, to know as much as possible about the precise state of arousal before attempting copulation. The application of the nose and tongue to the genital region provides valuable clues concerning odour, taste and texture. The actual stimulation of the partner by these contacts is probably of secondary importance.

In man, the situation is reversed, the stimulation element becoming more important. The mouth is employed to arouse the partner rather than to learn about his or her sexual condition. It is for this reason that, in man, rhythmic friction takes on a more important role than mere touching or licking, the female using her mouth as a pseudo-vagina and simulating the actions of pelvic thrusting by movements of her neck. The male may also use his tongue as a pseudo-penis, but he is more likely to employ clitoral stimulation, using rhythmic tongue pressure. Again, he will imitate the repeated massage of the female organ that occurs during the pelvic thrusting of copulation itself. The great advantage to the male of this form of mimic-copulation is that he can provide prolonged stimulation for the female without himself becoming orgasmically satiated. In this way he can compensate for the longer time the average female takes to reach the orgasmic level.

This last fact no doubt explains why the extensive use of this type of sexual intimacy is more common amongst males than females. A contrast, however, has been found in the portrayal of these acts in 'blue movies'. A recent study of the history of films of this type made over the past half-century reveals that here the female action is portrayed much more frequently than the male. There is a special reason for this. These films have traditionally been made for use at all-male gatherings, or 'stag-parties', and are often referred to as 'stag movies'. Such occasions have little to do with love, being concerned instead with sex as a status device. If male status is involved, the historians of blue movies have pointed out that it 'belittles' the man to show him in a subordinate posture to the female, but enhances his feelings of dominance to portray him in the superior role of being 'served' by the female. Here we are back to basic animal behaviour and the postures of inferior submissions. When kneeling and bowing are performed as submissive acts, their biological significance lies in the lowering of the inferior's body in front of the superior. It is significant that the slang expression for oral/genital contact in man is 'going down' on the partner. In order to apply the mouth to the genitals, the active partner must considerably lower his or her body in relation to that of the passive one. This applies in any position, but is particularly clear when the act is performed with the passive partner standing. The active male or female must then kneel or crouch in front of the standing body to apply the mouth to the genital region, thus entailing the adoption of an almost medieval posture of servility. It is little wonder, then, that the performance of this act by the female to the male appeals so strongly to the status sex gatherings of males at stag-parties. Between lovers in private, of course, the situation is entirely different. Unless the encounter is one of loveless sexual gratification, the act will be one of giving pleasure and not of status-boosting, and will show no such bias. Because of the time-lag difference in reaching orgasm that exists between the sexes, it will then, as we have already seen, become more commonly extended as a male action rather than a female one.

In considering variations in the basic sexual sequence, we have so far been dealing with some of the ways in which it has been reduced and elaborated, but I also mentioned a third possibility, namely shifts in the order of appearance of the acts. Clearly these are many, and the fixed sequence I outlined is often altered in some way. As it stands, it is no more than a rough guide to the general trend which the various actions follow, from the moment of the first encounter to the final pattern of copulation. It remains a true picture of the average sequence of events, but the formalization of certain specific elements will have a marked effect on the order in which they follow one another in many cases. Some examples will clarify this.

The first three acts listed were: eye to body, eye to eye, and voice to voice. These pre-tactile 'contacts' rarely change position in the sequence. Today, exceptions can occur in instances where the initial encounter takes place over the telephone, and one sometimes hears someone say, 'It's pleasant to meet after having spoken on the phone so often.' This implies that vocal exchanges on the telephone do not by themselves constitute a 'meeting'. Combined with eye contact, however, they do. The phrase 'we met last year' need not signify any tactile contact, but merely a combination of visual and verbal exchanges. Nevertheless, a 'meeting' does usually include at least the minimal body contact of the handshake. To 'meet someone' it does seem important to have displayed some degree of physical touching. Since, in modern life, we encounter so many strangers, it is not surprising to find that this initial touching is rigidly stylized in form. A more variable type of body contact would involve too great an intimacy at such an early stage in the time-scale of the sequence of a developing relationship.

Because it has become so formalized, the handshake can frequently jump almost to the front of the whole sequence. A third party says simply, 'Here is someone I want you to meet'; and, within seconds of making eye contact, skin contact has taken place, the two hands immediately stretching out and joining. The action may even occur slightly before verbal contact has been made.

This basic rule, that the more formalized a contact action becomes, the more it can jump forward in the sequence, is also particularly well illustrated by the mouth-to-mouth kiss. Although, strictly speaking, this is the first of the pre-copulatory arousal actions, and should belong to the second half of the sequence rather than the first, it often jumps forward in time by virtue of the accepted convention of the 'goodnight kiss' between young lovers. It is significant that the first kiss usually takes place as an act of farewell. The device employed here, which enables the kiss, combined with a full frontal embrace, to jump ahead of the less intimate semi-embraces of arm-around-shoulder and arm-around-waist, and possibly even hand-holding, is the way in which it borrows 'innocence' from the non-sexual kissing of family greetings and farewells. The young couple, having met and talked for some hours, may, at the moment of parting, go straight into a brief, formal embrace-and-kiss, even though they have not touched one another's bodies previously in any way. This contrasts sharply with the situation where a man visits a prostitute, when the kiss may drop back in the sequence to a point where genital contact has already been made, or where kissing may even be totally omitted.

It will have become obvious that, in discussing these sexual variations, I have been thinking primarily of modern 'civilized' societies. In other cultures and tribes the patterns vary to a certain extent, but the general principles of a sequence of escalating intimacy still apply. An American survey of nearly two hundred different human cultures revealed that 'unless social conditioning imposes inhibitions upon active foreplay it is very likely to occur'. Nearly all the arousal actions occur in most societies, but sometimes they take a slightly different form. The nose, for example, occasionally takes over from the mouth as a contact organ, nose-rubbing or -pressing replacing mouth-kissing. In certain tribes, mutual nose-and-face-pressing appears at the point where, more usually, mouth-to-face or mouth-to-mouth contacts would occur. In others, mouth-to-mouth and nose-to-nose contacts are performed simultaneously. Some males employ nose-rubbing rather than lip contact, to stimulate the female breasts. In other tribes, kissing takes the form of placing the lips close to the partner's face and inhaling. In still others, it is more a question of reciprocal lip-and-tongue-sucking. These variations of detail are interesting in their own right, but to over-emphasize their importance, as has sometimes been done in the past, is to obscure the fact that, in more general terms, there is a great similarity in the courtship and pre-copulatory patterns of all human beings.

Having looked at the sequence of human sexual intimacies, we now come to the question of their frequency. I have gone on record as saying that man is the sexiest of all the primates, a comment which has met with some criticism. The biological evidence, however, is irrefutable, and the argument that the high level of sexual activity observed in certain quarters today is the artificial product of civilized life is nonsensical. If anything, it is the remarkably *low* level of sexual activity in certain other quarters that can best be ascribed to the artificiality of modern living. As anyone who has been under severe stress will know, anxiety is a powerful anti-sexual influence, and, since there is a great deal of stress involved in the high-pressure existence of our modern urban communities, the fact that so much sexual behaviour still occurs is a remarkable testimony to the sexuality of our species.

Let me be more specific. If I put my statement in a slightly different way, namely that man is *potentially* the sexiest of all the primates, then there can be no argument. In the first place, other primates are limited in their sexual activities to a brief section of the female's monthly sexual cycle. At these times her external sexual organs undergo a change that in most species is clearly visible to the male. This makes her sexually attractive to him. At other times she will have little or no appeal for him. In the human species the active phase is extended throughout almost the whole of the monthly cycle, more or less tripling the time when the female will be appealing to the male. Already, in this respect alone, the human animal has three times the sexual potential of his near relatives, the monkeys and apes.

Secondly, the female human remains both sexually appealing and responsive during most of her period of pregnancy, when other primates are not. Also, she becomes sexually active again much sooner after giving birth than do the other species. Finally, the average human animal of modern times can expect to enjoy roughly half a century of active sexual life, a range that few other mammals can match.

Not only is there this enormous potential for sexual activity, but in the vast majority of cases it is fully realized, so that I see no reason to modify my original statement. Most human beings express themselves sexually by finding partners and indulging in frequent sexual interactions, but even those who do not, or who are temporarily sexually isolated, do not normally become inactive. For them, it is typically the case that masturbation at fairly high frequency will be employed to compensate for the absence of a mate.

Above all, the human sexual pattern is complex. It involves not only vigorous copulation, but also all the gentle subtleties of courtship and the intense arousal actions of pre-copulatory behaviour. In other words, it not only occurs with high frequency over a long period of years, and with few interruptions from 'dead periods' in female reproductive cycles, but, when it does occur, it is prolonged and elaborate. This enlargement of the sexual life of the species is achieved by the addition to its primate inheritance of a great variety of sexual body contacts and intimacies, of the kind we have been discussing. Here the contrast with other species is striking and, to clarify this point, it is worth pausing to look at the way in which monkeys and apes perform sexually.

Monkeys do not form deep bonds of attachment to their mates and there is little courtship or pre-copulatory behaviour. During the few days of her monthly cycle when she is in full sexual condition, the female approaches the male or is approached by him, she turns her rump towards him, crouching down slightly with the front end of her body, he mounts her from behind, inserts his penis, makes a few quick pelvic thrusts, ejaculates, dismounts, and they move apart again. The whole encounter is usually over in a few seconds. A number of examples will give a clear idea of the widespread occurrence of this extreme brevity. In the bonnet monkey, the male makes only 5 to 30 pelvic thrusts. In the howler monkey, the figure is 8 to 28 thrusts, with an average of 17, taking 22 seconds, with a preceding 10 seconds for 'body adjustment'. The rhesus monkey performs 2 to 8 pelvic thrusts, lasting a total of no more than 3 or 4 seconds. Baboons, in one report, made up to 15 pelvic thrusts, lasting for a total of 7–8 seconds; in another report, an average of 6 thrusts, lasting 8–20 seconds; in a third, 5 to 10 thrusts, lasting 10–15 seconds. Two reports for chimpanzees give the average male performance as 4 to 8 thrusts, with a maximum of 15 in one instance, and 6 to 20 thrusts in a total copulating time of 7–10 seconds in another.

These details plainly indicate that our hairier relatives do not linger at the business of mating. To be fair, however, they do perform these 'instant copulations' with a very high frequency during the short period of days while the female is in sexual condition. In some species, remounting occurs within a few minutes, and may be repeated a number of times in quick succession. In the South African baboon, for instance, there are usually from 3 to 6 mountings one after the other, with only two-minute intervals between them. In the rhesus monkey this figure rises, and there may be from 5 to 25 mountings with intervals of only a minute or so between each. It seems as if the male only ejaculates after the final mounting, which is more vigorous and intense, so that here the pattern does appear to be more complex. In all these cases, however, the mating activity differs markedly from that of the human animal.

In the human species, not only is there more sexual foreplay, but the act of copulation itself takes longer. In the pre-copulatory phase, over 50 per cent of human couples spend longer than ten minutes indulging in a wide variety of arousal techniques. After this, pelvic thrusting for the male could, in most cases, lead to ejaculation in only a few minutes, but typically he prolongs this phase. He does so because, unlike the monkeys, his female is able to experience a sexual climax, similar to his own in emotional intensity, but she usually takes from ten to twenty minutes to do so. This means that, for an ordinary human couple, the whole pattern, including both foreplay and copulation, takes roughly half an hour, which is more than a hundred times as long as for the typical monkey pair. Again, to be fair to the monkeys, they will be likely to repeat their brief encounter much sooner than the human pair, but against this must be set the fact that the female monkey will be receptive only for the few days of her period of heat.

To compare the situation for the female monkey and the female human, the former comes into heat as ovulation time approaches and stays in heat for nearly a week. During this time, copulation neither arouses nor exhausts her sexually. She remains permanently aroused during the whole mating period. For the human female it is as if each mating pattern is a short period of heat, now unrelated to the time of ovulation, but related instead to the pre-copulatory stimulations of the male. She has, in effect, become a mate-responder, rather than an ovulation-responder. Her physiological arousal is geared to the shared sexual intimacies with her male, rather than to the rigidly fixed sequence of the monthly cycle of ovulation and menstruation. This vital step, which represents a fundamental change in the usual primate sexual system, leads inevitably to a far greater degree and complexity of body contact between the mated pair and forms the basis of human sexual intimacy.

This leads us to the question of the origins of the more complex human sexual acts. What are the sources of all the additional body contacts? Since monkeys do little more than mount and copulate, the act of mounting, making rhythmic pelvic thrusts and ejaculating is virtually all we share with them. So from where do we derive all the gentle, hesitant touchings and hand-holdings of the courtship period, and all the passionate arousal actions of sexual foreplay? The answer seems to be that in almost all cases they can be traced back to the intimacies of the mother-infant relationship that were described earlier. Hardly any of them appear to be 'new' actions, specifically evolved in connection with sexuality itself. In terms of the behaviour involved, falling in love looks very much like a return to infancy.

In tracing the way in which the primary embrace of our earliest years gradually becomes restricted as we mature, we watched the decline and fall of close body intimacy. Now, as we observe the young lovers, we see the whole process put into reverse. The first actions in the sexual sequence are virtually identical with those of any other kind of adult social interaction. Then, little by little, the hands of the behavioural clock start to turn backwards. The formal handshake and small-talk of the first introduction grow back into the protective hand-holding of childhood. The young lovers now walk hand in hand, as each once did with his or her parent. As their bodies come closer together with increasing trust, we soon witness the welcome return of the intimate frontal embrace, with the two heads touching and kissing. As the relationship deepens, we travel still further back, to the earlier days of gentle caresses. The hands once again fondle the face, the hair and the body of the loved one. At last, the lovers are naked again and, for the first time since they were tiny babies, the most private parts of their bodies experience the intimate touch of another's hands. And, as their movements travel backwards in time, so too do their voices, the words spoken becoming less important than the soft tonal quality with which they are delivered. Frequently even the phrases used become infantile, as a new kind of 'baby-talk' develops. A wave of shared security envelops the young couple and, as in babyhood, the hurly-burly of the outside world has little meaning. The dreamy expression of a girl in love is not the alert face of an active child; it is the almost blank face of a satisfied baby.

This return to intimacy, so beautiful to those who are experiencing it, is often belittled by those who are not. The epigrams tell the story: 'The first sigh of love is the last of wisdom'; 'Love is a sickness full of woes'; 'Love is blind'; 'We are easily duped by what we love'; 'Love's a malady without a cure'; ''Tis impossible to love and to be wise'; 'Lovers are fools, but nature makes them so'. Even in the scientific literature, the term 'regressive behaviour' takes on the flavour of an insult, instead of an impartial, objective description of what is taking place. Of course, to behave in an infantile manner in certain adult contexts is an inefficient way of coping with a situation, but here, in the case of young lovers forming a deep bond of personal attachment, it is exactly the opposite. Extensive, intimate body contacts are the very best way of developing such a bond, and those who resist them because they are 'babyish' or infantile will be the losers.

When courtship advances to the stage of pre-copulatory behaviour, the infantile patterns do not fade. Instead they grow still younger, and the clock ticks backwards to the sucking at the mother's breast. The simple kiss, in which lips are gently pressed to the lover's mouth or cheek, becomes a vigorous, moving pressure. With muscular actions of their lips and tongues, the partners work on one another's mouths as if to draw milk from them. They suck and squeeze rhythmically with their lips, explore and lick with their tongues, like hungry babies. This active kissing is no longer confined to the partner's mouth. It seeks other sites, as if searching for the long-lost mother's nipple. In its quest it travels everywhere, discovering the pseudo-nipples of the ear-lobes, the toes, the clitoris and the penis, and, of course, the lover's nipples themselves.

Earlier, I mentioned the reward these actions bring from the knowledge of the sexual pleasure they give, but clearly that was only part of the story. There is also this more direct reward of re-experiencing the strongly gratifying oral contact of the suckling interaction in infancy. The effect is heightened where the pseudo-breast can be made to produce pseudo-milk. This can be obtained from the increased salivation of the lover's mouth, from the increased sexual secretions of the female's genitals and from the seminal fluid of the male's penis. If the mouthing of the penis by the female is prolonged until ejaculation occurs, it is as if the action has finally succeeded in starting the 'milk-flow' from this pseudo-breast, a similarity which was recognized as long ago as the seventeenth century, when the slang expression 'milking' for this activity first came into common usage.

Even when the pre-copulatory patterns are terminated and copulation itself begins, the infantile actions do not completely disappear. For the mating monkeys, the only body contacts, apart from actual genital interaction, are the mechanical holding actions by the male's hands and feet. He grips the female's body, not as an amorous intimacy, but to steady himself while he makes the rapid pelvic thrusts. Such graspings also occur between the human partners, but in addition there are many contacts that have no 'body adjustment' function. The hands clasp or hold the partner, not for mechanical reasons of thrust facilitation, but as tactile signals of intimacy.

Turning again to the illustrated sexual manuals discussed earlier, and taking only the cases where the male and female were shown actually copulating, it is possible to score the frequency of these non-genital contacts that accompany the pelvic thrusting. In no less than 74 per cent of the copulation postures depicted, the hand (or hands) of one partner clasps or touches some part of the other's body, in a 'non-steadying' way. In addition, there are many embracing acts, kissing acts and non-kissing head-to-head contacts; also a number of hand-to-head and hand-to-hand contacts. All these actions are basically embraces, partial embraces or fragments of embraces. They indicate that, for the human animal, copulation consists of the adult primate mating act *plus* the returned infantile embracing act. The latter pervades the whole sexual sequence from its earliest courtship stages right through to its final moments. The human animal does not merely copulate with a set of genitals belonging to a member of the opposite sex; it 'makes love' – a significant phrase – to a complete and special individual. This is why, in our species, all stages of the sequence, including copulation, can serve to enhance the pair-bonding process, and why, presumably, the female evolved an extended period of sexual receptivity, stretching far beyond the limits of the ovulation period. It could even be said that we now perform the mating act, not so much to fertilize an egg as to fertilize a relationship. There is no reproductive danger in this, for even the small proportion of mating acts that do happen to coincide with the time of ovulation will still be sufficient to produce an adequate number of offspring, and there are more than three thousand million of us alive today to prove the point.*

---

* The figure has now risen to more than five thousand million.

4

SOCIAL INTIMACY

TO STUDY HUMAN sexual intimacy is to witness the rebirth of lavish bodily contact between adults, replacing the lost intimacies of infancy. To study human social intimacy is, by contrast, to observe the restraint of cautious, inhibited contact, as the conflicting demands of closeness and privacy, of dependence and independence, do battle inside our brains.

We all feel overcrowded from time to time, and over-exposed to the prying eyes and minds of others. The monkish idea of shutting ourselves away from it all becomes appealing. But for most of us a few hours will do, and the idea of lifelong monastic solitude is appalling. For man is a social animal, and the ordinary healthy human being finds prolonged isolation a severe punishment. Short of physical torture or death, solitary confinement is the worst agony that can be inflicted on a prisoner. He is driven eventually, in near-madness, to talk into his lavatory pan so that he can enjoy the echo of his voice coming back to him. It is the nearest thing to a social response he can get.

A shy single person living in a big city can find him- or herself in almost the same situation. For such people, if they have left the intimacies of home behind and are now existing by themselves in a small room or apartment, the loneliness can soon become intolerable. Too timid to make friends, they may ultimately prefer death by suicide to prolonged lack of close human contact. Such is the basic need for intimacy. For intimacy breeds understanding, and most of us, unlike the solitary monk, do want to be understood, at least by a few people.

It is not a question of being understood rationally or intellectually. It is a matter of being understood emotionally, and in that respect a single intimate body contact will do more than all the beautiful words in the dictionary. The ability that physical feelings have to transmit emotional feelings is truly astonishing. Perhaps it is their strength that is also their weakness. In tracing the sequence of intimacies that occur through life, from birth to death, we saw the way in which the two phases of massive body contact were also the two phases of powerful social bonding, first between parent and child and second between lovers. All the indications are that it is impossible to be lavish and uninhibited with one's body-to-body contacts and not become strongly bonded with the object of one's attentions. An intuitive understanding of this is perhaps what inhibits us so strongly from indulging in the pure pleasure of more widespread bodily intimacies. It is not enough to say that it is unconventional to hug and embrace one's business colleagues, for example. That does not explain how the convention of 'keeping oneself to oneself' or 'keeping one's distance' arose in the first place. We have to look deeper than that to understand the extraordinary lengths we go to to avoid touching one another in ordinary day-to-day affairs outside the close family circle.

Part of the answer has to do with the great overcrowding we experience in our modern urban communities. We encounter so many people in streets and buildings every day that we simply cannot embark on intimacies with them, or all social organization would come to a halt. Ironically this over-crowding situation has two completely incompatible effects on us. On the one hand it stresses us and makes us feel tense and insecure, and on the other hand it makes us cut down on the very exchanges of intimacies which would relieve this stress and tension.

Another part of the answer has to do with sex. It is not merely that we cannot afford the time or energy to start setting up the endless social bonds that would result from widespread indulgence in extensive body intimacies. There is also the problem that, between adults, body intimacy spells sex. This is an unhappy confusion, but it is not hard to see how it has arisen. Since copulation, short of artificial insemination, is impossible without body intimacy, it has become in some respects synonymous with it. To indulge in the mating act, even the most 'untouchable' adult has to touch and be touched. At almost all other times he can avoid it if he wishes to, but then he cannot. Some Victorians went as far as they could to reduce contact by wearing nightgowns with small slits in the front, but even they had to make contact to the extent of inserting a penis into a vagina if they were to populate their world with children. And so it came to be that, in the year 1889, the expression 'to be intimate' became a euphemism for having sexual intercourse. During the present century it has become increasingly difficult for any adult, of either sex and with either sex, to indulge in intimate body contact without giving the impression that there is a sexual element involved in what is taking place.

It would be wrong to give the idea that this is an entirely new trend. The problem, of course, has always been there, and adult intimacies have always been curtailed to some extent to avoid sexual implications. But one gets a distinct impression that the situation has tightened up more in recent years. We no longer seem to be quite so free at falling on one another's necks in joy, or weeping copiously in one another's arms. The basic urge to touch one another remains, however, and it is intriguing to study how we go about this in our day-to-day affairs outside the bosom of the family.

The answer is that we formalize it. We take the uninhibited intimacies of infancy and we reduce them to fragments. Each fragment becomes stylized and rigidified until it fits into a neat category. We set up rules of etiquette (a word taken from the French and meaning, literally, a label) and we train the members of our cultures to abide by them. No training is necessary where an embrace is concerned. This, as we have seen, is an inborn biological act that we share with all our primate relatives. But an embrace contains many elements, and which particular fragment we are to use at which particular social moment, and in what rigidly stylized form, is something that our genetical make-up cannot help us with. For the animal, there is either behaviour or no behaviour, but for us there is either behaviour or misbehaviour, good behaviour or bad behaviour, and the rules are complex. This does not mean, however, that we cannot study them biologically. No matter how culturally determined they may be, or how culturally variable, we can still understand them better if we view them as pieces of primate behaviour. This is because we can nearly always trace them back to their biological origins.

Before surveying the whole scene, let me give a single detailed example to illustrate what I mean. I will use an action that does not appear to have received much attention in the past, namely the pat on the back. You may think that this is too trivial a piece of behaviour to be of much interest, but it is dangerous to dismiss small actions in this way. Every twitch, every scratch, every stroke and every pat has the potential of changing a person's whole life, or even a nation's. The warm caress that was withheld at the vital moment when it was desperately needed can easily be the act, or rather the non-act, that finally destroys a relationship. The simple failure to return a smile, between two great rulers, can in the same way lead to war and destruction. So it is unwise to sneer at a 'mere' pat on the back. These little actions are the stuff that emotional life is made of.

If you have ever had a close personal relationship with a chimpanzee, you will know that back-patting is not a uniquely human activity. If your ape is particularly glad to see you, he is likely to come up, embrace you, press his lips warmly and wetly to the side of your neck, and then start rhythmically patting you on the back with his hands. It is a strange sensation, because in one way it is so human and yet in another it is subtly different. The kiss is not quite like a human kiss. I can best describe it as being more of a soft-open-mouth-press. And the patting is both lighter and faster than human back-patting, with the two ape hands alternating rhythmically. Nevertheless, the actions of embracing, kissing and patting are basically the same in the two species, and the social signals they transmit appear to be identical. We can therefore start out with a reasonable guess that back-patting is a biological feature of the human animal.

I have already, in the first chapter, explained the probable origin of the activity, as a repeated intention movement of clinging that says, 'I will cling to you like this if necessary, but at the moment it is not, so relax, all is well.' In infancy we only get patted as an embellishment of the embrace, but later on the friendly pat may be executed by itself, without any embracing. The patter's arm simply reaches out towards the companion and contact is made with the hand alone. Already, with this change, the process of formalization has started to take place. Seeing only an embraceless pat would make it impossible to guess its true origin. Another change occurs at the same time: the area of the body patted becomes less restricted. A baby is patted almost exclusively on the back, but an older child is patted almost anywhere, not only on the back but also on the shoulder, the arm, the hand, the cheek, the top of the head, the back of the head, the stomach, the buttocks, the thighs, the knees and the legs. The message of the pat also becomes extended. The comforting signal 'all is well' becomes the congratulatory signal 'all is *very* well' or 'you have done well'. Since the brain that has done well is housed inside the skull, it is natural that the pat on the head should be the action that comes to typify the congratulatory message. In fact, this particular form of the action becomes so strongly associated with childhood congratulation that it has to be abandoned later on when patting occurs between adults, because it then acquires the flavour of condescension.

Other changes also occur as we move from the context adult-pats-child to adult-pats-adult. In addition to the head, certain other areas now become taboo. Patting on the back, shoulder and arm is still unhampered, but patting the back of the hand, the cheek, the knee or the thigh begins to acquire a slightly sexual flavour, and patting on the buttocks a strongly sexual flavour. The situation is highly variable, however, and there are many exceptions to this rule. Handback-patting and thigh-patting between two women, for example, may occur without any hint of sexuality being involved. Also it is possible, by comic over-exaggeration, to pat almost any part of the body without causing offence. The patter then makes joking remarks, as he pats his victim on the head or cheek, such as 'there, there, little man', indicating that the contact he is making is not sexual but mock-parental, and is not to be taken seriously. There is an element of offensiveness involved, of course, but it has nothing to do with the breaking of sexual taboos on touching certain areas in certain ways.

To complicate matters further, there is an intriguing exception to this last exception. It works like this. One adult, say a male, wishes to make sexual body contact with another, say a female. He knows she will not accept a direct, undisguised contact, which she would find distasteful. He knows, in fact, that she finds him sexually unattractive in general, but his urge to touch her is strong enough to ignore the disencouraging signals she transmits to him. His strategy therefore becomes one of pretending to behave like a mock-parent. He makes a great joke of patting her on the knee and calling her a funny little girl. He hopes that she will accept the contact as a joke action, even though the true reward he is getting is sexual. Unhappily for him he is not usually good enough at concealing other sexual signals, especially from his facial expressions, and the girl in question can normally see through the device and respond in an appropriately negative way.

The least sexually loaded patting action is the primary pat on the back. This somehow manages to retain its original quality and may often be observed between complete strangers, in contexts of either condolence or congratulation. Two specific situations which illustrate this are the road accident and the sportsman's moment of triumph. Following a road accident, if one of those involved is sitting slumped by the roadside in a state of numbed shock, he will soon be approached closely by one of the helpers who arrive on the scene. Typically, the helper will peer closely at the shocked person and ask some quite nonsensical question, such as 'Are you all right?', when clearly he is not. Almost immediately the helper realizes how meaningless his words are in such a situation, and reverts instead to the more powerful and basic communication pattern of direct body contact. The most likely form that this contact will take is a comforting, gentle patting on the back of the victim. The same response can be observed, but with much more vigour, when a sportsman has just achieved some sort of athletic triumph. As he returns cheerfully from the field or arena, his fans will compete with one another to get close enough to pat him warmly on the back as he passes by.

We have already come a long way from the primary situation of the mother lovingly patting her tiny baby, but there is still further to go, for amongst adults the action of patting has extended its range even beyond the tactile. The basic touch signal has, in two important contexts, become a sound signal and a visual signal. Both human clapping, when an audience applauds a performer, and human waving, during greetings and farewells, have been derived from the primary patting action. Let us take clapping first.

For years I was puzzled by the widespread use of hand-clapping as a method of rewarding a performer. The sharp slapping of one hand against another seemed an almost aggressive action, as did the harsh sound it produced. Yet clearly it was the exact opposite of aggressive in its effect on the happy performer. For centuries, actors have craved the applause of a sea of clapping hands, and have devised many a 'trap to catch a clap', thereby giving the English language its word 'clap-trap'.

To understand the potent reward of hand-clapping, we must search for its origins in childhood. Careful studies of infants in the second half of the first year of life reveal that at this age a hand-clap may often be given as part of the greeting towards the mother, when she returns to her baby after a brief absence. The action may be performed either just before, or instead of, reaching out with its arms towards the mother. It appears at about the same time as the act of holding on to the mother with the arms. It is as if the baby, seeing the mother approaching, makes a movement in which the arms are brought out and round as if to hold her. But her body is not there yet to be held, and so the arms continue in the arc of embracing until the hands meet with a clap. At this stage the clap is performed, as it were, from the arm, not from the wrist as in the adult version of hand-clapping.

Detailed observations have indicated that this occurs where there is no evidence of the mother's having taught a clapping response previously. The baby clap, in other words, can best be interpreted as the audible culmination of a vacuum-embracing of the mother. The rhythmically repeated clapping-from-the-wrist that develops later can then be seen clearly as a kind of vacuum-patting added to the vacuum-embrace. When we applaud a performer, we are, in effect, patting him on the back from a distance. It is inconvenient or impossible for us to all rush up and actually make physical contact with him, giving him a real pat to show our approval, so instead we stay in our seats and repeatedly pat him in vacuo. If you test this by clapping your hands as though you were applauding, you will find that you do not bring both hands together with equal force. One tends to take the role of the performer's back and the other does the vigorous vacuum-back-patting on it. It is true that both hands move, but one makes a much stronger action than the other. In nine people out of ten it is the right hand, with the palm facing half-downwards, that takes the patting role, and the left hand, with the palm facing half-upwards, that takes the role of the back to be patted.

Occasionally one gets an unexpected glimpse, even in the adult world, of the basic relationship that exists between the primary embrace and the action of hand-clapping. When the first Russian cosmonaut returned in triumph to Moscow and stood in Red Square with the Russian leaders, a vast crowd filed past paying homage, reaching up and clapping their hands to him as they went by. A film of the event clearly shows one man in the crowd so overcome with emotion that he keeps on interrupting his prolonged hand-clapping with vacuum embraces. He claps his outstretched hands, embraces the air in front of him and hugs it to him, then reaches out, claps again and embraces again. When the power of the emotion breaks down the formalization of the conventional pattern in this way, it provides us with an eloquent confirmation of the origins of the adult act.

Russia happens to provide us with another interesting variation in hand-clapping. In that country it is usual for the performers to clap the audience as the audience claps them. This does not mean, as has sometimes been cynically suggested, that Russian performers are so narcissistic that they even applaud their own performances. They are simply returning the audience's formalized embrace, as they would do if they met them body to body. In the West we lack this convention, although a variant of it can sometimes be seen in the wide-stretched arms of the performers seeking applause at the end of an act. Circus performers and acrobats are particularly prone to adopt this posture. At the completion of a difficult stunt, they stand proudly poised, face the audience, and fling their arms out wide. The audience immediately breaks into ringing applause. The opening of the arms in this way is an example of an intention movement of embracing. The arms are positioned ready to embrace the audience, but do not go on to consummate the act in vacuo. Some cabaret singers who specialize in highly emotional songs use much the same action whilst actually singing, arousing emotion in the audience by offering them an imploring invitation to embrace as an accompaniment to the imploring words of the song.

Hand-clapping is also used occasionally as an act of summoning a servant. In the harem fantasy, it is the signal that says 'bring on the dancing girls'. In these cases the clapping is not the typical fast, rhythmically repeated action of the applause pattern, but simply one or two hard slaps of one hand against the other. In this respect it is much more like the infant clapping that was performed as a greeting to the mother. The message is also similar. The infant's request, 'come closer', to the mother, becomes the adult's demand for the same thing from the servant.

I said earlier that the basic touch signal of patting has been extended both as a sound signal, which we have been examining, and as a visual signal, in the form of waving. Like clapping, waving is usually taken for granted, but it, too, has some unexpected elements, and it is worth analysing in detail.

To start with, it seems obvious that we wave when greeting or saying goodbye because, from a distance, it makes us more conspicuous. This is true, but it is not the whole answer. If you watch people who are really desperate to make themselves conspicuous, say when hailing a taxi, or when trying to make visual contact with a person in a crowd who has not yet spotted them, they do not wave in the usual, conventional manner. Instead, they raise one arm stiffly, straight up, and start swinging it from side to side, moving it from the shoulder. Under even greater pressure, they may raise and wave both arms in this way at the same time. This is the action that makes for maximum conspicuousness at a distance. It is not, however, the way we wave to one another when we are already in visual contact. If we are waving goodbye to someone, or if we are waving a greeting to someone who has already seen us but is still out of reach, we do not normally wave our arms. We raise the arm, but what we wave is the hand. We do it in one of three ways. One is to wave it up and down, with the fingers pointing away from us. When the hand is in the up position, the palm faces outwards; when in the down position, the palm faces downwards. Here again is the ubiquitous patting action. The greeting arm reaches out to embrace and pat, but, as with the clapping, the intervening distance forces us to perform the action in vacuo. The difference is that whereas in hand-clapping the long-distance embrace-and-pat is elaborated into a sound signal, here it is modified into a visual signal. The arm goes upward instead of forward, as it would in a true contact embrace, because this increases the visibility of the action. Otherwise there is little difference.

A second form of hand-waving reveals a further modification towards visibility. Instead of moving the hand up and down, it is waved from side to side, with the palm kept in the out-facing position. The speed is much the same, but the action is now one step further removed from the primary patting motion. It is significant that this form of waving is favoured more by adults than by children, who seem to prefer the primitive up-and-down version.

The third type of hand-wave is one that will not be familiar to most Western readers. I have myself observed it only in Italy, but apparently it also occurs in Spain, China, India, Pakistan, Burma, Malaysia, East Africa, Nigeria, and amongst gypsies. (This is, to say the least of it, a most curious distribution, for which I can as yet find no explanation.) It is reminiscent of a hand-beckoning action, but one only has to see it performed as a goodbye signal to realize that this is not what it is. Like the first form of hand-waving I mentioned, it is an up-and-down action, but this time the hand starts out palm uppermost (as in a begging posture) and is then moved repeatedly upwards towards the body of the waver. Again, it is basically a patting movement, and in true back-patting one often sees the hand adopt this position, with the fingers pointing upwards on the back, when the embracing arm has the elbow in a low position.

Two rather specialized waves are related to this last one. They are the Papal wave and the British royal wave. In both cases, for some reason, they are performed neither from the shoulder, as in the conspicuous arm-wave, nor from the wrist, as in the usual patting-wave. Instead they are done from the elbow. The Pope normally uses both arms at once and brings his hands and forearms slowly, rhythmically and repeatedly towards himself, palms uppermost, making a series of embracing intention movements. But it is not as simple as that, because his arms do not bend directly towards his chest. He does not hug the crowd to his bosom. Instead, the arc the arms perform is half-inward and half-upward, as though his action is a compromise, embracing the crowds partly towards himself and partly towards the heavens above, where one day they presumably all hope to be welcomed.

The British royal wave is also typically stiff from the elbow, but is normally one-handed and with the fingers pointing straight up. The palm faces inwards towards the royal body, emphasizing the embracing nature of the action, and the forearm is slowly and rhythmically rotated, with the emphasis on the inward part of the rotation. In this way the Queen, in a highly stylized manner, embraces her subjects and reassures them with a rather formal pat on the back.

As in the case of clapping, one is sometimes lucky enough to see the formality of waving break down under emotional pressure in a revealing way, laying bare its basic origins. A specific instance of greeting will illustrate this. At a small airport where I was making observations of waving behaviour, there is a balcony from which friends and relatives can watch the new arrivals descend from the incoming aircraft and walk across the tarmac to the customs entrance. This entrance is just beneath the balcony, so that although the new arrivals cannot touch the excited figures waving frantically to them from above, they do come very close before finally disappearing into the airport building. This, then, is the setting, and the action usually takes place as follows. After the aircraft doors open and the passengers start piling out, there is a great deal of distant eye-scanning from both the arrivals and the greeters. If one makes eye contact before the other, he normally starts vigorous arm-waving, moving the arm from the shoulder in the maximum-conspicuousness manner. After mutual eye contact has been made, then both sides tend to adopt the arm-raised hand-wave action. This goes on for some time, but it is a long walk to the building and after a while they usually break off. Their waving and smiling urges have become temporarily exhausted (like the person being photographed who, as time passes, finds it hard to maintain a natural smile for the lens-fiddling cameraman), but they do not wish to appear 'ungreetful', so both sides now take a sudden interest in other aspects of the airport scene. The new arrival glances round to survey the landscape of the airfield, or rearranges that suddenly awkward piece of hand-luggage that is mysteriously slipping from his grip. The greeters for their part start to exchange comments about the appearance of the new arrival. Then, as the latter comes nearer and his facial details can be made out more clearly, both sides start up the vigorous hand-waving and smiling again until the arrivals have disappeared into the building below. Half an hour later, with customs inspection over, the first body contact is made, with handshakes, embraces, pattings, hugs and kisses.

This is the basic story. Naturally, there are many minor variations, and on one occasion the pattern was exceeded in a most revealing way. A man was returning to the bosom of his family after a long spell abroad. From the moment he stepped off the aircraft both he and his group of family greeters exploded into an orgy of arm- and hand-waving. As he reached the building and saw the details of their faces clearly above him, he found the convention of hand-waving inadequate for his emotional needs. With tears in his eyes and his mouth shaping unheard words of love, he had to do something with his arm that would better express the enormous intensity of his feelings at being reunited with his family. At this moment, as I watched, I saw his hand actions change. The ordinary waving movements ceased and were replaced by a perfect miming of a passionate series of back-pattings. The arm was now held out towards the family group, rather than raised upward, which foreshortened it and reduced its conspicuousness. The hand curled round sideways and made vigorous, rapid patting actions in mid-air. The power of his emotions was so strong that all the secondary, conventionalized modifications of the primary embrace-and-pat actions, which help to improve the signal quality of this pattern from a distance by making it more clearly visible, were abandoned in the heat of the moment, and the original primary behaviour was once again laid bare.

The intensity of this encounter was confirmed by the tactile greeting behaviour that followed the customs interlude. When the man emerged into the body of the airport, he was embraced, hugged, kissed and patted with such vigour by all fourteen members of his family that, by the time they had finished, he was emotionally exhausted, his face flooded with tears, his body shaking. At one point a woman who appeared to be his mother augmented her embrace with vigorous face-kneading, taking both the man's cheeks in her hands and grappling with them as though she were in her kitchen kneading soft dough. While this was going on, the man's hands were embracing her and patting her back at high intensity. However, after about the tenth passionate greeting, it seemed as if the emotional exhaustion of the occasion was beginning to tell on him. As this occurred, his patting actions changed significantly. Once again, a signal convention was breaking down under emotional pressure, and once again the origins of a formalized pattern were being laid bare. Whereas, before, the waving had reverted to vacuum-air-patting, this time it went one stage further back to its original source. The repeated patting gave way to brief, repeated clinging actions. Each pat became a tightening of the hand contact, a sort of clinging squeeze, that was repeatedly relaxed and then tightened again. Here, without doubt, was the original clinging intention movement. This was the 'ancestral' pattern, the one from which all the others had descended by a process of signal specialization: to a tactile signal by modification to on-off patting, to a sound signal by using the other palm as the more noisily patted object in the act of hand-clapping, and to a visual signal by patting in mid-air with a raised arm in the act of hand-waving. Such are the ramifications that occur with our so-called 'trivial' acts of human intimacy.

In following this one small human-contact action through all its various developments, I have tried to show how it is possible to see old familiar activities in a new light. The need that we, as adults, have to make body contact with one another is basic and powerful, but, as we have seen, it is rarely fully expressed. Instead, it appears in fragmented, modified or disguised forms in many of the signs, gestures and signals we make to one another in our daily lives. Often the true meaning of the actions is hidden from us and we have to trace them back to their origins to understand them fully. In the examples I have just been describing, the primary contact action frequently became remote, operating at a distance, but there are also many ways in which we do still make actual body contact with one another, and it is interesting to survey these and see what forms they take. To do this it will help to go back for a moment to the primary embrace itself. This is not commonly seen today between adults in public, but it still does occur from time to time and it is worth studying the situations in which it appears.

The full embrace. If we make careful observations of as many full embraces as possible, then it soon becomes clear that between adults this action falls into three distinct categories. The biggest group, as we might expect, consists of amorous contact between lovers. This accounts for about two-thirds of all public embraces today. The remaining third can be split up into the two types that we can call the 'relatives' reunion' and the 'sportsman's triumph'.

Young lovers perform the full embrace, not only when they meet and part, but also frequently during the times they are together. Amongst older couples, after marriage, it is rare to see a full embrace in public unless one partner is going away for some time, or returning from a separation of at least some days. At other times, if the embrace occurs at all, it will be publicly expressed merely as a token contact of a rather mild kind.

Between adult relatives, such as brothers and sisters, or parents and their adult children, the passionate embrace is even less common. It does occur with remarkable predictability, however, whenever there has been some major disaster from which one of the relatives has escaped. If he or she has been hijacked, kidnapped, taken captive, or trapped by some upheaval of nature, then you can be sure that the 'relatives' reunion' that follows safe delivery and return will exhibit full embraces of the most intense kind. Under such circumstances the action may even extend to close friends of either sex, who would normally give only a handshake or a kiss on the cheek. Such is the emotional intensity of the situation that the passionate embracing of a man by a man, or a woman by a woman, or a man-*friend* by a woman-*friend*, creates no difficulties with regard to sexual taboos. At a lower emotional intensity there would be more of a problem, but at moments of high drama the taboos are forgotten. In triumph, relief or despair it is acceptable even for two adult males in our culture to hug and kiss one another, but if, in a less dramatic situation, they were to perform a mere fragment of an embrace such as holding hands, or pressing cheek to cheek, they would immediately create a homosexual impression.

This difference is significant and requires explanation. It tells us something about the way in which basic body contacts are fragmented and formalized. To begin with, the full embrace is natural between parent and baby, and therefore also between parent and older child, even though it becomes less frequent. Between adults it is typical of lovers and mates. Other adults who, for a variety of reasons, feel the urge to embrace one another, must therefore somehow make it clear that there is no sexual element in their contact. This they do by employing some formalized fragment of the full embrace, a fragment which by conventional agreement is non-sexual. A man, for example, can put his arm around another man's shoulder without running any risk of sexual misinterpretation, either by his contact partner, or by others who see him perform the action. If, however, he were to perform other simple fragments, such as, say, kissing the man's ear, a sexual connotation would immediately be placed upon the act.

The situation is entirely different when two men are seen employing the full embrace, complete with hugging and kissing, in a situation of great triumph, disaster or reunion. No sexual interpretation is made here because it is recognized that the response is not formalized, but basic. The onlookers recognize the situation as being one where the usual conventions are overpowered by the intensity of the emotions involved. They know, intuitively, that what they are witnessing is the return to the primary, pre-sexual embrace of infancy, with all the layers of later, adult stylization stripped away, and they accept the contact as being perfectly natural. In fact, if two male homosexuals wished to make body contact in public without arousing the usual heterosexual hostility or curiosity, they would do better to indulge in a wild hug rather than a gentle kiss.

By studying the various formal fragments of the basic embrace, we should therefore be able to see how convention has pigeon-holed them into different categories, so that each one now signals something quite specific about the nature of the relationship between the 'contacters'.

Before doing this, however, there is still the third category of the full embrace to be mentioned, namely the 'sportsman's triumph'. The embrace of two men following a major disaster has been with us for a long time, but the passionate hugging of football players after a goal has been scored is something comparatively recent. How is it that this occasion has suddenly been elevated to the ranks of a major emotional experience? To find the answer we have to go much further afield than the football pitch. We do, in fact, have to go back many hundreds of years.

Two thousand years ago, when the world was less crowded and the relationships between members of a community were more clearly defined, the full embrace was much more commonly used as an ordinary form of greeting between equals. The embrace-and-kiss was employed between men and men as well as between women and women and between non-amorous men and women. In ancient Persia it was even common for men of equal rank to kiss one another on the mouth, reserving the kiss on the cheek for someone of slightly inferior status. It was more usual in other places, however, for the cheek kiss to be employed between equals. This situation persisted for many centuries, and was still to be found in medieval England, where valiant knights would kiss and embrace one another at times when their modern equivalents would do no more than nod and shake an outstretched hand.

Towards the end of the seventeenth century the situation in England began to change, and the non-sexual greeting embrace went into a rapid decline. This began in the towns and slowly spread to the country, as we know from a line in Congreve's The Way of the World: 'You think you're in the country, where great lubberly brothers slabber and kiss one another when they meet. 'Tis not the fashion here; 'tis not indeed, dear brother.'

Social life in the cities was becoming more crowded and personal relationships more complex and confusing, and with the arrival of the nineteenth century further restrictions were imposed. Now even the elaborate bowing and curtsying that had survived through the eighteenth century became more and more limited to formal occasions and lost their everyday role. By the 1830s that minimal body contact, the handshake, had arrived, and it has been with us ever since.

Similar trends were taking place elsewhere, but not always to the same extent. The Latin countries tended to restrict their body contacts far less than the British, and, even into the twentieth century, friendly embraces between adult males remained far more acceptable. They do so to this day, and this is where we return to the case of the 'footballer's hug'. Football, which began as a British sport, spread rapidly in the present century to many parts of the world. In Latin countries it became especially popular, and before long international matches of great emotional intensity were being played. When Latin teams visited England, the passionate embracing of their members, following a successful goal, was at first met with astonishment and derision, but the excellence of their playing soon changed all that. As the years passed, the 'Well done, old chap' of the British players when one of their members scored began to seem almost churlish. Back-patting gave way to mild embracing, and mild embracing grew into wild hugging, until today spectators have become quite accustomed to seeing a goal-scorer almost submerged beneath a dense cluster of passionately hugging congratulators.

In this one specific context, then, we have gone full circle back to the times of medieval knights and the ancient world beyond. It remains to be seen whether this trend will extend to other spheres. It may do so, but there is one limitation we must bear in mind. The players embracing on their football field are in a strictly non-sexual context. Their roles are clearly defined and their physical masculinity is being strongly demonstrated by the toughness of the game they are playing. In a social situation of a less clearly defined type, the situation would be different, and the usual restrictions of our complex society will probably then continue to apply. Only in spheres where the expression of powerful emotions is part of the ordinary stock-in-trade, such as the acting profession, can we expect to find major exceptions. If the rest of us find the social embracings of actors and actresses somewhat excessive, we must remember three things. Not only are they trained to show passions easily, but they are also put under severe emotional strain by the nature of their work and, in addition, theirs happens to be a particularly insecure occupation. They need all the mutual reassurance they can get.

Leaving the full embrace now, we can start to look at its less intense forms of expression. So far we have been dealing with the maximal frontal embrace, in which the two partners are pressed close together with the sides of their heads in contact and their arms wrapped tightly around one another's bodies. When this action is performed at a lower intensity, there are usually three major changes. The bodies now make contact side to side instead of face to face; only one arm is wrapped around the partner's body instead of two; and the heads are usually apart instead of touching. My observations reveal that, between adults in public, a partial embrace of this type is six times as likely to occur as a full embrace.*

The shoulder embrace. The most common form of partial embrace is the shoulder embrace, in which one person wraps an arm around his partner so that the hand comes to rest on his far shoulder. This is twice as common as any other form of partial embrace.

The first difference to emerge, when comparing this with the full frontal embrace, is that it is predominantly a masculine act. Whereas the full embrace was given more or less equally by males and females, the shoulder embrace is five times more likely to be performed by a male than by a female. The reason is simple enough: men are taller than women, and women will always have to look up to them physically, no matter what their attitudes may be in other respects. The consequence of this anatomical difference is that certain body contacts are much easier for men than for women, and the shoulder embrace is one of these.

This fact gives the shoulder embrace a special quality. Since, when it is performed between a man and a woman, it is nearly always done by the man, this means that there is nothing effeminate about it. This in turn means that it is also available for use between males in casual, friendly situations, without giving any sexual flavour to the contact. About one in four shoulder embraces do, in fact, occur between males, and this is the only form of body embrace that does occur commonly in an all-male context. The difference with the full frontal embrace is striking. There, if two males were involved, the situation was typically one of high drama, or intense emotion, but here the context can be much more relaxed, the usual scene being one of team-mates, 'old pals' or 'buddies'.

---

* This, and other similar quantitative statements, are based on personal observations backed up by a detailed analysis of 10,000 photographs taken at random from a wide variety of recent news magazines and newspapers.

This 'safely masculine' rule does not apply to other types of partial embrace, such as putting the arm around the partner's waist. Since this is easier for either sex to do and since it also brings the hand closer to the genital region, it is rarely if ever employed between males.

If we now move still further away from the full embrace, shifting our attention from partial embraces to mere fragments of the complete act, we find similar differences. Some embrace fragments have a non-sexual quality and can be used freely between males, while others retain a more amorous flavour and are largely restricted to use between lovers and mates.

The hand-on-shoulder. A common action is placing one hand on the partner's shoulder, without involving any actual embrace. This is a simple reduction of the shoulder embrace and, as we might expect, is employed in similar contexts. Being slightly less intimate, it is even more common between males. Whereas only one in four of the shoulder embraces was done between two males, here the figure is one in three.

The arm-link. If we watch the embrace disintegrate still further, to a mere linking of arms, then the situation shows a striking change. Here, instead of increasing, the figure for males sinks to one in twelve, and we have to ask the question why, with an even less intimate form of body contact, men should become so much less inclined to link arms with other men rather than with women. The answer is that this action is basically feminine. When it occurs between males and females, it is five times more likely to be done by a female to a male than the other way around. This exactly reverses the position we found in the shoulder embrace, and means that if this contact is to be made between members of the same sex, it is going to have an effeminate quality. This leads to a prediction that if it is going to occur between friends of the same sex, it should occur more between women than between men, and observations do, in fact, bear this out.

If we look for cases where one man does link his arm through that of another, then we find that they fall into two categories: the Latin and the elderly. Latin males, with their culturally freer body contacts, often do it, and in non-Latin Western countries it can also be observed as the support-seeking act of an elderly male who is past the sexually potent phase of life.

The hand-in-hand. Continuing our anatomical progress away from the full embrace, via the shoulder embrace, the hand-on-shoulder and the arm-in-arm, we come finally to the hand-in-hand (not to be confused with the handshake, which is discussed separately later). Although this is a more remote form of contact than the last three, with the two bodies usually kept separate from one another, it does have something in common with the full embrace that the others do not. It is a mutual act. I can place my hand on your shoulder, for example, without you doing anything, but if I hold your hand, you are also going to be holding mine. Since it occurs frequently between a male and a female, and since they are always *both* doing it, it acquires neither a masculine nor a feminine quality, but rather a heterosexual one. This makes it, in effect, like a tiny version of the full embrace, and it is not surprising, therefore, to find that it is seldom used today between two males in public.

This was not always the case. Back in the days when the full embrace was freely employed between men, they could also be seen holding hands as an act of non-sexual friendship. To give one example, on an occasion when two medieval monarchs met, it is recorded that they 'took each other by the hand, when the king of France led the king of England to his tent; the four dukes took each other by the hand and followed them.' Before long this custom faded and 'leading by the hand' became restricted to use between males and females. In modern times the action has become modified in two different directions. On formal occasions, such as when a male escorts a female into a banquet, or down the aisle of a church, it has grown into the more reassuring arm-link. On less formal occasions it has changed into the typical hand-holding of mutually grasped palms. And sometimes, when greater intimacy is required, a couple can be seen to perform both acts at the same time.

Despite this general trend, there are certain specialized occasions when males in our modern world do still hold hands. One example is the multiple hand-holding that occurs when a whole group of people are joining hands with one another to do such things as sing community songs, or take curtain calls in the theatre. Even here the tendency is to alternate the positions of the males and females, so that each person is flanked by members of the opposite sex, but if the numbers are not equal, or if it is too difficult to jostle everyone into the correct positionings, then it is permissible to hold hands with your own sex. This is because you are not in any sense forming a pair with them. The very size of the group eliminates the potential sexual flavour of the hand-holding.

Another highly stylized version of hand-holding that can occur between males is for one of them to take the other's hand in his own and raise it high in the air as a sign of victory. Although this originates from the world of boxing, it is perhaps more frequently met with today between pairs of male politicians, who appear to fantasize imaginary boxing-gloves on the hands of their victorious colleagues. The hand-holding is permissible in this context because of the primarily aggressive nature of the arm-raising gesture. In its more original form, prior to the hand-holding embellishment, this movement of holding the raised fist aloft was undoubtedly a winning fighter's signal that he was still capable of hitting, at a stage when his rival was not. It is the frozen intention movement of delivering an overarm blow and is the same gesture that has been adopted as the modern communist salute. Studies of fighting behaviour between young children have revealed that this form of hitting, bringing the arm downwards from above, is very basic to our species and does not have to be learned. So it is interesting to see that the modern boxer still uses the intention movement of this action as a victory gesture, even though, in his actual fighting, he no longer employs it, but uses instead highly stylized and 'unnatural' frontal punches. It is also intriguing to notice how, in more informal fighting, such as that which occurs during street rioting, both the police and the rioters revert largely to the more primitive form of overarm hitting.

Returning now to the question of males holding hands in public, there is one final special context in which this occurs. It concerns priests, and especially those of high rank in the Catholic Church. The Pope, for instance, can frequently be seen to hold hands with his followers, both male and female, and this exception illustrates the way in which a well-known public figure can set himself outside normal conventions. The Pope's image is so totally non-sexual that he can perform a whole variety of fragmented intimacies with perfect strangers, intimacies which ordinary citizens could never contemplate. Who else, for example, could reach out and hold the cheeks of a beautiful girl in a completely non-sexual way? The Pope is, in fact, able to behave very much like the 'holy father' that he is called, and can confidently make intimate body contacts with adult strangers in the same way as a real father would do with his real children. By adopting the role of a super-father, the pontiff can strip away the body-contact restrictions that others must use, and return to the more natural and primary intimacies typical of the early parent-offspring phase. If he still appears more inhibited with his followers than a real father would be with his children, this is not due to the sexual confusion that restricts the rest of us, but simply to the fact that, in the face of a family of 500 million children, he has to conserve his strength.

Up to this point we have been moving away from the full embrace by travelling, as it were, across the shoulders and down the arm to the hand, and in that direction we can go no further. Instead, we can look at what other parts of the body come into contact with one another during the full embrace, and see if there, too, there are sources of useful fragments that can be employed in day-to-day encounters.

The pressing together of the trunks and legs during the full frontal embrace does not appear to be a very rich source and it is not hard to see why. For adults to touch one another in these regions, in public, brings them too close to the forbidden sexual zones. But there is another important contact region involved in the full embrace, and that is the head. At high intensities, the sides of the heads are pressed together, caressed with the hands or touched with the lips, and from these actions we do find the development of three important fragments that are widely used in everyday life. They can be labelled as the head-to-head contact, the hand-to-head contact and the kiss.

The head contacts. Touching the partner's head with the hand, and putting the two heads together, are both specialities of young lovers. This is especially true of the former. Hand-to-head contacts are four times as common between young lovers as between older married couples. Head-to-head contacts are twice as common with young lovers, and in both cases this contrasts with an intimacy such as the shoulder embrace, which is more common between the older couples.

Males rarely employ these head contacts with other males. When men 'put their heads together', they do not usually do it literally, the function being to indulge in intimate conversation rather than true body intimacy. If a male hand touches a male head, it usually does so for one of three special reasons: giving first aid, bestowing a blessing or delivering an attack. If a male (or a female) encounters an accident victim, the helplessness of the wounded person transmits strong infantile signals that are hard to resist. Photographs of the victims of assassination attempts, for example, nearly always show someone cradling the victim's head in their hands. Medically this is a somewhat dubious procedure, but medical logic has no place here. This is not a trained act of assistance; it is a more basic response related to the primary parental care of a helpless child. It is much too difficult for an untrained person to pause and make a reasoned assessment of the physical injuries the victim has sustained before taking first-aid action. Instead, he will reach out and touch or lift as a primary act of comfort, with no thought to the further damage he may be causing. It is too painful to stand by and coldly calculate the best steps to be taken. The urge to make comforting body contact is overpowering, but we have to face the fact that it can sometimes prove fatal. Once, as a small boy, ignorant of what was happening, I watched a man killed in this way. Following an accident, his injured body was cradled in the loving arms of anxious helpers who lifted him into a car to drive him away. The loving act destroyed his life by pressing his splintered ribs through his lungs. Had he been 'callously' left lying where he was until a stretcher arrived, he might have lived. Such is the power of the urge to make body contact when tragedy strikes, and this applies to males and females equally, for disaster knows no sex.

The bestowing of priestly blessings is equally sexless, as in the laying on of hands of a bishop in ordination or confirmation. Here we are back again to a copy of the primary parent-child relationship.

The delivering of an attack by the hand of one male to the head of another requires little comment in itself, but it does provide one possible source of inter-male intimacy. If a man feels the friendly urge to touch another man's head but is inhibited about making it a friendly caress, he can employ the simple device of mock-aggression. Instead of fondling his partner's head, which would have too strong a sexual flavour, he can deliver a playful 'pretend-attack', such as ruffling the hair or squeezing the neck in a mock-grasp. Just as play-fighting helped the parent to prolong intimacies with his growing children, so many a fragment of play-assault can be observed between male friends, enabling them to be both manly and intimate at one and the same time.

The kiss. This brings us to the last of the important derivatives of the primary embrace, namely the kiss, an action with an intriguing and complex history. If you feel that a kiss is a simple enough act, think for a moment about the many ways in which you do it, even in today's supposedly informal society. You kiss your lover on the lips, an old friend of the opposite sex on the cheek, an infant on the top of the head; if a child hurts a finger, you kiss it 'to make it better'; if you are about to face danger, you kiss a mascot 'to bring you luck'; if you are a gambler, you kiss the dice before you roll them; if you are the best man at a wedding, you kiss the bride; if you are religious, you kiss the bishop's ring as a sign of respect, or the Bible when taking an oath; if you are bidding someone farewell and they are already out of reach, you kiss your own hand and blow the kiss towards them. No, the kiss is not a simple matter, and to understand it we must once again turn back the clock.

The most sensitive areas of skin on the human body are the tips of the fingers, the clitoris, the tip of the penis, the tongue and the lips. It is not surprising, therefore, that the lips should be used a great deal in intimate body contacts. Their role begins in the act of sucking at the mother's breast, which provides a major tactile reward in addition to the reward of obtaining milk. This has been proved by studying the behaviour of unfortunate babies who have been born with an abnormal, blocked oesophagus, and who have to be fed by artificial means. It was observed that if they were given rubber teats to suck, this helped to calm them down and stopped them crying. Since they had never taken any food through the mouth, the reward of having a teat between the lips could have nothing to do with the pleasure of the milk supply that normally results from such an action. It had to be a case of contact for contact's sake. So the touching of something soft with the mouth is an important and primary intimacy in its own right.

As the child grows and exchanges head-to-head contacts with the mother, feeling her lips pressed to his skin and his to hers, it is easy to see how this early mouth contact can develop into a potent act of friendly greeting. In the embrace of childhood, the usual position for the lips when touching the parent will be the cheek or the side of the head. As I have already mentioned, in ancient times, when the full embrace was given more freely between adults of either sex, the kiss on the cheek was the usual form of mouth contact employed between equals. This was, in a sense, the primitive greeting kiss taken straight from childhood with little modification, and it has persisted through the centuries right down to the present day. In our culture, male and female friends and relatives still kiss in this way when meeting or parting, and the act can be performed without any sexual implication whatever. The same is true of adult females with adult females. Between adult males the situation varies considerably from country to country, with France, for example, remaining much closer to the ancient system than England.

Direct mouth-to-mouth kissing has taken a different course. At various times and in various places it has been employed to some extent as a non-sexual greeting between close friends, but the joining of two body orifices in this way has usually seemed to be an act of too great an intimacy even for close friends, and generally speaking it has become more and more restricted to contacts between lovers and mates.

Since the female breasts are sexual signals as well as feeding devices, the kissing of a female breast by an adult male has also become totally sexual in context, despite the similarity of the act to the primitive action of sucking at the breast in infancy. Needless to say, kissing of the genitals is also exclusively sexual, and so indeed is the kissing of many other parts of the body, especially the trunk, thighs and ears. Certain specific parts of the body, however, have been formally set aside for a special kind of non-sexual kissing – what we might call the subordinate kiss, or the kiss of reverence. This differs categorically from both the friendly kiss and the sexual kiss, and to understand it we must look at the way in which a subordinate human being presents himself in front of a dominant.

It is well known from studies of animal behaviour that one way to appease the wrath of a dominant animal is to make yourself seem smaller and therefore less threatening to him. If you threaten him less, then he is less likely to see you as a challenge to his superiority and therefore less likely to take damaging action against you. He will simply ignore you as being beneath him, both metaphorically and literally, which, if you happen to be the weaker animal, is precisely what you want (at least for the moment). And so we see all manner of cringings and crouchings, grovellings and hunchings-up, downcast eyes and lowered heads, in a wide variety of animal species.

It is the same with man. Where there are no formalities, the response takes the animal form of cringing low on the ground, but in many situations the response of the inferior man has become highly stylized, and these stylizations have varied considerably from place to place and from time to time. This does not put them outside the realm of a biological analysis, however, for they all, without exception, still reveal basic features that clearly relate them to the submissive behaviour of other species of animals.

The most extreme form of submissive body-lowering ever seen in man is full prostration, in which the whole body lies flat on the ground, face down. You simply cannot get any lower than that without an act of burial. The dominant, on the other hand, can, and often did, enhance the lowering effect by viewing it from a raised platform or throne. This total act of servility was common and widespread in the ancient kingdoms, performed by prisoners to their captors, slaves to their masters, and servants to their rulers. Between it and the act of standing fully erect, there is a whole range of formalized submissions, and we can scan them briefly in ascending order.

Next to the full prostration comes the kowtow of the Eastern world, in which the body does not lie, but kneels down and then bends the trunk low until the forehead is touching the ground. Coming one stage up from this is the full kneel, with both knees on the ground, but without the forward bending of the body. This, too, was frequently used in the ancient world when confronting an overlord, but by medieval times it had already risen to the half-kneel, with only one knee lowered to the ground. Men were then specifically instructed to reserve the full kneel for God, who by this time had to be given a little more respect than the rulers of the day. In modern times it is rare for us to kneel to any man at any time, except on certain state occasions in the presence of royalty, but worshippers in church have not changed the ancient full-kneel custom to this day, God having maintained his dominant status rather more successfully than modern rulers.

Coming one stage further up, we reach the curtsy (or courtesy), which was no more than an intention movement of the half-kneel. One leg was drawn back slightly, as if its knee was going to go down and touch the ground, and then both knees started to bend, but neither reached ground level. The body was not bowed forward. Up until the time of Shakespeare both men and women made the curtsy. In this respect, at least, there was equality between the sexes. The male bow had not yet appeared. With the arrival of the curtsy, the act of servility was further reduced, and the half-kneel started to fade from the scene, being given only to royalty.

In the seventeenth century the sexes split up, the men now bowing from the waist while the women retained the curtsy. Both actions lowered the body in front of the dominant individual, but in entirely different ways. From that day to this the situation has remained much the same, except that the extent of the actions has been reduced. The flowery male bowing of the Restoration period gave way to the much simpler and stiffer bow of Victorian times, and the curtsy dwindled to little more than a bob down and up. Today, except in the presence of powerful rulers or royalty, the curtsy is rarely given by women, and the male bow, if given at all, is seldom more than a mere lowering and raising of the head.

The one exception to this rule occurs at the end of a theatrical performance, when, for some reason, the performers slip back several centuries and indulge in deep bows and elaborate curtsies. It is amusing that here we sometimes also see an entirely new trend, with female performers bowing deeply as if they were males. It looks as if this return to sexual equality in the act of subordination is mirroring the new trend towards female equality in all other matters, but if this is the case, the males can at least claim that it was the females who changed to the male action, rather than that the males had to return to their medieval curtsying. It is just possible that there is another reason altogether for the actress's bow which has nothing to do with the masculinizing of the modern female in our culture. It may instead have to do with the precise opposite, dating back to the earlier times of play-acting, when all the actors were male, and half the men were feminized to play the female roles. Perhaps the modern actress when she bows is by force of tradition merely imitating her male transvestite predecessors. Even allowing for the persistence of ancient traditions, however, this explanation appears improbable. It seems much more likely that she feels she is joining the men.

All the bowing and scraping of yesterday's everyday greetings has now been almost universally replaced by the far more forthright and upstanding handshake. In this act, at last, there is no lowering of the body. We greet erect and, in so doing, have travelled the full distance from flat prostration. Today all men are not only 'born equal', but are still considered to be so, in greetings at least, when they are fully adult.

I have gone into these formalities of greeting at some length, despite the fact that, until we reach the handshake, they do not in themselves involve the intimacies of body contact. This digression was necessary because of their importance in relation to the kiss of reverence. I began by saying that, in ancient times, two equals kissed one another on the cheek, that is, at equal body height. But for an inferior to kiss a superior in this way would have been unthinkable. If he was to show his friendship by a touch of the lips, then that touch had to be performed at a level low enough to match his inferiority. For the lowest subordinates this meant the act of kissing the dominant one's foot. For an abject prisoner even this was too good, and he was forced to kiss the ground near the dominant shoe. In modern times these actions are rare, rulers not being what they once were, but even now the ruler of Ethiopia, for example, may find himself accorded this honour by one of his subjects in a public place. And slang phrases such as 'kiss the dirt', 'bite the dust' and 'boot-licker' are still with us to remind us of the humiliations of yesterday.

For those of slightly less inferiority, it was permissible to kiss the hem of a garment, or to kiss the knee of the dominant individual. A bishop, for instance, was permitted to kiss the Pope's knee, but a lesser mortal had to be content with kissing the cross embroidered on his right shoe.

Coming one step further up the body, we arrive at the kiss on the hand. This, too, was performed to many a dominant male, but today, apart from high-ranking priests, we reserve it entirely as a mark of respect to a lady, and even then only in certain countries and on certain occasions.

There were therefore four points on the body which were licensed, so to speak, for non-sexual kissing: the cheek, for friendly equality; the hand, for deep respect; the knee, for humble submission; and the foot, for grovelling servility. The action of touching with the lips was the same in each case, but the lower the point of its application, the lower was the expression of relative status. Despite all the pomp and ritual, nothing could be closer to a sequence of typical animal appeasement gestures. When stripped in this way of the fussy details of cultural variation and viewed as a whole, even the most courtly of human behaviour patterns come remarkably close to the patterns of animal behaviour we see all around us.

Earlier I listed a number of forms of modern kissing, some of which I may not appear to have explained: for example, kissing the dice before rolling them, kissing a lucky mascot, or a hurt finger to make it well. These and other similar actions, all of which are basically concerned with bringing good luck, are related to the kiss of reverence I have been describing. It is impossible to kiss God, the most dominant one of all, and so worshippers have to make do with symbols of God, such as crosses, Bibles, and similar objects. Since kissing them symbolizes kissing God, the act brings good luck simply because it appeases God. Any lucky mascot, therefore, is being treated as a holy relic. It may be odd to think of a gambler in Las Vegas kissing God when he blows on his dice during a crap game, but that is in effect what he is doing, just as when he crosses his fingers for good luck he is doing no more and no less than making a reverential sign of the cross to protect him from God's wrath. When we kiss our hands in farewell and blow a kiss to our departing friends, we are performing another ancient act, for in earlier days it was more servile to kiss one's own hand than the hand of the dominant person. The hand-kiss at the modern airport is the only survivor of this custom, even though it is now distance rather than servility that makes us perform the movement.

The handshake. With that farewell kiss, we leave the world of the fragmented embrace, with all its complexities, and come to the last of the adult body contacts that is important enough to be examined in detail, namely the handshake. I have already mentioned that this did not gain wide usage until about a hundred and fifty years ago, but its precursor, the hand-clasp, was employed long before that. In ancient Rome it was used as a pledge of honour, and this was to remain its primary function for nearly two thousand years. In medieval times, for instance, a man might kneel and clasp hands with his superior as an act of swearing allegiance to him. The addition of a shaking movement to the clasping hands is mentioned as early as the sixteenth century. The phrase 'they shook hands and swore brothers' appears in Shakespeare's *As You Like It*, where again the function is the binding of an agreement.

In the early part of the nineteenth century the situation changed. Although the handshake was still employed after the making of a promise or a contract, as an act of sealing it, it was now for the first time used in ordinary greetings. The cause of this change was the industrial revolution and the massive expansion of the middle classes, forcing an ever widening wedge between the aristocracy and the peasants. These new middlemen, with their businesses and their trades, were forever 'doing deals' and 'making agreements', and sealing them with the inevitable handshakings. Dealing and trading was becoming the new way of life, and social relationships began more and more to revolve around them. In this way the contractual handshake invaded the social occasion. Its message became the bartering one of 'I offer you an exchange of friendly greeting'. Gradually it ousted the other forms of greeting until today it has become universally used as the principal act performed, not only when meeting equals, but also when meeting both subordinates and superiors. Whereas once we would have had a wide range of alternatives to suit each type of social encounter, today we have merely this one. What a president does to a farm worker is now the same as what a farm worker does to a president – they both offer a hand, clasp it and shake it, both smiling as they do so. Furthermore, when a president meets another president, or a farm worker meets another farm worker, they will behave in precisely the same way. In terms of body intimacies, times have certainly changed. But if the ubiquitous handshake has simplified matters in one way, it has complicated them in another. We may know that it is the thing to do, but when precisely do we do it? Who offers the hand to whom?

Modern books of etiquette are full of conflicting advice, clearly indicating the confusion that exists. One tells us that a man never holds out his hand to a woman for a handshake, while another informs us that in many parts of the world it is the man who takes the initiative. One tells us that a younger man should never offer his hand to an older one, while another advises that, whenever we are in doubt, we should offer the hand, rather than risk hurting someone's feelings. One authority insists that a woman should rise to shake hands, another that she should remain seated. Further complications exist in respect of whether we are hosts or guests, male hosts offering their hands to female guests, but male guests waiting for a female hand to be offered to them. There are also separate rules for business and social occasions. One book goes so far as to say that 'There are no rules as to when to shake hands,' but clearly this is a statement of despair, the truth being that there are in fact far too many rules.

Obviously there is some hidden complication in the superficially simple act of handshaking which we must unravel if we are to understand these confusions. To do this we must look back at the origins of the act. If we go back as far as our animal relatives, we find that a subordinate chimpanzee will often appease a dominant one by reaching out towards it with a limp hand, as if making a begging gesture. If the action is returned, the two animals briefly touch hands in a contact that looks remarkably like an abbreviated handshake. The initial signal reads, 'See, I am just a harmless beggar who dare not attack you,' and the reply is, 'I will not attack you either.' Developing into a friendly gesture between equals, the message then becomes simply, 'I will not hurt you, I am your friend.' In other words, the chimpanzee hand-offering can be done either by a subordinate to a dominant, as a submissive act, or by a dominant to a subordinate, as a reassuring one, or it can be performed between equals as an act of friendship. Nevertheless, in this respect, it is fundamentally an appeasement gesture and, translated into the modern terms of the etiquette books, we would expect more emphasis to be placed on the inferior individual offering the hand first, to the superior.

Advancing now to the ancient human hand-clasp, we can see this in a similar light. Specifically, the offering of an empty hand revealed that there was no weapon in it, which would explain why we always use the right, or weapon, hand. Showing the hand in this way could be done either submissively, by a weaker to a stronger, or reassuringly, by a stronger to a weaker, as in the chimpanzee case. Developed into a strong, mutual hand-clasp, it became a vigorous pact-making device with two men accepting one another, momentarily at least, as equals. Essentially, however, it remains an act in which neither performer is asserting his dominance but, regardless of his relative status, is temporarily displaying himself as harmless.

This is one likely origin for the modern handshake, but there is another that confuses the picture. One of the important greeting acts of a male to a female was the kissing of the hand. To do this, the man took her offered hand in his before applying his lips to it. As this action became more stylized, the actual kissing element declined in intensity to a point where the mouth only approached the back of the lady's hand and stopped before making contact, the lips then forming a kiss in mid-air. Becoming even more fossilized, the act then sometimes occurred as a mere holding and raising of the lady's hand, accompanied by a slight bow of the head towards it. In this modified form it is little more or less than a weak handshake, but with the vigorous pumping action omitted. One writer has seen this as the sole source of the modern handshake: 'As a contact salutation the handshake would appear to be a late derivative of the "face-kiss", with the "hand-kiss" as a connecting link.' In this respect, offering the hand is essentially the act of asserted dominance towards a subordinate, and therefore differs fundamentally from the display of the male-pact handshake.

The truth appears to be that both the hand-clasp theory and the hand-kiss theory are correct, and that this double origin is the cause of all the confusion in the modern etiquette books. The point is that we do not today shake hands for a single reason only. We do it as a greeting, as a farewell, to make a pact, to seal a bargain, to congratulate, to accept a challenge, to give thanks, to commiserate, to make up after a squabble and to wish one another luck. There are two elements here. In some cases it symbolizes a friendly bond, in others merely that we are friendly at the moment of shaking. If I shake hands with a man when I am introduced to him for the first time, it is merely a courtesy and says nothing about our past or even our future relationship.

To put it another way, we can say that the modern handshake is a double act masquerading as a single one. The 'pact handshake' and the 'greeting handshake' have different origins and different functions, but because they have come to have the same form, we think of them both simply as the 'friendly handshake'. Hence all the confusion. Up to early Victorian times there was no problem. Then there was the pact hand-shake for males with males which said 'it's a deal', and the hand-kiss for males with females which said 'it's an honour to meet you'. But when the Victorians increasingly began to mix business with social life, the two became blended and muddled together. The vigorous pact handshake became softened and weakened, while the gentle clasping of the lady's hand in the already abbreviated hand-kiss became strengthened.

Although we accept this happily enough today, there was some resis-tance to it in nineteenth-century France, where the greeting shake was referred to as 'the American handshake', and frowned upon when it was done between visiting males and unmarried French girls. The reason for this was not so much the body contact involved, but simply that the French were still interpreting the handshake in its old masculine role. The visiting males were then seen to be 'making a pact' and establishing a bond of friendship with young girls they had only just met, which was considered highly improper. The foreign visitors, of course, thought that they were doing no more than offering a polite salutation.

This brings us back to the misunderstandings and confusions of the etiquette books. The big problem is who offers the hand to whom. Is it an insult to fail to offer the hand first and therefore to appear to be unfriendly, or to offer it first and therefore to appear to be demanding a modified hand-kiss? Careful observation of social occasions reveals that the confused greeters tend to solve the problem by watching for tiny clues. They look for the slightest sign of an intention movement of raising the arm on the part of the other person, and then try to make the contact appear to be simultaneous. Contributing to their confusion is the fact that with most other salutations the subordinate acts first to show his respect. The private salutes the officer before the officer salutes the private. In earlier days, it was always the junior who bowed first to the senior. But with kissing the hand it was different. The lady had to offer her hand first. No respectful male would grab it first without waiting for a sign from her. Because the hand-kiss is involved in the origin of handshake greetings, this rule still applies in most cases. The man waits for the woman to offer her hand for shaking, as if she were still offering it to be kissed. However, not to offer the hand to her first, now that the kissing has vanished from the act, is tanta-mount to saying that he is the officer and she the private, and that she must make the first sign of salute. Hence all the warnings and mum-blings of the etiquette experts.

The other origin of the handshake, concerning the making of pacts, further confuses the situation. The weaker male usually offers his hand first here, to show his eagerness to the stronger one. In a contest, it is usually the weaker loser who offers his hand to the stronger winner in the act of congratulation, to show that, despite his defeat, the bond of friendship is reconfirmed. So, for an eager young businessman to greet a senior colleague with an outstretched hand may be looked upon either as brashness ('you may kiss my hand'), or as humility ('you are the winner'). Again, as with the social occasions, the problem is usually solved by watching for small intention clues and trying to contrive a simultaneous act.

Given its complicated past and its confused present, one might expect to see the handshake on the decline in the increasingly informal world of today, and in certain contexts this appears to be the case. Social greetings are becoming increasingly verbal. Around the middle of the present century, the etiquette experts announced that 'Hand-shaking on introductions between men is nowadays on the wane in Great Britain.' Despite this, it is still much more common for a male/male shake to occur, rather than a male/female shake or a female/female shake. My observations suggest that two-thirds of all handshaking is done between males; in the remaining third, shaking between the sexes is three times as common as between females. These figures fit well with the history of the action, for men have inherited the handshake as a pact device and then added to it the greeting function, giving the all-male pattern double value, so to speak. Women with men have inherited it from the hand-kiss, but have not yet taken an equal role in business, so are poor on pact handshakes. And women with women never did hand-kiss, so are poor on both, and come at the bottom of the handshaking league.

A final point about this particular form of body contact, which may seem obvious but is significant nevertheless, is that lovers do not do it. Nor, in most countries, do married couples. Ask an Englishman who has been married for, say, twelve years when he last greeted his wife by shaking hands with her, and the answer is more likely to be twelve years than twelve days. This is, without any doubt, the least amorous of all friendly body contacts. In all the other cases mentioned in this chapter, from the full embrace to the kiss, there has always been a strong sexual element. They have all originated from the same primary source and they have all been performed more between lovers and mates than between adults in any other roles. When performed between males there have, in most cases, been special circumstances which make this possible. The handshake, by contrast, stemming originally not from a tender embrace but from a masculine act of pact-making, has avoided these difficulties. Even the later involvement of the hand-kiss in its history has not created any problems, because this was already a formalized, de-sexed kiss of reverence before it became incorporated. Strong men have therefore been able to shake one another's hands until they are blue in the palms without running the slightest risk of creating an amorous impression. The very act of shaking the clasped hands up and down in mid-air that typifies the action helps to make it more brusque and less gentle, and distinguishes it clearly, even at a distance, from the lovers' act of holding hands.

In this chapter we have looked at the way adults behave towards one another in public and we have seen how the all-enveloping, un-inhibited intimacies of infancy have become restricted, pigeon-holed and labelled. It can be argued that this has taken place because adults need greater independence of action and greater mobility than infants, and that more extensive body contacts would limit them in this respect. That would explain the reduction in the amount of time actually spent touching, but not the reduction of the intimacy of the touches that do still occur. It can be argued that it has taken place because adults do not need so much body contact; but if that is so, then why do they spend so much of their time indulging in second-hand intimacy in books, films, plays and television, and why is it that popular songs cry out the message hour after hour? It can be argued that our untouchability has to do with status, with not wishing to be touched by our inferiors and not daring to touch our superiors; but if this is so, then why are we not more intimate with our equals? It can be argued that we do not wish to have our intimate actions confused with those of lovers; but how does this explain the fact that lovers themselves, in public, restrict their intimacies so much more than they do in private?

All these arguments give partial answers, but there is something missing. This hidden factor seems to be the powerful bonding effect that close body intimacies have on those who perform them. We cannot be close physically without becoming 'close' emotionally. In our busy modern lives, we hold back from such involvements, even though we may need them. Our relationships are too profuse, too vague, too complex, and often too insincere for us to be able to risk the primitive bonding processes of body intimacy. In the ruthless world of business, we can dismiss a girl with whom we have only shaken hands, or we can betray a colleague with whom we have done no more than rest a hand on a shoulder; but what if the body contacts had been greater? What if, without any sexual involvement, we had experienced greater intimacies with them? Then, without a doubt, we would have seen our tough determination soften, and our competitiveness dwindle, when the moments for brutal decisions came. And if we dare not expose ourselves to these dangers, to these powerful reciprocal involvements that know no logic, then we certainly do not want to be reminded of them by seeing them flaunted in public by others. So the young lovers can keep to themselves and do it in private, and in case they ignore our request we will make it law. We will make it a crime to be intimate in public. And so it is that, even to this day, in certain sophisticated, civilized countries it remains a crime to kiss in public. A tender act of touching becomes immoral and illegal. A gentle intimacy becomes legally equated with an act of theft. So hide it away quickly, lest the rest of us see what we are missing!

It has sometimes been said that if only all the tight-lipped defenders of public morals would embrace one another lovingly, caress one another's faces, and kiss one another's cheeks, they might suddenly feel it was time to go home and leave the rest of society to go about its friendly, loving business without having to endure their desperate envy. But it is pointless to despise them, for society stitches its own strait-jacket. The teeming zoo in which we live is not the ideal setting for public intimacies. It suffers from people pollution; we bump into one another and apologize, when we should be reaching out to touch; we collide headlong and curse, when we should be embracing and laughing. There are strangers everywhere and so we hold ourselves back. There seems to be no alternative. Our only compensation is to indulge more heavily in private intimacies, but this we frequently fail to do. It seems as if our public restraint can spread to infect our conduct even in the bosom of our families. For many, the solution is to indulge in second-hand intimacies by spending the evening hours avidly watching the abandoned touchings and embracings of the professionals on our television or cinema screens, listening to endless words of love in our popular songs, or reading them in our novels and magazines. For some, there are other, more heavily disguised alternatives, as we shall see on the pages that follow.

5

SPECIALIZED INTIMACY

By STUDYING THE behaviour of infants and lovers, it becomes clear that the degree of physical intimacy that exists between two human animals relates to the degree of trust between them. The crowded conditions of modern life surround us with strangers whom we do not trust, at least not fully, and we go to great pains to keep our distance from them. The intricate avoidance patterns of any busy street bear witness to this. But the frenzy of urban living creates stress, and stress breeds anxiety and feelings of insecurity. Intimacy calms these feelings, and so, paradoxically, the more we are forced to keep apart, the more we need to make body contact. If our loved ones are loving enough, then the supply of intimacy they offer will suffice, and we can go out to face the world at arm's length. But supposing they are not; supposing we have failed as adults to form close bonds with either friends or lovers, and have no children; what do we do then? Or supposing we have formed these bonds successfully, but then they have broken down, or become fossilized into the remoteness of indifference, with the 'loving' embrace and kiss becoming as formalized as a public handshake; what then? The answer for many is simply to grouse and bear it, but there *are* solutions, and one of these is the device of employing professional touchers, a measure which helps to some extent to compensate for the shortcomings of the amateur and amatory touchers who are failing to supply us with our much-needed quota of body intimacy.

Who are these professional touchers? The answer is that they are virtually any strangers or semi-strangers who, under the pretext of providing us with some specialist service, are required to touch our bodies. This pretext is necessary because, of course, we do not like to admit that we are insecure and need the comforting touch of another human body. That would be 'soft', immature, regressive; it would assail our image of ourselves as self-controlled, independent adults. And so we must get our dose of intimacy in some disguised form.

One of the most popular and widespread methods is being ill. Nothing serious, of course, merely some mild sickness that will stimulate in others the urge to perform comforting acts in intimacy. The majority of people imagine that when they fall prey to some minor ailment, they have simply been unlucky in accidentally encountering a hostile virus, bacterium, or some other form of parasite. If they come down with a nasty bout of influenza, for instance, they feel it could have happened to anyone – anyone who, like them, has been shopping in busy stores, standing on tightly packed buses, or jamming themselves into stuffy corners at overcrowded parties, where coughs and sneezes can be heard incessantly wafting their eager pathogens through the air. The facts, however, do not support this view. Even at the height of a flu epidemic, there are still many people – equally exposed to the infection – who do not succumb. How is it that *they* manage to avoid taking to their sick-beds? How, in particular, does the medical profession manage to remain so remarkably healthy? They, more than anyone, are massively exposed to infection all day and every day, but they do not seem to become proportionally sick.

Minor ailments, therefore, do not appear to be entirely a matter of unlucky accident. In a modern city there are hostile microbes everywhere. Almost every day, and in almost every place we walk and breathe, we are exposed to sufficient of them to bring us down with some sort of infection. If we defeat them, it is not so much that we manage to avoid them as that our bodies are equipped with a highly efficient defence system which slaughters them by the million, week in and week out. If we succumb, it is not so much that we have been accidentally exposed to them as that we have, for some reason, lowered our body defences. One way we do this (apart from excessive hygiene!) is to let ourselves become overstressed and overstrained by the pressures of urban life. In our weakened condition, we soon fall prey to one or other of the wide selection of unfriendly microbes that fill the world around us. Luckily for us, the disease is its own cure, for, in putting us to bed, it provides us with the very comfort we were lacking before. We might call this the 'instant-baby' syndrome.

The man who is feeling 'poorly' begins to look weak and helpless and starts to transmit powerful pseudo-infantile signals to his wife. She responds automatically as an 'instant-parent' and begins to mother him, insisting on tucking him up in his bed (cot) and bringing him soup, hot drinks and medicine (baby food). Her tone of voice becomes softer (the maternal coo) and she fusses over him, feeling his forehead and performing other intimacies of a kind that were missing before, when he was fit and well but equally in need of them. The curative effect of this comfort behaviour works wonders and he is soon back in action again, facing the hostile world outside.

This description does not imply malingering. It is essential for the patient to be truly and visibly sick in order to stimulate fully the necessary pseudo-parental care. This accounts for the high frequency of strongly debilitating, but comparatively pain-free, minor ailments in cases of emotionally induced illness. It is important, not only to be sick, but to be seen to be sick.

To some, these comments will seem cynical, but that is not my intention. If the stress of life demands that we shall obtain increased comfort and intimacy from our closest companions, and forces us once again to sink into the warm embrace of the soft bedding of our 'cots', then this is a valuable social mechanism and must not be sneered at.

It is, indeed, so useful a device that it has come to support a major industry. Despite all the impressive technological advances of modern medicine and our so-called conquest of the environment, we still get sick at an astonishingly high rate. The majority of the victims do not see the inside of a hospital ward. They may be out-patients, pharmacy clients, or merely self-treating in the home. They suffer from a great variety of common ailments such as coughs, colds, influenza, headaches, allergies, backaches, tonsillitis, laryngitis, stomach-aches, ulcers, diarrhoea, skin rashes, and the like. The fashions change from generation to generation – once it was 'the vapours', now it is 'a virus' – but basically the list remains much the same. In terms of simple frequency of occurrence, these cases account for the vast majority of present-day illnesses.

In Britain, for example, over 500 million pharmaceutical purchases are made every year to treat minor illnesses, which works out at roughly ten ailments per year, per head of the population. Some 100 million pounds is spent annually on these products. Over two-thirds of all illnesses are not serious enough to involve the services of a doctor.

The reason for this situation is simple enough. All the time, our populations are increasing in size and our communities becoming more and more overcrowded and overstressed. The larger numbers of people involved means that there is more and more money available for medical research, which finds better and better cures. In the meantime, however, the populations have grown again, the social stresses have become greater and the susceptibility to disease has increased. Therefore more medical research is needed, and so on, neck and neck, into an imaginary, disease-free future that will never come.

But suppose for a moment that I am being pessimistic; suppose that some medical miracle has eventually appeared on the scene and defeated and exterminated all the parasites. Will we then finally have arrived at a condition where the downtrodden, emotionally bruised urbanite can no longer collapse with impunity into the comforting arms of his sick-bed? The chances are more than remote that this miracle will ever happen, but even if it did there are still several alternatives open to the would-be 'instant-baby'. These are already in frequent use. In the absence of suitable viruses or bacteria, he can always have a 'nervous breakdown'. Minor mental illnesses have the advantage that they can operate in the absence of acquired microbes, and they are equally effective as comfort-producers. Indeed, they are so effective that even a murderer can plead 'temporary insanity' as an excuse for his actions and have his sentence modified on the grounds of 'diminished responsibility' – again being treated as if he were a 'temporary infant'. Pleading that he was suffering from a cold in the head at the time of the murder would provide less comfort to him, so there is clearly a lot to be said for the power of mental breakdown as a survival device when stress becomes extreme. The main disadvantage here is that many of the milder versions of mental illness are lacking in the external symptoms necessary to provoke the much-needed comforting reactions. The emotionally bruised individual is driven to extremes to produce the required response. Internal agonizing is not enough, but after a good bout of screaming hysterics, his collapsed body stands a very high chance of feeling itself snugly enveloped in the embracing arms of an earnest comforter. If the breakdown is more violent, he may instead find himself encased in forcibly restraining arms, but even then all is not lost, for he will have succeeded, albeit in a desperate way, in making some kind of intimate body contact with another human being. Only if he loses control completely will he fail and find himself condemned to the solitary self-embrace imposed by the canvas sleeves of a strait-jacket.

A second alternative in the absence of foreign parasites is the use of the patient's own endogenous microbes, the ones that he has been carrying on his body all his life. To explain how this works, we must take a close look, in fact a microscopic look, at the surfaces of our bodies.

Many people seem to imagine that *all* microbes are nasty and that they automatically mean disease or dirt, but this is not true. As any bacteriologist will testify, this is nothing more than the modern myth of the new hygiene religion, the religion whose aerosol prayers keep its worshippers 'free from all known germs', whose holy water is anti-septic solution, and whose god is totally sterile. Of course, there *are* vicious, deadly germs that we do well to destroy as ruthlessly as possible. There is no denying that. But what about the 'germs' whose main activity in life is killing off other germs? Do we really want to kill all known germs?

The fact is that we are each of us protected by a vast army of friendly microbes that do not hinder us but, on the contrary, actively help us to keep healthy. On our healthy, clean skin there is an average of five million of them to every square centimetre. Ordinary saliva, spat from the mouth, contains between ten million and 1,000 million bacteria in every cubic centimetre. Every time we defecate we lose 100,000 million microbes, but their numbers are soon made up again inside the body. This is the normal condition of the adult human animal. If we managed to live 'germ-free' of our own microbes all our lives, we would be at a grave disadvantage. Amongst other things, we would be less resistant to the foreign, and really vicious, microbes that we would encounter from time to time. We know this from careful experiments with germ-free laboratory animals. Our natural load of body microbes is therefore of great value to us, but now comes the catch. We have to pay a price for their good services, for even they can get out of hand when we become unduly stressed. Some of our diseases are caused, not by acquiring infections from others, but by a sudden eruption and 'over-crowding' of our own 'normal' microbes. The usual measures of public hygiene that assist in cutting down cross-infection from one person to another cannot help in such cases: we do not 'catch' the diseases; we carry the makings of them ourselves all the time. This is particularly true of many of the alimentary upsets so common in the emotionally stressed patient. If we have 'stomach trouble' we put it down to 'something bad' that we ate, but it is amazing what a healthy, happy person can devour and get away with. Probably nearly all the mild stomach and intestinal upsets we suffer from are due instead to emotional disturbances resulting from failures to adjust to the stresses and strains of modern living. To remind ourselves of this we have only to watch a natural history film of a flock of healthy vultures on the plains of Africa, gobbling down the putrid flesh of a decaying carcass, an event which is more likely to turn our own stomachs rather than those of the birds concerned.

A third alternative for the human individual in need of comfort is a more drastic one. Failing mental illness or endogenous illness, he can, with a little agitated carelessness, become dramatically accident-prone. If he trips over and breaks an ankle, he will soon be able to curse that he is 'as helpless as a baby', and in no time at all find himself helped and supported just like one. But surely accidents are accidental? Of course they can be, but nevertheless it is surprising how much people vary in their susceptibility to 'accidental' injuries. In a recent hospital investigation into the emotional backgrounds of disease patients, a number of accident patients were used as a control group, because it was assumed that they must be in their hospital beds 'by accident', in both senses of the word. Results showed that this was far from being the case, the accident victims proving to be, if anything, more emotionally disturbed than the disease patients.

Our stressed urban comfort-seeker, therefore, has several ways in which he can become suitably helpless and promote calming intimacies from those who attend him. There is a considerable advantage in being mildly ill from time to time, and if the advantage cannot be gained in one way, there is always another open. This method of increasing adult intimacies does, however, have its drawbacks. In all cases it involves the sick individual in the adoption of a submissive role. To obtain the comforting attention that his ailment provokes, he is forced to become genuinely inferior, either physically or mentally, to his comforters. This was not so with the young lovers, who went 'soft' on a reciprocal basis that did not lower their social status. Furthermore, the patient's comfort-bath soon grows cold when he regains his health and strength, and the tender intimacies of those who have been caring for him cease abruptly. The reward was temporary, and the only way to prolong it is to become a chronic invalid who, as the saying goes, 'enjoys bad health'. Apart from prolonging the inferior status, this also introduces a new danger, that of ailment escalation. The comforting fire that has been lit may get out of control and burn down the house. Even when used as a short-term measure, there is always the risk of long-term damage to the organism, as ulcer-sufferers know to their cost. But for many who find the tensions of modern living hard to bear, the risk is worth it. Temporary respite is better than no respite. If they are lucky, it gives them time to recharge their emotional batteries, and in so doing it can be said, in biological terms, to have considerable survival value in today's crowded human communities.

Although much of the comfort obtained in this way is provided by the close companions of the patient, whose intimacy quotient becomes dramatically increased in most cases, the phenomenon of 'going sick' also provides the additional reward of obtaining the intimate attentions of a group of people who are comparative strangers – the members of the medical profession. Doctors are 'licensed to touch', and to do so with a degree of intimacy forbidden between most adults. Intuitively aware of this important element in their work, they know well the curative value of the 'bedside manner'. The reassurance of the softly spoken word, the confident touch of the hand that takes the pulse, or taps the chest, or turns the head to examine eyes and mouth, these are the body-contact actions that, for some, are better than a hundred pills.

Sometimes a doctor will order the removal of a patient to a hospital bed on emotional grounds alone. For an individual whose source of stress lies solely in the outside world, such a move is unnecessary. By staying at home and taking to his bed, he escapes the tension that is damaging him. But if the tension lies in the home itself, there is no such escape. If the emotional pressures are coming from inside the family unit, then even his bedroom may not provide the necessary hiding-place, where he can curl up and find the comfort he needs so badly. Then the only solution is the hospital cot, and pray God for short visiting hours.

The medical solution for the adult intimacy-seeker is, as we have seen, a mixed blessing, and he would clearly do better to look elsewhere. If he is religious, he can perhaps enjoy an unmixed blessing from the hands of a priest, but, failing that, there are several other soothing contacts he can enjoy.

There is the whole lush world of body conditioning and beautifying to indulge in, where an army of professional touchers is waiting to rub, slap, stroke, smooth and pluck almost any part of your body you wish to indicate. This is like a kind of 'healthy medicine', the unpleasant stigma of sickness being replaced by a mood that is predominantly athletic or cosmetic. Or so it seems; but once again there is a powerful element of body-contact-for-contact's-sake underlying all these activities. To be massaged from head to toe by a young masseuse is, for a man, almost as intimate a procedure as if he were to make love to her. In some ways it is more so, since by the time she has finished she will have made active body contact with nearly every part of his body, applying to each section of it in turn a rich variety of pressures, touches and tactile rhythms. Herein, we might dare to say, lies the rub, for the interaction, although it involves no direct sexual contact, is far too close for some men's comfort.

Perhaps it would be more correct to say that it is too close for the comfort of Western society. Privately, the massaged body would no doubt enjoy itself greatly, but the public image of the massage parlour is, in our culture, not what it might be. One trend has been to reduce the imagined eroticism of the activity by introducing sexual segregation, so that men massage men and women massage women. Even this step has failed to give this intrinsically harmless form of soothing body contact a widespread acceptance in modern society. In removing the heterosexual contact, the way was inevitably paved for dark murmurings about the homosexual element. Only intensely athletic males can, with ease, overcome this slur. For the boxer or the wrestler there is no problem. Like the triumphant footballers who could embrace passionately in public without criticism, because of their obviously aggressive, masculine role, the prize-fighter can luxuriate on his massage table without any adverse comment. In theory, the rest of the adult population could follow his lead and do so without the slightest sexual involvement, regardless of the sexes involved, but in practice this plainly has not happened, and so, for the unmassaged majority, we must look elsewhere for adult body intimacies.

One way in which the problem has been solved is to multiply the numbers involved and to eliminate the atmosphere of an intimate 'pair'. This is done in many gymnasiums and health farms, where groups of people gather to indulge in a variety of exercises which may include a great variety of body contacts without creating the flavour of two 'consenting adults in private'. Another method is to replace the human masseur or masseuse with a strictly sexless machine that embraces them, not with loving arms, but with an impersonal canvas belt which then proceeds to be mechanically intimate with them.

A more commonly employed solution is to restrict the body contacts to the less private parts of the human body. Here we move into the totally acceptable world of hairdressers and beauty experts, pausing only to cast a last sympathetic glance at the massage world, where some practitioners have attempted a similar restriction by coyly advertising that they provide only 'arm and leg massage'.

Since, in Western society, we all expose our heads to one another's public gaze, the hairdresser is automatically excused the stigma of increased nudity during the course of his professional body contacts. What he or she handles, we all see. Nevertheless, touching the head, as we saw in an earlier chapter, is normally reserved for only the closest of intimates and particularly characterizes the amorous contacts of young lovers. Between adult strangers it is almost taboo, and so the hairdresser, in the guise of a cosmetician, can fill an important gap for a contact-starved adult. This does not mean that the cosmetic role is unimportant, but merely that there is more to hairdressing than meets the mirror's eye.

Head-grooming, in the dual cosmetic/intimate role, has been with us for thousands of years. If we care to include our primate ancestors, we can safely put the figure at millions of years. The detailed and tender fingering that can be seen in any zoo monkey-house, as one monkey or ape works lovingly over the head-hair of its companion, leaves little doubt about the intimacy factor involved. Cleansing alone cannot account for the relaxed ecstasy of the primate groomee. And so it is with us, except that we, of course, cannot extend the interaction over our whole bodies like the furry monkey or ape. Where we cover our naked skins with clothing, we must rely on the deft, delicate touch of the tailor's fingers as he adjusts our new garments to rekindle – faintly, very faintly – the long-lost sensation of intimate body-grooming.

For the monkey, hair-grooming by another is an act of social bonding, so it is not surprising to find that in earlier periods of our history the professional hairdresser was a rarity. Hair was groomed by close intimates, rather than by comparative strangers. In the days when we lived in small tribes this was, of course, inevitable, since everyone in the social group knew everyone else on a personal basis. Later, when the urban revolution came and we found ourselves increasingly surrounded by strangers, the tendency was to restrict hairdressing and its associated activities to interactions between close personal contacts. Much later, with the increasingly complex coiffure that appeared after the Middle Ages, more expert attention was needed by the high-ranking members of society, and the professional hairdresser began to make his mark. At first, where ladies were concerned, his intimate operations were confined to the privacy of his clients' homes, but, gradually, more efficient public salons were opened and ladies of fashion began to flock to their doors. Even so, it was not until the second half of the last century that this became a common practice. Then the rush was on. In 1851 there were already 2,338 hairdressers operating in London, but fifty years later, in 1901, this figure had shot up to no less than 7,771, a dramatic rise that far outstripped the general increase in the city's population. Part of the reason for this change was undoubtedly economic, but perhaps, too, there was another factor, for the Victorian female was severely restricted in the other ways in which she could make adult body contacts. The rules of conduct were so tightened during this period that the caress of the hairdresser's hands must have provided a welcome intimacy in an era of such rigid restraint. Not only did more and more women venture forth, but they did so with increasing frequency. In the present century the pattern has spread out from the great cities and down to the smallest towns, involving almost the entire female population.

Aware that their modern clients craved more intimacy than the mere dressing of the hair could offer, this new army of professional touchers expanded the nature of their activities. Wherever there was exposed skin, they applied their delicate attentions. Manicures became popular. The 'facial' appeared on the scene. Mud-packs were applied, wrinkles smoothed and caressed, soft skin 'toned-up', the latest style of make-up demonstrated by a professional hand. 'Beauty', cried *Vogue* in 1923, 'is a full-time job.' There is no denying that the primary motive was visual, but the increased tactile intimacies involved in obtaining the desired visual effect were also undoubtedly of great importance. To visit a modern beauty parlour is nothing if not a touching experience.

By comparison, the modern male is poorly supplied with intimacies of this kind. Some men indulge in manicure and scalp massage, and a few still have their faces shaved occasionally, but for most the visit to the barber's is a quick snip-snip and home again to wash the hair themselves. It is interesting that the barber does his best to increase the intimacy of this simple snipping by employing a ritual device. If you are a male, the next time you visit your barber, listen to the snipping sound of his scissors and you will find that for every hair-snip there are a number of 'air-snips', the scissors snapping together rapidly in mid-air before closing in for the next actual cut. There is no mechanical function to these air-snips, but they create the impression of great activity in the proximity of the scalp and thereby effectively increase the impression of 'contact-complexity'.

For all that, the intimacy involved is a remarkably limited one, and it is surprising that today's males should accept such restrictions. Perhaps with the return of longer male hair-styles we shall witness some changes. So far, it must be admitted, there is little sign of any general increase, rather the reverse. If anything, long male hair now means that there is a rapid decline even in the simple snip-snip, with the hair-washing still done largely in the home. Only in the more sophisticated urban centres is there any indication that the new hair-styles are leading to greater barbering activities, and it remains to be seen whether this development will spread. But the fashion is new and, if it survives, it will take some time for it to regain the widespread respectability it once had. There is an unjustified stigma of 'effemi-nacy' attached to it by the older males in the population, who have still not woken up to the fact that their close-cropped styles arose primarily as anti-louse devices and that to insist on all males retaining such styles in a post-lousy era is the height of irrationality. As long as this slur persists, there will be a reluctance on the part of many of the younger males to continue their trend to its logical conclusion and once again luxuriate in more elaborate tonsorial intimacies.

Just about the only 'cosmetic' intimacy that the modern male enjoys more than the female is the use of a public shoe-shine and, as a trade, even that has been losing ground of late. In most big cities now it has become little more than a curiosity, found only at one or two special points. Apart from the oral-genital contacts discussed earlier, this is probably the only time in a modern man's life when he will see other human beings going on their knees before him to perform an act of body contact, and it is certainly the only time it will happen in public. (The shoe-shop attendant avoids the posture by sitting and leaning forward.) The kneeling posture of the shoe-shine creates such a strik-ing impression of servility that this feature has perhaps been his undoing. In the past, a man could more easily accept a display of humility of this kind, so that the humble intimacy performed was doubly rewarding, but with a growing respect for human equality such an overt submissiveness becomes almost embarrassing. A symbolic kissing of our feet is too much for us, and the shoe-shine is fast becoming a vanishing breed. It is not that we have ceased to be responsive to humiliating services – that would be too congratulatory a thought – but rather that we no longer wish to be *seen* to be so responsive to them.

In this survey of professional touchers, we have so far covered the doctor, the nurse, the masseur, the gymnastics and health-and-beauty instructors, the hairdresser, the tailor, the manicurist, the beautician, the make-up specialist, the barber, the shoe-shine and the shoe-shop attendant. To this list we could add many other related occupations such as those of the wig-maker, the hatter, the chiropodist, the dentist, the surgeon, the gynaecologist and a whole variety of medical and semi-medical specialists. Of these, few warrant special comment. The dentist usually causes too much stress for his oral intimacies to provide any contact reward. The surgeon, whose body intimacies go so very much deeper than those of even the most passionate lover, also has little impact on us emotionally, thanks to the use of anaesthetics.

The actions that must take place during a gynaecologist's examination of a patient are so similar, at a descriptive level, to the hand-to-genital contacts of a lover that here, too, paradoxically, there is no comfort in the intimacy. Embarrassment is reduced today by an intensely professional atmosphere, with both sides strictly on their guard against any misinterpretation of the anatomically sexual contact. Whereas holding a woman patient's hand while taking her pulse may provide the secondary benefits of soothing bodily intimacy, touching her genitals is inevitably *so* intimate that the emotional barriers clamp down immediately and no such benefits are possible.

In the past, the special nature of genital examinations has caused endless trouble for well-meaning gynaecologists. Extraordinary anti-intimacy procedures have been insisted on. Three hundred years ago he was even, on occasion, required to crawl into the pregnant woman's bedroom on his hands and knees to perform the examination, so that she would be unable to see the owner of the fingers which were to touch her so privately. At a later date, he was forced to work in a darkened room, or to deliver a baby by groping beneath the bed-clothes. A seventeenth-century etching shows him sitting at the foot of the labour bed with the sheet tucked into his collar like a napkin, so that he is unable to see what his hands are doing, an anti-intimacy device that made cutting the umbilical cord a particularly hazardous operation.

Despite these bizarre precautions, the male midwife was forever under fire, and just over two hundred years ago a learned textbook on the theory and practice of midwifery was openly condemned as 'the most bawdy, indecent and shameful book which the press ever brought into the world'. Needless to say, it was usually the men who complained and always the women who suffered. For centuries the sexual nature of the intimacies involved in assisting at the birth of a child stood in the way of efficient medical attention. Usually, properly qualified men were banished altogether from the labour bed, and the duties were performed by unskilled and often highly superstitious female midwives. (The word 'midwife' means simply 'with-the-wife', and makes no reference to the sex of the person concerned, although today we automatically think of it as indicating a woman, a fact that reflects this early ban on men.) As a result of this, an enormous number of women died in childbirth and many thousands of children succumbed at birth or in the first month of life. A large number of these cases were due entirely to the anti-intimacy rules that prevented skilled aid from being provided.

Here, then, is an instance of the sexual taboos on bodily contact creating a major social disaster and influencing the whole course of history. Year after year was to pass, and countless human miseries were to be heaped one on top of the other, before sanity prevailed and science was able to sweep away the ancient prejudices. Only by obeying the strictest possible code of conduct has the profession gradually been able to eliminate these early stupidities. Even so, the echoes of ancient fears can still be felt, and the modern gynaecological examination remains comfortless in the sphere of bodily contact.

There is only one area of social activity where sexual contacts do not suffer in this way, and that is the theatrical profession. Actors and actresses, including ballet dancers, opera singers and photographic models, all enjoy a professional life where they are widely licensed to touch one another in a sexual manner. In their performances they kiss and fondle, embrace and stroke, as the director demands. If it is in the script, it is within the social 'law', and the actor or actress can, during his or her working day, enjoy many bodily-contact comforts. For such an insecure profession this is undoubtedly a major benefit, although the extremes sometimes demanded can lead to difficulties. It is hard to pretend to make love to someone, even a professional colleague, time and time again, without the basic emotional reactions beginning to creep into the relationship, and this often happens, to the detriment of other intimate relationships in the 'real' world outside. If sexual intimacies are mimicked well enough, it is not easy to suppress the true biological responses which normally accompany them.

Another hazardous contact reward for the stars who dazzle us in the entertainment world is the physical acclaim of their more ardent followers. In public places they may find themselves hemmed in by eager fans, desperate to touch their idols. At a mild level this can provide a pleasant emotional reward, but occasionally it can lead to bruises and even injury. The powerful urge to touch the bodies of

certain star musicians and singers – and even some of the more glamor-
ous politicians – has recently reached staggering proportions. For the
groupie girls who follow the more famous pop stars, there are literally
no holds barred. Perhaps the most intimate example is that of the
'plaster-casters', groupies who persuade their pop idols to permit them
to take plaster casts of their erect genitals, so that these effigies can be
touched later at leisure, after their gods have departed.

In dealing with these interactions between pop stars and their fans,
we have moved away from the situation in which touching is an
inherent part of the professional activity itself. A masseur or a hairdresser *has* to touch his client or he cannot perform his task, but a
singer does not have to touch or be touched in order to perform his
songs. The fact that his special role in society makes him more touch-
worthy is a secondary factor. A similar condition applies in other
spheres, an obvious example being the police.

It is not the policeman's job to touch people, but he is nevertheless
licensed to do so with much greater freedom than the rest of us. He can
lay hands on us in a way we would resent in a member of the general
public. He can take a child's hand in the street without causing
comment. In a crowd he can push against us to keep us back, and we
accept his contact role with equal ease. If he manhandles us when we
are violent, again we are less likely to lash out wildly at him than
we are at someone else who treats us in a similar manner. Only at the
extremes of violence, where his own restraint breaks down and he
begins to behave, under intense provocation, like a uniformed thug, do
we fully disinhibit our reactions to him. Then, by contrast, our fury
knows no bounds, as recent riot-scenes have testified all too often. It is
as if, having given him a limited licence to touch us, we find abuse of
that licence particularly unacceptable, as when a choir-master behaves
improperly with a choirboy, or a schoolmaster with a pupil. The result
is that, if driven to repeated breakdown in restraint, the police rapidly
become dubbed as hated men and violently persecuted whenever angry
crowds gather. Only in countries such as Great Britain, where the
police are deliberately sent out into the streets completely unarmed,
have there been any signs at all of slight restraints being applied on
both sides during the worst civil rioting of recent years. It is as if the
fact that both sides are forced to indulge in the greater body intimacy
of hand-to-hand grappling, rather than the remoter savageries of over-
head club- and stick-beating, or the totally remote brutalities of
firearms, has some kind of restraining influence on the hostilities.
There is nothing inherently less vicious about such encounters; even
without weapons, eyes can be gouged out and genitals kicked in, but
such cruelties are extremely rare. When compared with the cracked

and bleeding skulls of other riot scenes, the hand-to-hand battles of London and other British cities begin to look almost civilized, and it is ironic that they do so by returning to the more intimate forms of pre-civilized, pre-weapon combat.

There is a well-known film-sequence cliché in which two tough and otherwise admirable men set about one another with their fists to settle some long-standing quarrel. A sophisticated movie audience knows full well that, if the two men both begin to lose, each beating the other into total physical exhaustion, they are about to witness the birth of a great new friendship. As the two bruised hulks sprawl weakly on the ground, sure enough, one pair of cracked and bleeding lips spits out a loose tooth, and grins admiringly at his equally beaten opponent. In no time at all, our heroes are helping one another up and crawling to the bar (there is usually one nearby) to share a reviving drink. After this we can be sure that nothing will ever separate them again, and that they will become indomitable partners in righting all wrongs, until, at the end of the film, one of them will die bravely saving the life of the other, breathing his last gasp cradled in the loving arms of the man whose face he once succeeded in beating to a pulp.

The moral of this highly coloured story is, of course, that a warm enemy is better than a cold friend, and it bears some investigation in terms of the body intimacies involved. It is almost as if any form of intimacy, even violent intimacy, providing it is performed on a sufficiently personal basis, can produce a bond of attachment between two antagonists. Needless to say, it is dangerous to generalize, and it can certainly not be offered as a general excuse for violence, but to ignore the phenomenon completely because it frightens us is equally unwise.

The difficulty is that impersonal violence has in recent times reached such a horrific scale that an almost total taboo has descended on the subject. For the sexually permissive society, violence, all violence, regardless of scale or context, has become the new philosophical restriction. In the broad context in which it is intended, the creed that we should 'make love not war' is unassailable, but the message underlying the ritualized film fight may perhaps lead us to consider a possible exception to this general rule. Clearly I am not thinking of anything as savage as the brawl I described above. I am imagining instead a situation in which certain people have so suppressed their aggressiveness that, even under intense provocation, they will 'not so much as lay a finger on' their partners' bodies. To take non-violence to such an extreme in every instance can create a new form of anti-intimacy. Let me give an example.

If, unavoidably, two individuals have grown cold towards one another, for whatever reason, the relationship can finally freeze to death in an atmosphere of hypocritical restraint. The thin hard smile of inhibited anger can cut sharp as any knife. Sometimes, under such conditions, an explosion into a flaming row, accompanied with mild but nevertheless aggressive interaction, can clear the air like a long-awaited thunderstorm, and release the damaging tension. Perhaps for the first time in months, a bickering couple actually take one another in their arms and, even though it is to shake the partner violently by the shoulders rather than to embrace lovingly, the result is the feel of the first truly meant body contact in ages. It is, of course, a desperate situation to have arrived at, when to touch at all means to touch in this hostile way, and it may very well fail. But just occasionally it may succeed, and to ignore this fact because it is out of step with the current cultural mood is to disregard another facet of the powerful emotional impact that body intimacy can have on the bonds of attachment between two human beings.

A related pattern of behaviour is the rough-and-tumble play of children, or the 'horseplay' or 'rough-housing' that can sometimes be observed between friendly adults. Again, the body contacts involved make their emotional impact, and they do so because they are accompanied by the unspoken message, 'Even though I am being aggressive, you can see that I am not *really* aggressive.' The message is a subtle one, however, and play-fighting at any age can become a delicately balanced interaction. The man who playfully slaps a companion on the back can easily reverse the signal, so that it becomes, 'Even though I am pretending to be only playfully aggressive, you can tell by the way I am doing it that I am not.' He uses the slap because it has become formalized as an accepted play-fighting pattern, but by his accompanying actions and by the hardness of the slap it becomes instantly apparent to his companion that he has twisted the message back to front.

A similar complexity exists in the case of the bickering couple mentioned above. If, under extreme provocation, the action is no more than a mild slap on the cheek, or the shaking of the partner's shoulders, then the message reads, 'Although you have made me want to kick your teeth in, this is all I am doing to you.' But if the provocation is less than extreme, then even the most moderate of aggressive contacts transmits a signal that is merely surly and unpleasant.

The subtle dangers of play-fighting can sometimes be observed very clearly when two boys start idly wrestling on a street-corner. At first they both obey the conventions of playful aggression. Each body-push and arm-lock is performed with exactly the right intensity – strong enough to make it forceful, but not so strong that it becomes truly violent. If this delicate balance is accidentally upset and one of them is hurt, the mood changes. Now he retaliates more powerfully and, if the situation is badly handled, a real fight can slowly grow out of the playful one. The changes that signal this are difficult to analyse, because even the playful wrestling may look real enough. Usually the tell-tale signs begin to show in the facial expressions, which, instead of being relaxed and smiling, or exaggeratedly mock-savage, become hard and set, often with accompanying changes in pallor and flushing.

Where professional wrestlers are concerned, a mimic of this change-over can be seen. The 'villain' deliberately fouls the 'hero', who then becomes expansively outraged, protesting to the referee and demanding sympathy from the crowd. Lunging wildly at his opponent, he appears to switch from the conventional combat techniques to uncontrolled violence, returning foul for foul, and the audience roars its approval. But here, even the 'uncontrolled' aggression is itself formalized, and the audience, joining in the game, knows this perfectly well. Should one wrestler genuinely hurt a rival, the bout is immediately called off and, instead of 'savage reprisals', ill-concealed concern is shown on all sides.

Leaving this dangerous subject, we can turn now to the safer and more tender intimacies of the dance-floor. As a sphere of activity in which there are professionals who are licensed to touch, dancing offers limited possibilities. True, the adult who is seeking some form of body contact can achieve it by using the services of a dancing instructor, and a male dancer can, in certain localities, visit a dance-hall which supplies professional dancing partners at a set fee per dance, but the world of social dancing is today largely one for the amateur. At parties, discotheques, dance-halls and ballrooms, adults who are strangers to one another can come together and move around the room in an intimate frontal embrace. Individuals who are already friendly can also use the situation to escalate a non-touching relationship into a touching one. The special role that social dancing plays in our society is that it permits, in its special context, a sudden and dramatic increase in body intimacy in a way that would be impossible elsewhere. If the same full frontal embrace were performed between strangers, or partial strangers, outside the context of the dance floor, the impact would be entirely different. Dancing, so to speak, devalues the significance of the embrace, lowering its threshold to a point where it can lightly be indulged in without fear of rebuff. Having permitted it to occur, it then gives a chance for it to work its powerful magic. If the magic fails to work, the formalities of the situation also permit retreat without ignominy.

Like so many other aspects of body intimacy, dancing has a long history stretching back into our animal past. In behaviour terms, its basic ingredient is the repeated intention movement. If we look at the dancing displays of various birds, we find that the rhythmic movements they perform are mostly made up of movements that start to go one way, then stop and go another, then stop again and repeat the first action, and so on. Turning from side to side, twisting back and forth, or bobbing up and down, the bird displays vigorously in front of its mate. It is in a state of conflict, one urge pulling it forward and another holding it back. During the course of evolution, the rhythm of these intention movements becomes fixed and the display becomes a ritual. The form the ritual takes varies from species to species and in each case becomes characteristic of their particular sexual preliminaries.

Most of our dance movements have originated in the same way, but in us they have not evolved into a fixed form. Instead, they have been culturally developed and are highly variable. Many of the actions of human dancers are no more than intention movements of going somewhere, only instead of carrying the action through, we check it, move back or round, and start again. In earlier centuries, many dances were like little parades, with the couple demurely holding hands and stepping round the floor, pausing every so often, turning round, and then going on again, to the rhythm of the music. Because the pattern was essentially one of going on a journey, it also frequently included mock-greetings towards the partner, with formal bowings and curt-syings, as though the two dancers had just met. In both folk-dancing and the courtly ballrooms, there was typically an intricate weaving round and round and in and out of other pairs on the floor, or arena. The body intimacies involved in such performances were so strictly limited that they gave rise to no sexual problems. They simply permitted a general social intermingling. The fact that the leading of the female by the male, around and around the floor, was so formalized, stopped any awkward questions about where he was really supposed to be leading her, or for what purpose.

The situation changed dramatically at the beginning of the last century, as a new dance craze swept across Europe. The waltz had arrived. For the first time the dancing couple embraced as they moved, a public intimacy that immediately created widespread scandal and concern. Such a major advance required a subterfuge, and it is one we have met before. When discussing the first way in which a simple hand-to-hand contact can be effected, I mentioned that a much-used trick is the intimacy-disguised-as-aid. The hand that reaches out does so ostensibly to support or steady the other person, to guide them or to prevent them from falling. In this way it can cross the vital threshold of making body contact without causing alarm. So it was with the waltz. At the very beginning of its history it was an incredibly rapid and athletic dance, so that the partners were forced to clutch at one another's bodies to prevent themselves from spinning apart. This was the 'supporting' device and, once it had enabled the waltz to gain an entrance into the ballroom, it was then only a matter of slowing down the speed of the performance to convert these actions of mutual physical aid into the more tender intimacies of a true frontal embrace.

The older generation, who had not known such delights, were outraged. The waltz, which today seems quaintly old-fashioned, was, in its early years, described as 'polluting' and 'the most degenerate dance that the last or present century can see'. The early Victorian author of *The Ladies' Pocket-Book of Etiquette* devoted ten pages to an all-out attack on this abominable new public intimacy. Among her comments: 'Ask any mother . . . can she consent to commit her daughter promiscuously to the arms of each waltzer? Ask the lover . . . could he endure the sight of the adopted of his heart . . . reclining in the arms of another? . . . Ask the husband . . . will you suffer your wife to be half-embraced by every puppy who turns on his heel or his toe?' The attacks persisted and, less than a hundred years ago, an American dancing-master in Philadelphia pronounced the waltz immoral because it involved the hugging of a lady by a gentleman she might not previously have met. But the battle was gradually lost, and the wicked waltz reigned supreme, bringing in its wake a whole variety of dances involving the full frontal embrace. These, in their turn, caused further scandalized mutterings.

The importation of the tango from South America in 1912 was again greeted with outrage. Because this dance included 'suggestive lateral movement of the hips', which reminded the hawk-eyed guardians of morals of the actions of copulation, it was instantly dubbed as depraved.

No sooner was that battle lost than the Jazz Age burst upon the scene, and the frantic dancing-teachers of the 1920s called urgent meetings to discuss this new threat to their respectability. They issued strong official protests about this new craze, pointing out that all the jazz dances had originated in Negro brothels.

Perhaps the most extraordinary attack on jazz dancing came in a newspaper report which claimed that 'The dance, and the music, with its abominable rhythm and copulative beat, was imported from Central Africa by a gang of Bolshevists in America, their aim being to strike at Christian civilization throughout the world.' Perhaps this puts into true perspective the recent claims that the current wave of student revolt, dropping-out and drug-taking is also a 'Red plot'.

Since its early days, jazz has given birth to several lusty offspring, and each in turn has caused the inevitable raised eyebrows as the dancers have taken to the floor with more and more variations of the public embrace. In the 'forties it was jitterbugging and in the 'fifties rock-and-roll, but then something strange happened. For some reason that it is perhaps still too early to understand, the couples separated. With the 'sixties, the dancing embrace went into a rapid decline. Now only the older, more staid couples clung to one another as they rotated around the floor. The younger dancers pulled apart from one another and danced more or less on the spot where they stood. It began with the twist and before long involved a confusingly large number of alternatives such as the hitch-hiker, the shake, the monkey and the frug. More and more styles were specified until eventually, as the decade drew to a close, the situation became so confused that they all merged into one more or less nameless amalgam, and became simply the dance that was danced to 'pop'. All had the same important feature – no touching. Presumably the significance of this change lies in the marked increase in sexual permissiveness. If young Victorian couples were not allowed to enjoy extensive private intimacies, then the embrace of the waltz had great meaning for them, but if matters are freer today, then who cares about a specially 'licensed' context for a mere standing embrace? It is as if the young dancers of today are publicly stating, 'We don't need it, we have the real thing.'

This brings us to the end of this brief survey of the way in which we, as adults, find specialized methods of indulging in bodily intimacy. All through the chapter, from doctors to dancers, there has always been something other than pure contact involved. At no point has there been touching merely for touching's sake. In every case there has been some excuse that provides us with a licence to touch or be touched. And yet, frequently, there is the distinct impression that it is the contact that is more important than the official activity. Perhaps one day, as the stresses of modern living increase, we shall see the appearance of an undisguised professional toucher, who will sell embraces like beads. Or perhaps to buy his wares will always be too great an admission of failure on our part, a failure to achieve the longed-for intimacies with a family unit of our own.

Whatever happens, we can always fall back on that perpetual substitute for body intimacy, namely verbal intimacy. Instead of exchanging embraces we can exchange comforting words. We can smile and talk about the weather. It is a poor substitute where emotional interchanges are concerned, but it is better than total emotional isolation. And if we still yearn after a more direct form of contact, there are other alternatives open to us: we can touch some non-human animal, or an inanimate object, using it as a stand-in for the human body we would really like to approach, or, if there is no other solution, we can always touch ourselves. The ways in which we employ animals, objects and our own bodies as substitutes for human intimates are discussed in the next three chapters.

6

SUBSTITUTES FOR INTIMACY

IN THE ADULT human world, a world full of stress and strangers, we reach out to our loved ones for comfort. If, through their indifference or through their preoccupation with the complexities of modern living, they fail to respond, we are in danger of becoming starved of the primary reassurance of bodily contact. If, through the moralizing of a warped minority, they have become inhibited in their intimacies and have been driven to accept the view that indulgence in the tactile pleasures of the body is somehow sinful and wicked, then, even in the midst of our nearest and dearest, we are liable to become touch-hungry and body-lonely. We are, however, an ingenious species, and if we are denied something we badly want or need, our resourcefulness soon urges us on to find a substitute to replace it.

If we cannot find love inside the family, we soon start looking for it outside. The ignored wife takes a lover; the husband, a mistress. Body intimacies reblossom. Unhappily, these particular substitutes do not always add to the surviving intimacies of family life; they compete with them, and perhaps eventually replace them altogether, causing varying degrees of social havoc as they do so. A less damaging alternative was the one discussed in the last chapter – the use of contacts with specialists who are licensed to touch. These have the great advantage that they do not usually compete with the relationships inside the family unit. The extensive intimacies of the masseur, providing they are applied with a strict professionalism, cannot be cited as grounds for divorce. But even a professional toucher, no matter how valid his official excuse for touching may be, is still a physiologically functional adult being, and as such is inevitably seen as a potential sexual threat. The 'seeing' of this threat is seldom spoken of openly, except occasionally in jest. Instead, society quietly imposes more and more restrictions on the nature and context of the specialist intimacies. To begin with, they are rarely admitted to exist. One goes dancing, not to touch, but 'for fun'. One goes to the doctor because of a virus, not because one needs comfort. One goes to a hairdresser to have the hair styled, not to have the head caressed. These official functions are, of course, all perfectly valid and important. They have to be so in order to mask the fact that something else is going on at the same time, namely the seeking of friendly body contact. The moment they cease to be important, this unfulfilled need becomes too obvious, and some basic questions about our way of life start demanding answers we would rather not be forced to consider.

Unconsciously, however, we are all aware of the game that is being played, and so, indirectly, we tie the hands that we would have caress us. We do this by applying conventions and codes of conduct that reduce our sexual fears. Usually we do not say why. We simply accept the abstract rules of good etiquette, and tell one another that certain things are 'not done' or 'not nice'. It is rude to point, leave alone touch. It is impolite to show one's feelings.

So where do we turn? The answer is as soft and cuddly as the kitten in your lap. We turn, in fact, to other species. If those humans closest to us cannot supply us with what we want, and if it is too dangerous to seek intimacies with strangers, then we can make tracks to the nearest pet shop and, for a small sum, buy ourselves a piece of animal intimacy. For pets are innocent; they cause no questions and they ask no questions. They lick our hands, they rub softly up against our legs, they curl up to sleep on our thighs, and they nuzzle us. We can cuddle them, stroke them, pat them, carry them like babies, tickle them behind the ears, and even kiss them.

If this seems trivial, consider the scale of the operation. In the United States, more than 5,000 million dollars is spent on pets every year. In Britain the annual figure is 100 million pounds. In West Germany it is 600 million Deutsche marks. In France, a few years ago it was 125 million new francs, and estimates already indicate that this figure has by now doubled. Trivial is not the word for figures such as these.

The most important pets are cats and dogs. In the United States there are 90 million of them. Puppies and kittens are born there at the rate of 10,000 every hour. There are over 16 million dogs in France, eight million in West Germany and five million in Britain. Precise information on cats is not available, but there are certainly as many cats as dogs and probably more.

Putting these figures together, one can say that, at a rough guess, there are approximately 150 million cats and dogs in these four countries alone. Making another rough guess, let us say that each owner of one of these animals stroke, pats or caresses it, on the average, three times a day – or about 1,000 times a year. This adds up to a total of 150,000 million intimate body contacts per year. What is astonishing about this figure is that it represents for Americans, Frenchmen, Germans and Englishmen intimacies performed not with other Americans, Frenchmen, Germans or Englishmen, but with alien species belonging to the order Carnivora. Viewed in this way, the phenomenon looks even less trivial.

As we have already seen, we pat one another on the back when we embrace, and we stroke one another's hair and skin when we are lovers, or parents with children. But clearly we do not get enough, and those thousands of millions of animal caresses are there to prove it. Blocked in our human contacts by our cultural restrictions, we redirect our intimacies towards our adoring pets, our substitutes for love.

This situation has led to violent criticism from some quarters. Dubbed 'petishism' by one author, it has been condemned as reflecting a decadent failure of modern, civilized human beings to communicate intimately with one another. In particular it has been stressed that more money is usually forthcoming to support the prevention of cruelty to animals than to prevent cruelty to children. The answers given in support of modern pet-keeping are rejected as illogical and hypocritical. The argument that it teaches us the ways of animal life is considered nonsensical, in view of the gross anthropomorphism of the relationship in almost every case. The pets are humanized – they are seen as furry people, not real animals at all. The argument that animals are innocent and helpless and need our aid is seen as hopelessly one-sided in an era of battered babies and napalmed peasants. How is it that, in this enlightened age, we can have permitted a million children to be killed or wounded in Vietnam, while our cats and dogs have been provided with expert and immediate attention whenever they have needed it? How is it that in the twentieth century we can have licensed our adult males to murder 100 million members of their own species in warfare, while we have spent more millions on stuffing food into our luxuriating pet animals? How is it, to sum up, that we have come to be kinder to other species than to our own?

These are strong arguments and they cannot be dismissed lightly, but they contain a vital flaw. The answer, put very simply, is the old one that two wrongs do not make a right. Undeniably, it is monstrous to cuddle a pet and ignore a child, and it is true that in extreme cases this does happen. But to use this as an argument for not cuddling a pet is a folly. It is doubtful if, even in extreme cases, the pet 'steals' the caress from the child. If, for some neurotic reason, the child is not receiving love from the parent, it is doubtful whether the absence of a cuddlesome pet would help to improve the situation. In almost every case, a pet animal is being used either as an additional source of intimacy, or as a substitute for intimacies that are already lacking for some reason. To say that more caring for animals is actively causing less caring for other humans seems to be totally unjustified.

Imagine for a moment that a freak disease exterminated all pet animals tomorrow, and effectively eliminated all those millions of tender intimacies that would have occurred between them and their owners. Where would all that loving go? Would it magically be re-redirected, back on to other human companions? The answer, sadly, is that it would probably not. All that would happen is that millions of people, some of them lonely and incapable for a variety of reasons of enjoying any real human intimacies, would be robbed of a major form of tender body contact. The old lady who lived alone with her cats would hardly start stroking the postman. The man who fondly patted his dog would be unlikely to pat his teenage son more in its absence.

It is true that in an ideal society we should not need these substitutes or additional outlets for our intimacies, but to suggest banning them because of this is to attempt to cure the symptom and not the cause of the trouble. And even in the ideally loving and body-free society, we would probably always have plenty of intimacy to spare for our animal companions, not because we would then need such contacts, but simply because they would give us additional pleasures that would in no way compete with our human relationships.

A final word in defence of pets: if we are capable of tenderness towards animals it does at least reveal that we are capable of such tenderness. But, the answer comes back, even the commandants of concentration camps were kind to their dogs, so what does that prove? It proves, in short, that even the most monstrous of human beings is capable of some kind of tenderness, and the fact that its juxtaposition to callous brutality in this particular case offends us so deeply, and makes the brutality even more horrific, must not blind us to this fact. It serves as a constant reminder that the human animal, when not warped by what must paradoxically be called the savageries of civilization, is fundamentally endowed with a great potential for tenderness and intimacy. If witnessing the gentle, friendly touching that occurs between pet-owners and their pets does no more than bring home to us that man is basically a loving, intimate animal, then this alone is a valuable lesson to learn and relearn, all the more so in a world that grows yearly more impersonal and cold-hearted. When, under pressure, men become merciless, it is then that we need all the evidence we can muster to prove that this need not be so – that this is not the natural condition of man. If our capacity to love our pet animals serves to demonstrate one facet of this, then well-meaning critics must think twice about launching an attack on it, no matter how unreasonable it may seem when viewed from certain angles.

This said, what of the nature of the animal intimacies themselves? Why, for example, do we pat a dog and stroke a cat, but rarely stroke a dog or pat a cat? Why does one kind of animal draw forth one type of intimacy and another another? To answer this we have to look at the anatomy of the animals concerned. In their roles as pets they are, of course, acting as stand-ins for human companions, and their bodies are therefore substitutes for human bodies. Anatomically, however, there are striking disparities. The stiff legs of a dog cannot embrace us. We cannot fling our arms around a cat. Even the largest cat is no bigger than a human baby, and its body is soft and pliable. We therefore adjust our actions accordingly.

First, the dog. As our loving companion, we want to embrace him, but because his legs make this difficult, we isolate the patting element from the embrace-and-pat complex and apply it direct. Reaching out, we pat the animal's back, or perhaps its head or flanks. In a typical large dog, the back is broad and firm and a suitable substitute for the human back which we are patting by proxy.

The cat is a different matter. Being smaller and softer to the touch, it does not feel right as a back-substitute to be vigorously patted. Its soft, silky fur is more like human head-hair to the touch. We tend to stroke a loved one's hair, and so it follows that we tend to stroke a cat. As the dog was a back-substitute, so the cat is a hair-substitute. In fact, we often treat a cat as though its whole body is a stand-in for a silky-haired human head.

Extending this argument, it might be thought that patting is something we automatically do to all canines, and that stroking is an action for all felines, but it is not as simple as this. It has much more to do with the typical body quality of the domestic dog and the domestic cat. Anyone who has enjoyed the exotic luxuries of body intimacies with a tame cheetah, lion or tiger will know that there the pattern changes. Although they are true felines, they have broad, firm backs more reminiscent of the domestic dog than of the family cat. Like the typical dog, the hair is also coarser. The result is that they are patted, not stroked. By contrast, a tiny lap-dog with long flowing hair is stroked and caressed more like a cat.

Moving up the scale in size, the horse-lover is also a patter, but there is a subtle change. The original human back – where the patting began, so to speak – was a vertical surface, but the back of a horse is horizontal and therefore less satisfying as a site for the substitute action. The horse's neck, however, comes to the rescue, being both the right height and, what is more, providing the ideal vertical surface, and it is here that the majority of horse-pattings are delivered. In this respect, the horse goes one better than the dog, whose neck is generally too small to be of much use in this respect. Again, the horse's height makes it ideal for head contacts which, in the dog, force us to lower ourselves to his level, or raise him up in our arms. And so many a horse-lover can be seen with her head pressed to her animal's neck or face, while her arm embraces and her hand pats the firm, warm flesh.

For many people a pet is not merely a substitute companion, but more specifically a substitute for a child. Here the size of the animal becomes important. Domestic cats are no problem, but the typical dog is too large, and so certain types have been progressively reduced in size by selective breeding until they have been successfully scaled down to human baby proportions. Then they, like cats and various other creatures such as rabbits and monkeys, can be scooped up in their owner's pseudo-parental arms without undue exertion. This is by far the most popular form of body contact to occur, where pet animals are concerned. An analysis of a large number of photographs depicting owners in contact with their pets reveals that the act of holding the animal in the arms, as if it were an infant, accounts for 50 per cent of all cases. Patting is the next most common action (11 per cent), followed by the semi-embrace, in which one arm is wrapped around the animal (7 per cent), followed closely by the pressing of the cheek to the pet's body, usually in the region of its head. Another intimacy that appears with rather surprising frequency is the mouth-to-mouth kiss (5 per cent), the species involved ranging from the budgerigar to the whale. The whale, one might think, leaves something to be desired as an animal intimate. Captain Ahab would certainly have been startled at the idea of a girl kissing one on the mouth, but the recent trend in oceanarium displays has changed all that. Both tame whales and their smaller relatives, the dolphins, have become front-line favourites in recent years, and since their bulbous, swollen foreheads give a baby-like shape to their heads, they create a strong urge in their human companions to pat, tickle and caress them when they protrude their apparently grinning faces from the sides of their pools.

Birds that are hand-tame, such as parrots, budgerigars and doves, are frequently brought up to the face and held against the cheek, where the soft smoothness of their plumage can be felt against the skin. The intimacy is often elaborated with mouth-to-mouth feeding of morsels of food. Because of their small size, which rules out embracing and patting, the hand intimacies are limited to finger-stroking and gentle tickling 'behind the ear'.

If we move further away on the evolutionary scale, the possibilities for intimacies decline rapidly. For most people, reptiles, amphibians, fish and insects are singularly unrewarding to the touch. The tortoise, with its smooth, hard shell, rates an occasional pat on the back, but its scalier relatives lack the essential qualities for friendly body contact. Perhaps the only exceptions worth mentioning are the giant constricting snakes. When suitably tamed, pythons, for example, can provide their owners with something that even the cats and dogs cannot offer – an all-enveloping embrace. Wrapping their strong coils around their human companions' bodies, tightening and relaxing their muscles, undulating their many ribs, and flickering their gentle tongues across their owners' skins, they create a sensuous impact that has to be felt to be believed. However, because of their difficult feeding habits and the bad press they have received ever since the fracas in Eden, not to mention our horror of their smaller and highly poisonous relatives, the big snakes have never enjoyed wide popularity as close intimates, even for the most embrace-hungry of humans.

Fish-touching, if we draw a discreet veil over the treacherous human intimacy of trout-tickling, is virtually non-existent. Perhaps the only exception here is the voluptuous hand-kissing sometimes performed by tame giant carp when sticking their gaping heads out of water as they beg for food. These fish can gape and gulp with such energy at the edge of a carp pond that even a passing bird may be coerced into a brief act of intimacy. There is an extraordinary photograph in existence which shows a small finch, its beak full of luscious insects for its hungry nestlings, pausing in front of the inviting gape of a tame carp's mouth and impulsively ramming its precious catch down the wide open throat of the fish. If a bird can be attracted in this way to make a thoroughly unnatural body contact, then it is little wonder that human visitors to carp-ponds react in much the same way.

Up to this point we have considered only friendly and parental intimacies, but for some humans the contacts go further and include full sexual interaction. These cases are rare, but they have a long and ancient history, references to them being scattered throughout art and literature from the earliest times. They take two main forms. Either a human male copulates with an animal, usually a domesticated farm animal, or masturbation occurs. In the latter case, a natural tendency on the part of a particular species to lick or suck is directed towards the human genitals, either male or female, as a device for producing sexual arousal. It says a lot for the degree of alienation and body-contact frustration that must exist in human societies that such aberrant intimacies occur at all. However, when we remember the millions of lesser intimacies, in the form of cuddlings, kissings and strokings, that take place in our modern cultures between pet-owners and their vast army of pets, it is not so surprising that, in a small minority of cases, greater intimacies such as these do occasionally arise.

In surveying the whole question of human-animal contacts, mention has so far been made only of pets and farm animals, but there are two other spheres of interaction that deserve some comment. Human-controlled animals exist not only in private homes and on farms; they are also found in large numbers in zoos and research laboratories. Here, too, frequent contacts occur and they are not always ones that meet with general approval.

Visitors to zoos not only want to see the captive creatures held there; they also want to hold the captive creatures seen there. The urge to touch is so strong that it constitutes a constant hazard for the zoo authorities. The first-aid department register of any major zoological gardens bears witness to this. For every sprained ankle or cut finger, there is a bitten hand or a scratched face. Sometimes the injuries sustained by the eager animal-gropers are serious, but they are seldom caused by carelessness on the part of the zoo staff. Two examples will suffice to illustrate this. The first concerns a woman who arrived at the first-aid department of a major zoo, holding her screaming child, who had a badly mauled hand. While it was being treated, it emerged that he had begged to be allowed to touch the body of the zoo's adult male gorilla. Complying with his wish, the woman had lifted him laboriously over the safety barrier, past the large warning sign indicating that the animal was extremely dangerous, and had thrust him forwards so that he could push his arms around the edge of the protective armoured glass screen and through the bars into the cage. The gorilla, misinterpreting this friendly act, had promptly sunk its teeth into the boy's hand. Unrepentant, the woman now presented herself, outraged, to the helpless zoo authorities.

The second case concerns the tragic affair of the 'tiger-toucher', an elderly gentleman who repeatedly clambered over the barrier at the same zoo's big cat house in order to caress one particular tigress. Removed, protesting, time and again by the zoo staff, he finally leapt over the barrier in such desperation that he broke a leg and was removed to a hospital bed. During his absence the tigress in question was dispatched to another zoo for breeding purposes. On his return to health, the man went straight back to the cage, only to find it occupied by a strange leopard. Furious at this, he marched across to the zoo office and demanded to know what they had done with his wife. At first the authorities were nonplussed by this extraordinary accusation, but after quiet questioning it emerged that the unhappy man had recently lost his real wife, after a lifetime of close companionship, and had since transferred all his emotional attachments to the tigress in question. Because the animal had, in his mind, become the embodiment of his late mate, it was only natural that he should want to continue to make intimate contact with her body in its new form, even at considerable risk to life and limb.

If these examples seem outlandish, it is worth remembering that they are only extremes of actions which, at a more moderate level, are occurring in zoos throughout the world in large numbers every day. When the urge to touch another human being is blocked, either by personal tragedy or by cultural taboo, it will nearly always find a way of expressing itself, no matter what the consequences. One is inescapably reminded here of the pathetic cases of child-molesters who are arrested for supposedly sexual assaults on infants. Unable to make proper contact with adults, they turn to children, who are innocent of the strictness of adult taboos. Frequently all that such men want is some kind of gentle, friendly body intimacy, but always the cry for blood goes up and the actions are interpreted as inevitably sexually motivated. This they may of course be, but it is by no means inevitable, and many a harmless old man has suffered heavily as a result. Needless to say, the children in such cases always suffer too, not from the original intimacies, which even in the specifically sexual cases they probably did not understand, but from the parental panic that follows and, above all, from the trauma of the court proceedings through which they are shamefully dragged.

Returning to the animal situation and leaving the zoo gates behind us, we come now to the fourth major category of man-animal contacts, namely those that exist in the world of science. Millions of laboratory animals are bred and killed annually in the course of medical research, and the contacts that occur between research workers and their experimental subjects have given rise to much heated debate. To the scientist, the interaction is a totally objective one. He admits to no emotional bond, either positive or negative, either loving or hating, with the animals he must handle while carrying out his investigations. The decision is simple enough: if he can reduce human suffering by sacrificing the lives of laboratory animals, he sees no other choice. He would avoid it if he could, but he cannot, and he refuses to place the lives of animals on a higher plane than the lives of fellow humans. That, briefly, is his case, but it is frequently and vociferously contested.

The opponents have been many, and their general attitude can best be summed up in the words of George Bernard Shaw, who said that 'If you cannot attain knowledge without torturing a dog, you must do without knowledge.' A more moderate view is expressed by those who feel that many animal experiments are pointless and that the results they obtain are worthless in any humanitarian sense, doing no more than satisfy the idle curiosity of the academic world. Surprisingly enough, such a view was voiced by the great Charles Darwin himself, in a letter to another famous zoologist, in which he said, 'Physiological experiment on animals is justifiable for real investigation, but not for mere damnable and detestable curiosity.' More recently, it has been pointed out by a respected experimental psychologist that 'One consequence of the obsessively behaviouristic and mechanistic approach is the apparent callousness of much of the experimental work carried out on the lower animals, often without any worthwhile aim.'

It is certainly true that the number of licensed animal experiments performed each year has risen sharply as the twentieth century has grown older. In Britain the figure for 1910 was 95,000; by 1945 it had exceeded 1,000,000; more recently, in 1969, it was in the region of 5,500,000, involving 600 separate research establishments. The vast scale of the operation has started to cause comment in political circles. One member of the British Parliament, speaking in 1971, protested: 'I know that the object is to preserve human life; but it does make me wonder whether a human race that can take such morally degrading practices in its stride is really worth preserving.'

It is important to separate two distinct elements in these and other criticisms of the large-scale use of animals for research. First, there is the extreme, anthropomorphic element, which sees the animals as symbolic people and therefore dislikes the idea of causing them pain for whatever purpose. Second, there is the humanitarian element, which sees animals as *similar* to people, in that they are capable in their own ways of feeling fear, pain and distress, and dislikes the idea that they should be caused any unnecessary suffering at human hands. This second element accepts, however, that it is necessary to cause some degree of suffering, but only if it is kept to an absolute minimum and only if the research is directly aimed at reducing a greater suffering.

The research scientist responds to these two criticisms in the following way. To the first critic he says, 'Tell that to the mother of a thalidomide baby.' If more extensive animal experimentation had been carried out, she might have had a normal child. Or he may say, 'Tell that to the mother whose child died of diphtheria.' Only a few years ago this disease killed thousands of children annually, but now, thanks to the development of a vaccine developed entirely by experiments on living animals, it has practically disappeared. Or he may say, 'Ask the mother of a polio child how she feels about the fact that it costs the life of an experimental monkey for every three doses of the polio vaccine that could have saved her child.'

In other words, what the out-and-out anti-vivisectionist is proclaiming is that it is better for a child to die or suffer agonies than for living animals to be used for experimental research. Whilst this may reflect an admirable concern for the welfare of animals, it also reveals a startlingly callous attitude towards human children. This putting of animals before people takes us back again to the pet-keeping situation, but here there is an important difference. Where pets were concerned, it was perfectly possible to be kind both to pets and to people. One did not automatically exclude the other, and the anti-pet argument to the contrary was shown to be false. But here the situation does demand that in order to be kind to the child it is unhappily necessary to be unkind to the experimental animal. We simply cannot have it both ways. An unpleasant choice has to be made.

To the second and more moderate critic, the research scientist says, 'I agree; animal suffering must be kept to a minimum, but there are problems.' A great deal of detailed study has been made in recent years of ways in which experimental procedures can be made less painful for the animal subjects, and everything is done to devise tests which use fewer animals, which cause them the minimum of distress and, where possible, replace them altogether. On this basis we might expect to see the number of laboratory animals killed annually declining steadily. As the figures I quoted show, however, this is not the case. The research scientist's answer is that this does not mean that more wasteful methods are being used, but rather that research programmes are becoming increasingly extensive and investigating more and more ways of alleviating human suffering. Furthermore, he will point out that one of the great problems with research is that it is impossible to limit it to areas which are directly and obviously connected with specific forms of suffering. Many of the greatest and ultimately most beneficial discoveries are made as a result of animal experiments in 'pure' rather than 'applied' research. To say that an animal experiment must not be done because, at the moment, it has no obvious application in such spheres as medicine or psychiatry is to stifle the whole progress of scientific understanding.

This is the point at which some of the least emotional and most educated critics begin to get worried. How far, to use Darwin's words, does 'real investigation' have to go before it becomes 'mere damnable and detestable curiosity'? This involves a much more difficult and delicate argument. Reading some of the scientific journals, especially those concerned with experimental psychology, it is difficult to escape the conclusion that many research workers in recent times have, by any reasonable standards, gone too far. By so doing they are endangering the public acceptance of scientific endeavour as a whole, and many authorities believe that it is high time that a drastic revision was made of the direction that many research projects are taking. If this is not done there may be a large-scale public backlash that will, in the long run, do untold harm to scientific progress.

Having made these general points, it now remains to ask why the man/animal contacts that occur in the laboratory should cause so much heated debate and concern. The obvious – too obvious – answer is that, even when we accept that it is justified and necessary, we do not like the idea of a man causing pain to the animal he handles. But what about the man who finds mice in his kitchen, or the slum-dweller who finds rats in his bedroom, and beats them to death with a stick or condemns them to a slow and painful death by putting down poison? He does not receive our criticism, only our sympathy. There are no protection societies formed to protect the wild rats and mice that infest our dwelling-places, and yet these are the same species that are used in the laboratory experiments which cause so much comment. Killing a wild rat is approved of because it may spread disease, but killing a laboratory rat is disapproved of, even though its death may also help to prevent the spread of disease, via the agency of scientific discovery.

How can we explain this inconsistency? Clearly it has little to do – whatever we may say – with our objective concern for the welfare of rats, wild or tame. If we really cared about the laboratory rat for its own sake, as an exciting form of animal life, we would not treat its wild counterpart so brutally. No, what is happening is that we are responding in a much more complex and subtle way than we imagine. We respond to the wild rat in a very basic way as an invader of our private territory, and we feel justified in defending that territory with any means at our disposal. No treatment is too harsh for a dangerous intruder. But what of the tame white rat in the laboratory? Is this not the creature whose ancestors brought the great plague into our midst? Certainly it is, but now it appears in a new role, and we must understand what that role is if we are to understand the strong emotions its experimental death causes in us.

To start with, the white rat is no longer a pest, but a servant of man. He is gently handled, well fed, well housed and cared for in every possible way. The attitude of his human companion is that of a doctor tending a patient before an operation. Then he is experimentally infected with cancer. Later he is killed by the same hands that cared for him. Except for the cancer element, this sequence could also apply to the relationship between a farmer and his domestic stock. He cares for them, then kills them. Yet we do not complain about the behaviour of the average farmer towards his animals, any more than we complain about the man who poisons a wild rat in his kitchen. Where does this leave us? The laboratory sequence involves tender handling, then causing pain, then killing. The farm sequence involves tender handling, then killing. The pest sequence involves causing pain and killing. In other words, we do not object to killing after caring, or to killing after causing pain, but we do object to causing pain after caring. The symbolic role that the white rat plays in the research laboratory is that of the humble and faithful servant who is loved by his master until, one day, without warning or provocation, this loving master starts to torture his servant and does so, not for the servant's own good, but for the benefit of the master himself. This is the allegory of betrayal that causes all the trouble.

The critics of animal experiments will hotly deny this, claiming that it is the rat they are thinking about and not this symbolic relationship, but unless they are full-time vegetarians who literally would not swat a fly, they are deluding themselves. If ever they have received any kind of medical aid, they are hypocrites. If, however, they are honest, they will admit that it is the *betrayal of intimacy* inherent in the symbolic man-rat relationship that really concerns them.

Now it should become clear why I have gone at some length into a pattern of human behaviour that, at first sight, does not appear to have any close connection with the subject of this book. The whole essence of the experimentalist's dilemma is that, to allay fears, he must emphasize over and over again how well he treats his laboratory animals: how gently he handles them, how relaxed and contented they are in their hygienic cages where they await the important part they have to play in his research. It is the contrast between this tender intimacy and what he then proceeds to do to them that is the crux of the passionate antagonism he arouses in his critics. For, as we have seen throughout this book, intimacy means trust, and the symbolic rat-servant is made to trust his master totally, only then to be subjected to pain and disease at his gentle, caring hands. If this betrayal of intimacy occurs only occasionally and for very special reasons, then most of the critics can reluctantly accept it, but when it takes place millions of times every year, then they begin to get the creepy feeling that they belong to a nation of emotional traitors. If a man can inflict deliberate pain on an animal that trusted him and which, a moment before, he was handling so gently and carefully, then how can he be trusted in his human relationships? How, when in all other respects of his social life he behaves in a perfectly reasonable and friendly way, can we ever be sure again that reasonable friendliness is any true guide to the nature of the members of the society in which we live? How can he behave so well towards his real children, when he constantly double-crosses his symbolic laboratory 'children'? These are the fears that run unspoken through the minds of his critics.

There is a similarity here to the case mentioned earlier of the concentration camp commandant who was kind and gentle to his pet dogs, whilst brutally torturing his prisoners. There, the kindness to his animals reminded us that even such a monstrous human being was not totally devoid of tender feelings. Here, the position is reversed, with a man who is capable of being kind to his fellow men nevertheless being able to spend his working days inflicting pain on his experimental animals. It is the contrast that frightens us. If we see a friendly-looking soldier patting his dog on the head, we cannot help wondering whether he, too, would be capable of gassing helpless human victims. If we see a friendly-looking father playing lovingly with his children, we cannot help wondering whether, beneath the surface, he is capable of cruel experiments. We begin to lose our sense of values. Our faith in the bonding power of body intimacies begins to waver, and we rebel against what we call the callousness of science.

We know perfectly well that this rebellion is unjustified because of the immense benefits that scientific research has brought us, but it hits so hard at our basic concepts of what gentle, caring intimacy means that we cannot help it. We still rush to the pharmacy when we get sick and quickly swallow our pills and tablets, but we try not to think of the trusting, betrayed animals who suffered to give us these antibiotic blessings.

If the situation is bad for the general public, what must it be like for the experimentalist? The answer is that it is not bad at all, for the simple reason that he has trained himself specifically not to see his relationship with his animals as a symbolic one. In applying a ruthlessly objective approach to his subject, he overcomes the emotional difficulty. If he handles his animals with gentle care, he does it to make them better subjects for experimental procedure, not to satisfy his emotional needs for substitute body intimacy like the ardent pet-keeper. This often requires considerable restraint and self-discipline, because, of course, even the most intellectually controlled act of body contact can begin to work its basic magic and start to form bonds of attachment. It is not unknown for a large laboratory to house, in a corner cage, a fat, lop-eared rabbit that has become the departmental mascot, a pampered pet that no one would dream of using for an experiment, because it has slipped into a totally different role.

For the non-scientist it is difficult to make these rigid distinctions. For him, all animals belong in Disneyland. If, through the modern educational media of film and television, he broadens his horizons and begins at last to forget the toy-animal images of his childhood, he does so not at the deft hands of experimentalists, but in the company of naturalists, whose basic approach is that of the observer, rather than the manipulator, of animal life.

The plight of the serious experimentalist therefore remains unsolved. Like the surgeon who operates to save his patients' lives, he strives to improve our lot, but unlike the surgeon he gets little thanks for it. Like the surgeon, he remains strictly objective and unemotional throughout his operations. In either case, emotional involvement would be damaging. For the surgeon this is less obvious, for he must put on a bedside manner outside the operating theatre. Once inside, however, he treats the bodies of his patients as coldly and objectively as the experimentalist, carving them up like a master chef performing with a choice joint of meat. If this were not so, we would all suffer for it in the long run. If the experimentalist became emotionally involved with his animals and treated them all like beloved pets, he would soon be incapable of carrying on his arduous research projects that bring us so much widespread relief from disease and agony. He would be driven to drink by the enormity of what he was doing. Likewise, if the surgeon allowed himself to become emotionally aroused by the plight of his patients, his knife might waver as it sliced, and vital damage would be done. If hospital patients could hear the conversations that take place in many operating theatres, they would probably be horrified by the sometimes jocular, sometimes matter-of-fact tones, but their response would be misguided. The terrible intimacy of entering another person's body with a sharp instrument demands a dramatic switching-off of the emotional impact of the act. If the action is performed as a piece of desperate, loving care, then the patient's next piece of body intimacy is liable to be at the cold hands of an undertaker.

In this chapter we have been looking at the use of living substitutes for human bodies in a contact-hungry world. Where the contacts have been loving, as with cuddly pets, the intimacies involved have caused considerable pleasure; where they have been strictly non-loving, as with experimental animals, they have caused considerable displeasure. In sum total they account for a vast number of tactile interactions, and animals are clearly of great importance to us in this respect. We have been considering mostly cases of adult human activity; but pet-keeping is also a significant pattern for the older child, when it starts to imitate its parents by showing intense pseudo-parental care for small animals, cuddling them, carrying them, nursing them and caring for them as if they were totally dependent infants. Since cats and dogs are often already stamped as the pseudo-infants of the real parents in the family group, the young pseudo-parents frequently become more devoted to other species of a type that adults normally scorn, such as rabbits, guinea-pigs and tortoises. These species, being uncontaminated by parental involvements, then provide a separate and more private world for the substitute intimacies of the juvenile pseudo-parents.

For younger children the problem is solved by the use of toy animals – substitutes for the substitutes for love. These are cared for and loved exactly as though they were living beings, and the attachment to a favourite Mickey Mouse or Teddy bear is as passionate and powerful as that of any older child to a favourite rabbit or, later, to an adored pony. For many girls the attachment to a large cuddly toy animal survives right into adulthood, and a newspaper photograph of recent hijack victims shows a teenage girl returning to safety 'still clutching the Teddy bear that comforted her through her ordeal in the desert'. When we are badly in need of some kind of reassuring body contact, even an inanimate object will do, and this is the subject of the next chapter.

7

OBJECT INTIMACY

ON A HOARDING in Zurich, Switzerland, there is a large poster showing a man's head reproduced twice, one beside the other. The heads are identical except for one detail: between the lips of one there is a cigarette; between the lips of the other there is instead a baby's dummy, or pacifier. It is assumed that the message is obvious, since not a single word accompanies the picture. Without realizing it, the designers of this poster have said far more about the importance of smoking than they intended. In one simple visual statement they have explained why so many thousands of people are prepared to risk a painful death, coughing and spewing as their lungs clog with cancerous cells.

The poster is, of course, supposed to put adult smokers to shame by making them feel immature and babyish, but it can also be read backwards. If the man with the dummy in his mouth is gaining some comfort from it, just like a baby, then all that is wrong with that part of the picture is that it looks so infantile. Now switch to the other head – here the problem is solved. Like the dummy, the cigarette gives comfort, too, and in one stroke the babyish element is gone. Seen this way, it might almost be an advertisement to encourage smoking in those who have not yet discovered the basic comfort of this activity. Smoke a cigarette and you can be pacified without feeling immature!

Even if we do not perversely twist the well-intended message in this way, it nevertheless provides us with a valuable clue concerning the world-wide smoking problem that faces society today. It is a problem that has been dealt with recently for the first time. A large-scale campaign to alert smokers to the dangers of filling the lungs with carcinogenic smoke has been undertaken in many countries. Cigarette promotions have been banned on television in several major areas, and there has been endless discussion on how to discourage children from taking up the habit. Gruesome films are shown of pathetic hospital patients in the advanced stages of lung cancer. Some smokers have responded intelligently and given up, but many others have become so alarmed that instead they have been forced to light up an extra cigarette to calm their shattered nerves. In other words, although the problem is at last being dealt with, it is by no means solved. Simply to tell people they must not do something because it is harmful may be a wise step to take, but it is also a short-term one. It is like using war to solve the population problem. War kills millions, but as soon as it is over there is a post-war birth bulge and the population growth goes soaring on again. Similarly, every time there is an anti-smoking scare, thousands of people stop smoking, but after the scare is over, the shares of the cigarette companies start to soar again.

The great error of the anti-smoking campaigners is that they rarely stop and ask the basic question: why do people want to smoke in the first place? They seem to think it has something to do with drug addiction – with the habit-forming effects of nicotine. There is an element of this, certainly, but it is by no means the most important factor operating. Many people do not even inhale their smoke and can be absorbing only minute amounts of the drug, so that the causes of their addiction to cigarettes must be sought elsewhere. The answer clearly lies in the act of oral intimacy involved in holding the object between the lips, as the Zurich poster so beautifully demonstrates, and this answer almost certainly applies as the basic explanation for the full inhalers as well. Until this aspect of smoking is properly investigated, there will be little long-term hope of eliminating it from our stressed, comfort-seeking cultures.

What we are plainly dealing with here is a case of an inanimate object being used as a substitute for a real intimacy with another human being. In examining this phenomenon, we are moving one step further away from the original source – namely, intimacy with intimates. The first step away took us to intimacy with semi-strangers (the professional touchers), the second step took us to intimacy with live substitutes (pet animals), and now the third step takes us into the world of dummies – objects with a hidden intimacy factor. There are many of them besides the cigarette, but it helps to start with this one because it leads us naturally back to the start of the whole story, at the point where a distraught mother jams a rubber substitute for her nipple into the mouth of her screaming infant.

The baby's dummy, sometimes called a pacifier or a comforter, is usually described as a 'blind' nipple, since, unlike the teat of a feeding-bottle, it has no hole in it. The description is a little misleading because no mother can boast such a huge bulbous nipple as that found on the average commercial dummy. This is a super-nipple, milkless, but with a greatly magnified tactile quality. At its outer end there is a flat disc to simulate the mother's breast and to stop the rubber super-nipple being sucked right into the mouth.

Dummies of this sort have been in use for centuries, but not so long ago they fell into disrepute because they were considered a dangerous source of infection. More recently they have started to make a come-back, and today they are recommended in many cases by medical authorities. Babies given dummies in their early months are much less likely to become thumb-suckers (the obvious alternative if no nipple is available to give comfort when comfort is needed). Also, it is no longer believed that dummies deform the mouth or damage the developing teeth, and recent experiments have shown the experts what many mothers knew already, namely that dummies do have a really dramatic calming effect upon a distressed infant. 'Non-nutritive sucking', as it is officially termed, was studied carefully in a large number of babies and their responses recorded. It was found that after only thirty seconds with the dummy in the mouth, crying was reduced to one-fifth of its previous level, and agitated hand and foot movements to one-half. It was also pointed out that, even without active sucking, the presence of the super-nipple between the baby's lips has a calming effect. If a baby is half asleep and has stopped sucking, the removal of the dummy can easily start it crying again.

All this adds up to the fact that having something between the lips is a comforting experience for the human animal, since it spells reassuring contact with the primary protector, the mother. It is a powerful form of symbolic intimacy, and when we look at an old man sucking contentedly on the stem of his pipe, it becomes abundantly clear that it is one that stays with us all our lives.

The important thing for the adult 'sucker' is that he should not appear to be doing what he is doing; hence the message of the Zurich poster. The use of a baby's dummy by a stressed adult would probably be as calming as anything else, if only it did not carry the 'infantile' stigma. Since it does, however, he is forced to adopt disguised dummies of various kinds. The cigarette, in this respect at least, is ideal, because it is so totally adult. Being prohibited for children means that it is not only non-infantile, but also non-childlike, and therefore completely removed in context from the baby-sucking that is its true origin. The object feels soft between the lips and the smoke warms it, which makes it even more like the genuine mother's nipple than a rubber dummy. Furthermore, the sensation of something being sucked out of the end of it and drawn down the throat adds to the illusion. A new symbolic equation is set up: warm inhaled smoke equals mother's warm milk.

Many smokers, when putting a cigarette to their mouths, or when taking it away, let their fingers fall on the outsides of their lips, simulating in this way the touch of the mother's breast. Some put the cigarette between their lips and leave it there for long periods of time, only drawing on it occasionally. When they do this, the non-drawing moments are similar to those of the half-asleep baby who still held the dummy in its mouth after it had stopped sucking on it. Other smokers, when they take the cigarette from the mouth, continue to fondle it between their fingers, even though it would be easy to put it down on an ashtray or some other surface. Deeply stained 'nicotine fingers' bear silent testimony to this urge to hold on to the comforting tobacco-nipple, even when it is not in oral use.

Variations on this theme include the businessman's super-nipple, the cigar, the tip of which is suitably rounded and smooth where it touches the mouth. With quiet ceremony this smooth 'blind' nipple is pierced and snipped with special gadgets, to ease the comforting flow of warming smoke-milk. For some, the soft touch of the cigarette or cigar is sacrificed to increased smoothness in the form of a cigarette-holder, a cigar-holder or a pipe. Here the tongue can play with a surface as smooth and slippery as a nipple of flesh or a teat of rubber. It is surprising that some device has not been used that is both soft and slippery – say a rubber holder – but perhaps this would not be sufficiently disguised, and would begin to look too much like the real thing to maintain its adult respectability. It would certainly make it more difficult for pipe-smokers to employ one of their favourite 'devices, namely sucking an empty pipe. That is already getting dangerously close to the obvious, and a rubber pipe-stem would be the final give-away.

The enormous amount of tobacco-smoking that takes place around the world today bears evidence to the vast demand that exists for comforting acts of symbolic intimacy. If the damaging side-effects of this pattern of behaviour are to be eradicated, it will be necessary either to de-stress the population to the appropriate degree, or to provide alternatives. Since there is no sign of any great or immediate hope for the former, the solution will have to be the latter. Plastic cigarettes have been suggested and even tried, but there seems little hope for them. The suggestion is valid enough in itself, but it overlooks the important factors of the warmth and true 'suckability' of real cigarettes. Also, it fails to provide any official excuse for the action. There must be a disguise of some kind if the activity is to be readily acceptable. It is true that many people suck the ends of pencils, pens, matchsticks, and the tips of the side-pieces of spectacles, but all these objects have other 'official' functions. A plastic cigarette would fail in this respect and would therefore appear too much like the baby's dummy in the Zurich poster. Some other solution will have to be found, and it looks very much as though this will have to come from the cigarette manufacturers themselves, in the form of a synthetic or herbal tobacco that does not damage the lungs. Research is already progressing in this direction, and perhaps the most valuable contribution made by the recent lung-cancer scares and propaganda campaigns will be to force a drastic speeding up in these investigations. Bearing in mind the deep significance of smoking, as I have outlined it here, this is probably the only long-term way in which these campaigns will be able to help.

Those people who have given up smoking, or who have attempted to give it up, complain that they start getting fatter soon after they abandon their non-nutritional tobacco-nipples. This immediately gives a clue about certain kinds of feeding. A great deal of the nibbling and food-sucking we do is primarily concerned with symbolic oral intim-acies, rather than true adult food-intake. The cigarette-hungry ex-smoker, when in sudden need of added comfort, grabs a sweet food morsel and stuffs it into his nipple-empty mouth. Sucking candies and sweets is yet another of our disguised breast-feeding substitutes. For most of us it is the pattern of behaviour that fills the gap between the dummies of infancy and the cigarettes of adulthood. The confectionery shop is the world of the child. Too old for rubber pacifiers, he takes to sucking gob-stoppers and bull's-eyes, lollipops and sticks of seaside rock. They may rot the teeth, but they help to replace the lost comfort. As adults we largely turn our backs on these delights, but many a young lover still brings to his 'sweetheart' the comforting gift of a box of assorted chocolate nipples. And many a bored housewife dips into a box of soothing candies. A trick sometimes used to give these objects adult respectability is to fill them with anti-childish alcohol and pop them into our mouths in the form of 'liqueur chocolates'.

Although these food objects do not last as long as nipples, they do have the important qualities of softness and sweetness to help them in their symbolic role. One special form overcomes this drawback of being short-lived, and that is chewing-gum. Chewing-gum consists of an elastic substance known as chicle gum, sweetened and flavoured. (One part of chicle gum to three parts of sugar, warmed and kneaded together and flavoured with cloves and cinnamon, wintergreen or peppermint.) It can be chewed for hour after hour and is advertised as something to 'calm your nerves and help you concentrate'. Symbolic-ally, it is nothing short of a rubbery, detachable nipple. Because of its special properties it should enjoy enormous success, but it is badly hindered by the conspicuous jaw movements that accompany its use. These cause no problem for the chewer, but for those near him they create the impression that he is incessantly eating. Since he never swallows the 'food' in his mouth, this conveys the feeling that the object in his mouth is in some way unpleasant, like a tough piece of gristle, and as he becomes soothed, his observers become irritated. The result has been that, in many social settings, chewing a piece of gum has become looked upon as a 'dirty habit', and the activity has therefore remained a restricted one.

Since mother's milk is a warm, sweet liquid, it is not surprising that adults employ a variety of warm, sweet drinks to soothe themselves at moments of tension or boredom. The millions of gallons of tea, coffee, drinking-chocolate and cocoa that are consumed annually have little to do with the real demands of thirst, but again thirst is there to provide the vital official excuse. The cups and mugs from which we sip these milk-substitutes so eagerly also provide a pleasantly smooth, slippery surface to press against our comfort-seeking lips, and the outcry when modern 'disposability' demands the use of non-smooth, non-slippery paper cups is easy to understand.

Once more, it is interesting to see the way we avoid the obvious: we drink tea hot, but milk cold. To drink hot milk is too overtly babyish. Only invalids drink hot milk, but that is permissible because, as we have already seen, the invalid has given up the adult struggle and has become an 'instant-baby' in other ways as well, so for him one more baby pattern makes no difference.

Apart from cold milk, or milk-shakes, which significantly are usually sucked through a straw, there are many other types of cold, sweet drink that we employ as comforters. They are nearly always advertised as thirst-quenchers, but in this respect they always fall far short of simple, plain water. They do, however, provide that vital sweet taste, and the increasingly acceptable habit of drinking them straight from the bottle helps to improve their symbolic value. The bottles in question have therefore shrunk in size from the traditional dimensions down to something remarkably close to that of the baby's bottle. In fact, if someone were to emulate the Zurich cigarette poster and show a man drinking from a cola or lemonade bottle with a rubber teat on it, the game would be up.

Many other objects, such as the stems of plants, or the beads of a necklace worn around the neck, are often brought up to the lips in fleeting moments of self-comfort, but enough has been said now to show that the oral intimacies of infancy remain an important part of our adult lives, even outside the more obvious spheres of friendly or sexual kissing, and we can move on to consider other parts of the adult body.

Another basic form of contact in babyhood is the pressing of the cheek against the mother's body when resting. Cheek-pressing with soft substitute objects is rare amongst adult males, but it remains fairly common with females. Many advertisements for soft bedding, blankets and linen display a serenely smiling female hugging to her body the cuddly product, her head tilted to one side and her cheek pressed lovingly to the smooth surface of the cloth. This is particularly common with blanket advertisements, to the extent that it is almost the only pose employed, despite the obvious fact that, once on the bed, the blanket will be prevented from making such a contact by the intervention of the inevitable bed-sheets.

Fur coat advertisements follow a similar course, frequently showing the fur collar turned up, or pushed up with the hands, so that its ultra-soft surface caresses the wearer's cheeks. Fur rugs offer a more extensive contact surface, like a giant maternal body flattened out on the floor or bed.

Perhaps the most widespread and common form of soft cheek contact, and one that is employed by both males and females, is the use of a down-filled pillow when sleeping at night. The caress of this tender pillow-breast provides a major soothing element at the end of the day, helping to calm us into a condition where we are prepared at last to sink into a deep slumber and give up the adult battle of the day. Great subtlety has been employed by pillow manufacturers in producing exactly the right balance between springiness and softness, and at any large bedding store it is possible to select a new pillow from a wide range of slightly varying tactile qualities. For many adults, one particular pillow, or pillow 'strength', becomes extremely important as an aid to falling asleep, and if they are faced (in both senses of the word) with the wrong type of pillow when trying to sleep in a strange bed, at a hotel or in a friend's house, they may find it difficult to drift off into a peaceful sleep as quickly as they can at home. This phenomenon is much more pronounced in the case of 'home-lovers' who travel little and who, over a period of years, become fixated on a specific pillow quality, such as resilience, thickness or sagginess.

A similar development occurs with the rest of the bed. In addition to sensitive pillow responses, adults come to prefer a particular softness or hardness in the mattress beneath them, and a certain lightness or heaviness, a looseness or a tight 'tucked-in-ness' in the bedding that covers them, as they settle down to the vitally important nocturnal bed-embrace that will envelop them for a total of one-third of their entire lives.

In 1970 a new type of bed appeared on the market in America – the 'waterbed'. Essentially, this is a vinyl mattress filled with water. Lying on it, the sleeper sinks gently into its liquid embrace as if returning to a semi-womb. A thermostat and heating element inside it keeps the water at an appropriately soothing temperature. In the second half of 1970, over 15,000 of these beds were sold, and the demand soon outstripped the supply. The advertisers encouraged their prospective buyers with significant phrases such as 'Live and love in liquid luxury' and 'You can make them rock-and-roll you to sleep'. The only hazard, to use a gynaecological expression, is rupturing the membrane. Accidentally puncturing a waterbed is almost as messy and comfortless as being born. Perhaps this slight but nagging fear will, in the end, keep most of us wrapped in the safer embrace of our old-fashioned cloth-beds.

Examined objectively, our sleeping habits, with our soft pillows, bedding and mattresses, begin to take on a special significance. They are more than a device for acquiring dream-time, in order for our computer-brains to sort out and file away the confusing bombardment of new thoughts from the past day, and much more than the mere act of obtaining physical rest for the exertions of the new day that is coming. They represent also a massive, world-wide indulgence in abandoning ourselves to the comforting intimacy of an inanimate envelopment that is part cloth-womb and part cloth-mother embrace.

Even during our waking hours we do not entirely reject these primal delights, as the modern furniture industry can demonstrate so clearly. 'Easy' chairs and sofas, of a voluptuous softness and bed-like snugness unknown in previous centuries, have become the almost inevitable centre-piece of every drawing-room, sitting-room and lounge. There, at the end of the hard working day, we sink gratefully into the soft intimacy of our favourite piece of soft furniture, whose 'arms' may not actually embrace us, but whose yielding surfaces nevertheless provide great body comfort. Cuddled snugly on the symbolic laps of our chair-mothers, we then settle down with childlike security to view at a safe distance the chaos of the harsh adult world outside, as symbolically portrayed on our television screens or between the covers of our novels.

If, in describing the act of watching television from the soft comfort of an easy chair in this way, as an infantile act similar to looking out of a window while safely held on a mother's lap, I appear to be condemning it, I hasten to add that this is not my intention. On the contrary, it is an added advantage to this now world-wide pattern of behaviour. In addition to providing entertainment and education, the act of watching television can, as I have shown, provide a vitally important soothing element in our stressful adult world. The glass screen that covers the pictures we watch traps them safely inside the television box where they cannot harm us. This helps to compensate for the fact that our chair-mothers only provide one of the two vital security factors that the real mother gives to her infant. The real mother provides both the intimacy of soft body contact *and* protection against the outside world. Our chair-mothers provide only the soft contact – they cannot protect us. But this is where the inpenetrable glass surface of the television screen comes to our rescue, compensating for the missing protection by safely walling us off from the adult dramas unfolding inside the box. The symbolic equation is therefore simple enough: real mother that protects and comforts = screen that protects + chair-mother that comforts.

Viewing our home life in this way, it is not surprising to find that when we travel or go on a vacation most of us prefer to stay in hotels which simulate in almost every way the conditions we once knew in the nursery. As in our infancy, everything is done for us and we do not need to lift a finger. Our food is prepared by the chef-mother, served to us by the waitress-mother, and our beds are made and our rooms cleaned by the maid-mother. At the best hotels, the use of room service can take us back virtually to the cradle, with our baby-crying replaced by the simple act of pressing the wall-button or lifting the house-phone. And frequently one of the first things that people do when they become rich is to introduce these nursery conditions into their own homes by employing personal staff-mothers. Also, as I pointed out in an earlier chapter, the sick-bed and the hospital provide a similar condition for the invalid who has temporarily given up the adult struggle completely.

Sometimes we indulge ourselves briefly in the even more basic luxury of a return to a womb-like condition by the act of taking a hot bath. It is no accident that nearly all of us prefer to do this at womb-temperature, floating blissfully in our mock-amniotic fluid and feeling beautifully secure inside the curving walls of our bath-wombs, with the bathroom door safely locked against the adult world outside. Sooner or later, however, we are forced to remove the cervical bath-plug and reluctantly face the trauma of a new birth. As if knowing of our fears at this dreaded moment, the towel manufacturers compete to provide us with the softest embrace they can produce. As one towelling advertisement puts it, 'Our towels just hug you dry!'; and the girl in the accompanying picture is shown clutching the object in question ecstatically to her body and face, as if her very life depended on it.

When this towel-hugging girl finally gets dressed, she need not fear that these tender intimacies will cease. Advertisers of body clothing – underwear, sweaters, skirts, and the rest – all promise her similar rewards. Those brief panties are much more, it seems, than a matter of mere modesty, for we learn that they also offer you a 'bare hug' which 'gently, caressingly . . . stretches to follow every curve of your body'. And those tights – they are 'silky soft and sensual' and 'hug you snugly from top to toe', not to mention those stockings which 'embrace your legs in a gentle, lingering caress', or those jersey dresses with that 'clinging feeling'. The lucky girl can therefore walk about fully dressed and apparently alone, but symbolically clad in a whole mass of caressing, embracing, hugging cloth-lover intimacies. If all the clothing advertisements put together had a cumulative effect, it would be surprising if she could perform the simple act of crossing a room without experiencing a multiple orgasm. Luckily for her real lovers, however, the impact of her assorted cloth-lovers is much milder, in most cases, than the advertisers would have us believe. Nevertheless, mild though it may be, it is still a genuine and important part of the body reward of wearing the soft and comfortable clothing of today.

This intimacy between clothing and wearer is more than a one-way affair. Not only do the clothes embrace the wearer – in addition, the wearer also embraces the clothes. This is, after all, a fair return for all that snug hugging and gentle caressing. The favourite way of repaying the compliment is to thrust one or both hands deep into some suitable fold of cloth. Napoleon's characteristic pose, with one hand inserted into his jacket, immediately comes to mind, but today the most widespread version is the hands-in-pockets action. Pockets are officially there to carry small objects, and if we put a hand into one, it is supposedly in the process of taking something out. But the vast majority of hand-in-pocket poses have nothing to do with object-retrieving. Instead, they are prolonged contact actions in which we, so to speak, hold hands with our pockets. Schoolboys and soldiers are often ordered to 'take your hands out of your pockets', with no explanation given other than that it is slovenly or untidy. The truth is, of course, that the posture indicates that they have relaxed into a symbolic act of intimacy, and this conflicts with their official roles as attentive, subordinate males. For males who are not restricted in this way, there are several alternatives open, and the choice made in any particular instance follows a rather curious rule. It is this: the higher up the body the hand/clothing contact is made, the more assertive it is. The most assertive of all is the grasping of the lapels. Coming a close second is the thumbs-in-waistcoat action. Next is the Napoleonic hand-in-jacket-front posture. Further down there is the hands-in-jacket-side-pockets pose, and further still the very common hands-in-trouser-pockets. Going any lower, with a hands-grasp-trouser-legs action, becomes appropriately low on the assertiveness scale.

The reason for this rule seems to be that the higher up the hand goes in making the contact, the more it adopts what amounts to an intention movement of striking a blow. Whenever a real blow is struck, it must be preceded by a raising of the hitting arm, prior to lashing out at the opponent. As we have already seen, this action becomes frozen as a formal signal in the case of the raised fist of the communist salute. The firm grasping of the lapels goes a long way towards this – as far, in fact, as a hand-to-clothing contact can go – and it is natural therefore that this should be the most truculent message of the various alternatives. Along with the thumbs-in-waistcoat posture, it has become almost a caricature of assertiveness, and a serious dominant male today is much more likely to adopt the lower-level hands-in-jacket-side-pockets posture when he finds himself displayed in a public place. This latter action is particularly favoured by tycoons, generals, admirals and political leaders, and it also became a cliché posture for the big-time gangsters of the roaring 'twenties. Such men are much more reluctant to adopt the lower-level posture of hands-in-trouser-pockets, at least when they are in a context that demands the assertion of their dominant rights.

An intriguing exception to the above rule is the thumbs-hooked-in-belt posture. Although this occurs rather low down on the body, it conveys a decidedly truculent flavour. It is popular with 'he-men', cowboys, pseudo-cowboys and mock-aggressive girls. Its assertive qualities appear to stem not only from a quick-on-the-draw intention movement, but also from the fact that it has become the modern, waistcoatless version of the old-fashioned thumbs-in-waistcoat posture. Sometimes the whole hand is slipped beneath the belt, or into the top of the trousers, but it then immediately loses much of its aggressiveness and fits more suitably on to the scale outlined above.

In addition to these actions, there are many small ways in which the hands perform minor intimacies with different parts of the clothing. All of them appear under stress, and many of them seem to represent symbolic versions of grooming acts that we would like someone else to be applying to our bodies to soothe us. Men can frequently be seen adjusting their cuff-links or smoothing their ties. President Kennedy frequently fingered his central jacket button at moments of public stress. Winston Churchill was often pictured at times of tension with his hand pressed flatly against the lower part of his jacket, as if engaged in a fragmentary self-embrace.

With the female sex, bracelets and necklaces come in for a great deal of handling and fingering at moments of strain, just as nuns no doubt obtain soothing comfort from the physical actions of telling their beads. At other times, the smooth caress of lipstick on lips, or powder-puff on cheeks, will provide a reassuring sensation of touch for a nervous female taking time off from a stressful social engagement. At more private moments, the repeated combing or brushing of hair, far beyond the demands of 'hair adjustment', can also have a marked calming effect, playing the role of a self-directed lover's caress.

In some instances, the act of making contact with a companion is performed indirectly, through an intermediate object of some kind, as when we clink our glasses together in making a toast, instead of making direct skin contact. A classic example can be found in any old Victorian scrap-book where a family group photograph has been taken. Typically, the mother sits in a central chair, with the latest addition to the large family nestled on her lap. Her husband, whose natural inclination is to put his arm around her shoulder, is too inhibited to do this in so public a situation and instead embraces the back of the chair in which she is sitting. The modern version of this can often be seen when two friends sit together informally and one stretches his arm along the back of the sofa they are sharing, aiming it in the direction of the other's back. Similarly, if a person is sitting alone in a chair, he may embrace the arms of it lovingly while talking animatedly to a companion in a chair opposite. Occasionally, additional chair-comfort is obtained by the use of a rocking-chair – another favourite action of President Kennedy's when under stress. The rocking comfort, needless to say, relates directly back to the rocking of the cradle or the mother's arms.

Finally we come to those objects that provide, quite specifically, substitutions for sexual intimacies. At the mildest level there are the photographs of loved ones, or the 'pin-ups' of those we would like to make love to, which can be kissed and touched in the unavoidable absence of the real thing. The use of life-size 'pillow-posters' is a new trend in the direction, it now being possible to buy a pillow-slip imprinted with a picture of the face of a favourite film star, to fit over the pillow that graces your bed. Then, at bedtime, you can lie cheek to cheek with the adored one, and fall gently asleep in this surrogate, cloth embrace.

Moving on to copulation itself, it was claimed during World War II that enemy soldiers (it is always enemy soldiers) at the front line were supplied with inflatable rubber dummy-females, complete with sexual orifices, for purposes of relieving sexual tensions. Whether this was merely propaganda to show how sex-starved and badly off the enemy were, or whether it actually happened, I have not been able to ascertain.

Inanimate substitutes for the male penis have, by contrast, a long and factual history, and even rate a mention in the Old Testament. Usually called dildoes, but also referred to as godemiches, consolateurs, bijoux indiscrets and dil-dols, they were known even before biblical times, and appear in ancient Babylonian sculptures dating from hundreds of years before Christ. In ancient Greece they had the name 'olisbos', meaning 'slippery bull', and they were apparently particularly popular amongst the Turkish harems. As the centuries passed, their use spread to practically every land in the world. Their popularity waxed and waned, apparently reaching a peak in the eighteenth century, when they were sold openly in London, a phenomenon not encountered again until the second half of the present century. Great care and skill is said to have been put into their manufacture 'so as to enhance realism in a coition fantasy'. In the 1970s they are now on sale in several versions in the 'sex shops' of a number of Western countries. Those that are not purchased by males out of sheer curiosity are used by lesbians or by solitary females for the purpose of masturbation.

Two forms of mechanically operated dildo have also appeared in recent times. One sort was of a highly technical nature, designed especially for an American research investigation into the nature of human copulation. Devised by radio-physicists, electrically powered, made of plastic with the optical properties of plate glass, equipped with cold-light illumination to facilitate intra-vaginal film-making, and fitted with masturbator-operated controls for varying both speed and depth of thrust, this was, by any standards, a truly remarkable instrument, a sensitive and tireless dummy lover, the sex-surrogate to end all sex-surrogates. A less ambitious and much less expensive mechanical device, and one that has gained widespread popularity in recent years, is the comparatively simple 'vibrator', or 'vibro massager'. It is a small, smooth-surfaced, battery-operated, plastic object, long and thin, with a rounded tip, the original and official function of which was localized muscle massage. It soon found a new and more sexual function as a gently vibrating masturbation dildo, and since it could be bought in its official role as a simple massage machine, had the added advantage that it could be obtained without undue embarrassment by purchasers who would have hesitated to acquire the more obvious forms of sexual equipment. Even in the outspoken underground press, the charade is maintained. A typical advertisement reads: 'Personal Massagers – penetrating, stimulating massager. Throbs away aches and frustrating pains. 7 in. long by $1\frac{1}{2}$ in. Standard batteries included.' The coyness employed in this advertisement is completely out of step with the rest of the text of underground papers, where the bluntest and most uninhibited forms of sexual comment are to be found. Once again we see the operation of the rule we have met so many times before, namely that adult intimacies require some sort of disguise, either to ourselves or to others, to obscure the real purpose of what is going on.

A most unusual and ingenious form of sex-surrogate sometimes used by females in Japan is the rin-no-tama, also known as the watama or ben-wa. This consists of two hollow balls, roughly the size of pigeon's eggs, which are inserted into the vagina. Originally made of leaf brass, but nowadays probably of plastic, one ball is empty and the other contains a small quantity of quicksilver (mercury). The empty ball is inserted first and pushed up to the end of the vagina, next to the cervix. The second is then placed against it and the opening of the vagina plugged with paper or cotton. Thus equipped, and with no embarrassing outward signs of her peculiar condition, the female proceeds to amuse herself with apparent innocence by swinging on a swing or rocking in a rocking-chair. The rhythmic back-and-forth motions then produce shifting pressures inside the vagina which simulate the thrusting of a male penis. Although, as a sexual 'toy', the rin-no-tama has the great advantage of permitting private enjoyment in public, it has not achieved the widespread popularity of the ubiquitous vibrator, presumably because, unlike the latter, it lacks a non-sexual, 'official' function.

Toys themselves, of completely non-sexual types, should also, incidentally, be a medium where tactile rewards are made available to us through inanimate objects. The possibilities are enormous, but few are attempted and even fewer succeed. When they do appear, they are usually presented as some kind of athletic exercise. The trampoline was one. The main reward here was the strange sensation of being embraced by the springy surface, flung into the air and then embraced again in a new posture. But the whole process had to be carried out under the cover of a highly muscular and sporting atmosphere, which ruled it out for many people. The short-lived hula-hoop was another case, combining the rotating embrace of the hoop around the performer's waist with an undulating action of the hips. Its appeal, however, was strictly limited and did not survive past the novelty stage.

The art world has several times attempted to present intimacy objects to an intimacy-hungry world, but with little success. In 1942 the Museum of Modern Art in New York exhibited for the first time a new type of sculpture called 'handies' or hand sculpture. They consisted of small, smoothly rounded pieces of polished wood in abstract shapes that would fit comfortably into the human hand and could be squeezed and turned this way and that to vary the tactile sensation. The artist who created them stressed that they were meant to be felt rather than looked at, and suggested that they would make an excellent substitute for cigarettes, chewing-gum or doodling for those who tended to be fidgety in committee meetings. Unhappily, it was not to be, and handies have hardly been heard of since. Once again, the message was too obvious, no committee member wishing it to be known that he was so obviously in need of a little comforting pseudo-body contact.

More recently, in the 1960s, certain artists have attempted more ambitious assaults on the bodies of art-lovers by creating 'environmental sculptures'. These have taken many forms, some of which have included a kind of play-space into which the visitor walks, there to be assailed by a series of varying tactile impressions as he passes through tubes, tunnels and passageways, walled and hung with a wide variety of textures and substances. Again, success has been short-lived and great possibilities have been wasted.

A final example neatly sums up the whole situation. One particular artist devised a simulated copulation capsule, into which the 'art-lover' was placed and wired up in various ways. The capsule was then shut and the machine switched on, with the idea of producing a massive sensory experience. At an art institute, the creator of this machine delivered a lecture about his concepts to an engrossed audience, who listened with interest as he explained that, owing to technical hitches, he had now devised a much simpler version of the machine, in which he had great faith. The modified device consisted basically of a large vertical sheet of rubber, or some such material, with a small hole at genital height, through which a male art-lover could insert his penis. For the female art-lover there was a similar vertical sheet, with a penis-shape protruding through it. In serious tones he then explained that, in addition to its simplicity, this new exhibit had the advantage that it could be used simultaneously by a male and female art-lover, with one standing on each side of it.

The absurdity of this story brings us back inevitably to the inherent absurdity of many of the examples given in the present chapter. It *is* absurd that an adult human being should have to coat his lungs with carcinogens in order to enjoy a crude substitute of the pleasures he once knew at his mother's breast, or when a baby's bottle was held to his lips. And it *is* absurd that grown men should endlessly have to mouth a disembodied, rubberized nipple in the form of chewing-gum, or that adult females should have to use a plastic massager instead of a live penis to achieve sexual gratification. But although these actions may seem absurd, pathetic or even downright repulsive to some, to many they are the only solution that seems to be available, and it must always be borne in mind that any intimacy, no matter how far removed it becomes from the real thing, is still better than the frightening loneliness of no intimacy at all. In other words, we must stop attacking the symptoms and take a closer look instead at the causes of the problem. If only we can become more intimate with our 'intimates', then we should need less and less in the way of substitutes for intimacy. In the meantime, almost any dummy-touch is better than no touch.

8

SELF-INTIMACY

THE WOMAN standing on the railway platform, about to board a train, is horrified. Her husband has just asked her if she remembered to lock the kitchen door and she has realized that she did not. What does she do? Before uttering a word, her mouth drops open and she clasps a palm to one of her cheeks. Even as she starts to speak, the hand stays there, pressed against the side of her face. Then, after a few moments, it descends, and the next phase of the behaviour sequence begins. We will not follow it further, however; instead we will concentrate on that hand, for it is the clue to a whole new world of body intimacies – intimacies with oneself.

In her fleeting moment of horror, the woman on the platform gave herself the instantaneous self-comfort of a swift caress – the clasping of a cheek. Her sudden feeling of emotional distress drove her, unconsciously, to provide the soothing contact which, under other circumstances, a loved one's hand might have offered, or which, long ago, her parents would have provided when she was a tiny, hurt child. Now, in place of a lover's or a mother's hand reaching out to touch her cheek, it is her own hand that flies up to make the contact. It does so automatically, unthinkingly, and without hesitation. In performing this act, her cheek has remained *her* cheek, but her hand has symbolically become someone else's – the lover's or the mother's.

Self-contacts of this kind are a form of body intimacy that we hardly recognize as such, and yet they are fundamentally the same as the others discussed in previous chapters. They may appear to be 'one-person' acts, but in truth they are unconscious mimes of two-person acts, with part of the body being used to perform the contact movement of the imaginary companion. They are, in other words, pseudo-interpersonal.

In this respect they provide the fifth, and final, major source of body intimacies. The five can be illustrated as follows. (1) When we are feeling nervous or depressed, a loved one may attempt to reassure us by giving us a comforting hug or a squeeze of the hand. (2) In the absence of a loved one, it may have to be one of the specialist touchers, such as a doctor, who pats our arm and tells us not to worry. (3) If our only company is our pet dog or cat, we may take it in our arms and press our cheek to its furry body to feel the comfort of its warm touch.

(4) If we are completely alone and some sinister noise startles us in the night, we may hug the bedclothes tightly around us to feel secure in their soft embrace. (5) If all else fails, we still have our own bodies, and we can hug, embrace, clasp and touch ourselves in a great variety of ways to help soothe away our fears.

If you spend some time as an observer, simply watching the way people behave, you will soon discover that acts of self-contact, or auto-contact, are extremely common, much more common than you might at first suppose. It would be wrong, however, to consider all these contacts as substitutes for interpersonal intimacies. Some of them have other functions. A man scratching an itch on his leg, for instance, is not doing it as a mime of someone else doing it to him. He is doing it as a simple act of self-cleaning, performed in its own right, with no hidden intimacy factor. It is important, therefore, not to overstate the case for self-intimacies. In order to put them into their true perspective, it is best to start out with a basic question, namely how and why do we touch our own bodies?

With this question in mind, I analysed several thousand examples of human actions involving self-contact. The first fact to emerge was that the head region was the most important area for *receiving* these contacts, and the hand the most important organ for *giving* them. Although the head is only a small part of the total surface area of the human body, it nevertheless received approximately half the total number of self-contacts.

Surveying these head contacts first, it was possible to identify 650 different types of action. This was done by recording which part of the hand was used, how it made the contact, and which part of the head was involved. It soon became clear that there were four major categories. (The first three, although interesting in their own right, do not directly concern us here and will only be mentioned briefly. Their inclusion is important, however, in order to make it clear that they must be kept separate and not confused with the true self-intimacies.) The four categories are as follows.

1. *Shielding actions*. The hand is brought up to the head to cut off or reduce input to the sense organs. The man who wants to hear less puts his hands over his ears. The man who wants to smell less holds his nose. If the light is too bright, he shields his eyes, and if he cannot bear the sight in front of him, he covers them completely. Similar actions are used to reduce output, as when a hand comes up to cover the mouth and thereby conceal a facial expression.

2. *Cleaning actions*. The hand is brought up to the head to perform a scratch, rub, pick, wipe, or some similar action. A variety of hair-tidying actions also come under this general heading. Some of these

movements are genuine attempts to clean and tidy the head region, but in many instances they are 'nervous' actions, caused by emotional tensions, and are similar to the 'displacement activities' described by ethologists in other species.

3. *Specialized signals.* The hand is brought up to the head to perform a symbolic gesture of some kind. A man who says 'I am fed up to here' holds the back of his hand to the underside of his chin, indicating that he is so full of symbolic 'food' that he cannot take any more. A boy who 'thumbs his nose' presses his thumb to his nose and spreads his fingers out in the shape of a vertical fan. This insult originates from the symbolic act of imitating the comb of a fighting cock, which is how it has become a threatening gesture. This is also the reason why it is sometimes called 'cocking a snook'. Another animal symbolism used as an insult in certain countries is making a pair of horns by holding the hands to the temples, with the forefingers raised and slightly curled. A common form of self-insult is aiming a forefinger at the temple and firing an imaginary gun.

4. *Self-intimacies.* The hand is brought up to the head to perform some action that copies or imitates an interpersonal intimacy. Surprisingly, no fewer than four-fifths of the different hand-to-head actions fall into this self-intimacy category. It seems as if the main reason we have for touching our heads is one of obtaining comfort from unconsciously mimed acts of *being touched by someone else.*

The most common form that this takes is resting part of the head on the hand, with the elbow of the arm in question in contact with a supporting surface, and the forearm acting as a prop to take the weight of the head. It could, of course, be argued that this simply indicates that the neck muscles are tired. A little close observation of these actions soon reveals, however, that physical exhaustion cannot account for the majority of cases.

In this action, the hand is being used as more than a hand. By providing it with support from the elbow, it has become something more solid, and seems instead to be acting as a substitute for the shoulder or chest of the imaginary 'embracing companion'. When, as a child or a lover, we are held in another's arms, we frequently rest the side of our face against their body and feel their soft warmth through the skin of our cheek. By resting the side of our face on our supported hand, we are able to re-create that feeling in their absence, and thereby give ourselves a welcome sensation of comfort and intimacy. Furthermore, since the origin of the act is suitably obscure, we can do this in public without any fear of being thought of as infantile. Sucking a thumb in imitation of childhood breast-feeding might do as well, but there the disguise would wear too thin, and so we tend to avoid it.

Clasping an unsupported hand to the head is also a common act, like the one in the example given of the woman on the railway platform. When this is done, the head cannot lean so heavily, and it appears as if this type of action is more related to the caressing or clasping of the face or hair that is often performed by the embracing companion as an embellishment of the general intimacy. Here, the hand is acting as a symbolic companion's hand, rather than as a symbolic chest or shoulder.

The mouth is a region that receives a great deal of attention, but here the most common action is to touch it in some way with the fingers or thumb, rather than with the whole hand. When making oral contact, the fingers or thumb are being used as substitutes for the mother's breast and nipple. Full thumb-sucking, as I have said, is rare; but modified, less obvious versions of it are common. The simplest modification, and one that is frequently seen, is the pressing of the tip of the thumb between the lips. It is not inserted into the mouth or sucked, but the comforting contact is there nevertheless. The tip, side or back of the forefinger is also used a great deal in this way, and it is often held in contact with the lips for a considerable period of time, while its worried owner gains reassurance from its presence, as dim, unconscious echoes from the infantile past make themselves felt in the brain.

As an elaboration of this form of mouth contact, the finger or thumb is sometimes gently and slowly rubbed across the surface of the lips, re-creating the movements of the baby's mouth on the mother's breast. At more intense moments of anxiety, knuckle-biting and nail-biting put in an appearance. When frustrated aggression is added to the act in this way, it can, in the case of nail-biting, become so persistent as to cause near-mutilation, with the nails bitten down to tiny stumps and the nearby skin chewed raw.

Of all the many different kinds of hand-to-head contact, the most common, in order of frequency, are: (1) jaw rest, (2) chin rest, (3) hair clasp, (4) cheek rest, (5) mouth touch and (6) temple rest. All are performed by both adult males and females, but in two cases there is a strong sexual bias. Hair-clasping is three times as common in women as men, and temple-resting is twice as common in men as in women.

If we leave the head and move down the body, we soon find other forms of self-intimacy. We are all familiar with the tragic newsreel scenes of the aftermath of a disaster such as an earthquake or a mine collapse. A distraught woman in such a situation does not merely clasp one hand to her cheek. The act would be inadequate under the circumstances. Instead she goes much further, hugging her body with her arms and rocking herself pathetically from side to side, as she sits outside the ruins of her home or waits desperately at the pit-head. If she and another sufferer do not find comfort in a mutual embrace, she responds by embracing herself and by rocking herself gently back and forth as her mother once would have done when she was a frightened infant.

This is an extreme case, but we all use a similar device almost every day of our lives, when we fold our arms across our chest. Because the situation is less intense, so is the action, and the folding of arms on the chest is a much weaker form of self-embrace than the full self-hug of misery. It nevertheless provides a mildly comforting sensation of self-intimacy and is typically seen in moments when we are slightly on the defensive. If we are talking in a group of semi-strangers, for example, at a party or some other social gathering, and one of them is coming rather 'too close for comfort', we regain some of our lost comfort by bringing up our arms and folding them across our chest. Usually we are hardly aware that we have performed the act, or that it has any relation to the movements around us, but the fact that it operates in this way has led to its use as an unconscious social signal. For instance, a man who wishes to block a doorway against intruders may stand in front of it, fold his arms across his chest and say, 'No one is allowed inside.' The act of arm-folding in this case, which comforts the man in question, begins to look positively threatening to those in front of him. It signals the fact that he is shutting them out of his embrace, and that he finds self-sufficient strength in his own private act of self-embrace.

Another act of intimacy we all indulge in daily is what can be described as 'holding hands with ourself'. One hand acts as our own, while the other, which clasps or grasps it, acts as the hand of an imaginary companion. We do this in several ways, some more intense than others. When, for example, we are in a particularly strong hand-holding mood with a real companion, we often interlock our fingers with theirs, making the interaction somehow more binding and complex. Similarly, in the absence of such a companion, we can re-create this sensation by interlocking the fingers of our left hand with those of our right. At moments of tension this is sometimes done with such force that the flesh shows white with the great pressure we are unconsciously exerting.

Similar pressures are exerted lower down on the body when we sit with one leg twined tightly around the other. Leg-crossing again seems to provide us with a remarkable degree of self-comfort, providing, as it does, the reassuring pressure of one part of the body against another, and reminding us perhaps of the comforting pressure we felt on our legs when, in a clinging embrace, we straddled the bodies of our parents.

In Victorian times, ladies were expressly forbidden – by the official rules of etiquette then applying – to cross their legs in public or social situations. Victorian males were less restricted in this way, but they were, nevertheless, requested not to hug their knees or feet when performing the act. Today there are no such restrictions, and a random count of a large number of leg-crossings revealed that 53 per cent were female and 47 per cent male, so that no sex difference has survived the passage of time from the last century into this. Two sex differences do exist, however, in the form which the act takes. If it is done by placing the ankle of one leg on the knee or thigh of the other, then it is nearly always a male performance, presumably because for the female this means an undue amount of crotch-exposure. It is intriguing that this applies even where women are wearing trousers, so that it would appear that a trousered woman is still mentally wearing her skirt. The second difference concerns the position of the feet of the crossed legs. If the foot of the 'upper' leg remains in contact with the surface of the 'lower' leg after the legs have been crossed, then the performance is almost always a female one. (The exception to this rule is the low-level ankle/ankle cross, where there are no sex differences, and where the feet are almost bound to be touching one another because of the nature of the act.)

A more intimate form of leg contact is leg-hugging. At its highest intensity this involves bringing the thighs up and the chest down until the two meet. The pressure is increased by embracing the knees or lower legs with the arms. As an addition, the head is lowered on to the knees and the chin or side of the face rested there. In such cases, the bent-up legs are being used as the substitute for the trunk of the imaginary companion, with the knees acting as the chest or shoulders. This is predominantly a female act – of a number of cases recorded at random, 95 per cent were female and only 5 per cent male.

Another typically female action is the clasping of the thigh with the hand, a survey of a large number of such contacts revealing that 91 per cent were female and only 9 per cent male. There appears to be an erotic element present here, the female hand acting as if it were a man's hand placed on her thigh in a sexual context, an act more typical of a courting male than a courting female.

In this survey of self-intimacies, it has nearly always been the hands and arms, and sometimes the legs, that have performed as the active organs, the ones making the contact, but there are a few exceptions to this rule. Sometimes, and again this is typically a female movement, the head is actively lowered on to one shoulder and pressed or rested there, the contact being made by the cheek, jaw or chin. Here it is the shoulder that is being used as the symbolic chest or shoulder of the imaginary companion. Another example concerns the tongue, which may be used to caress the lips, or some other part of the body, certain females even being capable of making contact with their own nipples in this way.

In addition to all these varied methods of making bodily contact with oneself, there is one important aspect of self-intimacy that remains to be discussed, and that is the auto-erotic stimulation usually referred to as masturbation. The word itself appears to be a corruption of *manustuprare*, 'to defile with the hand', and reflects the fact that the most common method of sexual self-stimulation involves a hand-genital contact. For males, this usually means grasping the penis with one hand and rhythmically raising and lowering the arm. The hand then takes on two simultaneous symbolic roles. Its movements up and down the penis mimic the male's own pelvic thrusts, whilst with its grip it acts as a pseudo-vagina. For females, the equivalent action is the stroking of the clitoris with the fingers. Here the fingers are acting as substitutes for the rhythmic pressure applied indirectly to the clitoris by the pelvic thrusting of the male during copulation. Alternative methods for the female are the stroking of the labia or the rhythmic insertion of the fingers into the vagina, with the fingers then acting as a substitute penis. Another technique is thigh-rubbing, in which the thighs are squeezed together, with an alternating tightening and relaxing of the inner muscles to produce a rhythmic pressure on the compressed genitals.

Surveys carried out in the middle of the present century revealed that masturbation is an extremely common form of self-intimacy and is indulged in by the vast majority of individuals at some time in their lives. Although it has always been little more than a harmless substitute for the interpersonal act of copulation, social attitudes towards it have varied considerably at different times. It appears to be widely practised amongst so-called 'primitive tribes', but is usually referred to as something of a joke, indicating that the masturbator is a failed copulator.

An entirely different and much less healthy view was prevalent in our own cultures in earlier centuries, when serious attempts were made to suppress the activity completely. In the eighteenth century, masturbation was denounced as 'the heinous sin of self-pollution'. In the nineteenth century, it became 'the horrid and exhausting vice of self-abuse', and young Victorian ladies were forbidden to wash their genitals in case the gentle friction of such an act, when regularly performed, 'might induce impure thoughts'. The wicked French bidet was not allowed to cross the English Channel. In the early part of the twentieth century, masturbation declined in horror to the level of a 'nasty habit', but religious authorities were still seriously concerned that it might actually give some sensual reward to the masturbator. They did, however, allow that 'the effusion of semen would be legitimate for medical purposes if only it could be achieved without causing pleasure'. By the middle of the twentieth century, attitudes had undergone a dramatic change, and it was at last boldly announced that masturbation is 'a normal and healthy act for a person of any age'. In the past two decades this new approach has continued to gain ground to the point where, in 1971, a respectable women's magazine was able to publish the following words of advice, words which would have astonished a Victorian reader: 'Masturbation . . . is wholesome, normal and sound . . . you are training your body to become a superb instrument of love. Masturbate to your heart's content.'

Today's adolescent who, in the absence of copulatory opportunities, feels inclined to indulge in this form of sexual self-intimacy is lucky indeed. The adolescent of yesterday, far from being freely permitted to perform this activity, was often severely punished for doing so. During the past two centuries all kinds of harsh restraints have been applied, some of which we now find hard to believe. In some cases the young male offender was fitted with a silver ring that was slotted through holes pierced in his foreskin. Alternatively, he might have been equipped with a small penis-belt armed with spikes that automatically pricked the penis if it started to become erect. Blistering the penis with red mercury ointment was another 'remedy' that was sometimes recommended. Both sexes of maturing children were occasionally forced to sleep with their hands tied together or to the bed-posts, to prevent them from 'playing with themselves' at night, or were equipped with modern versions of chastity-belts. Young females might be forced to suffer the mutilation of having the clitoris cauterized or completely removed by surgery, and circumcision for males was advised by some medical authorities as an imagined aid to stamping out the 'evil act' of self-stimulation.

Happily, with the single exception of male circumcision, none of these painful hazards has survived to the present day as a common practice. Society's age-old urge to mutilate its growing juveniles seems, at long last, to be under control. Bearing this in mind, it is worth digressing for a moment to consider why the curious ritual of circumcision should have escaped this general change of attitude. Today the anti-masturbatory excuse is no longer given. Instead, the foreskin of the male infant is amputated for 'religious, medical or hygienic' reasons. The frequency of the operation varies from country to country; in Britain it is thought to be performed on fewer than half the male babies born, whereas in the United States a figure as high as 85 per cent has been quoted.

The medical reason given in favour of foreskin-removal is that it eliminates certain (extremely rare) disease dangers. These only occur, however, if the unmutilated adult male fails to keep his penis reasonably clean by the simple act of pulling back the foreskin and washing the tip of the organ. If this is done regularly, there is, according to medical authorities, no more of a health risk for an uncircumcised male than for a circumcised one. Since the vast majority of foreskin removals are not performed for religious reasons, and since the medical grounds are hardly worth considering, the true reason for the thousands of sexual mutilations carried out on male babies each year remains something of a mystery. Referred to recently by one doctor in America as 'the rape of the phallus', it appears to be a hang-over from our distant cultural past. It has, since early times, been a common practice in most African tribes and was adopted by the ancient Egyptians, whose priest-doctors made sure that no self-respecting male retained his foreskin. Because of the social stigma attached to an attached foreskin, the Jews borrowed the circumcision ritual from the Egyptians and made it even more obligatory for the male members of their religion. In becoming a social or religious 'law', the original significance of the operation had already been forgotten, and it is not easy today to trace it back to its source. Even amongst the African tribes where it is part of elaborate initiation ceremonies, it is usually merely referred to as being 'the custom', but a number of explanations have been forthcoming from modern investigators. One suggestion is that the male foreskin was considered to be a feminine attribute, presumably because it covered up the head of the male organ in the way that the female labia cover the female genital opening. By the same argument, the female's clitoris was considered to be a masculine organ, so that when boys and girls reached sexual maturity, they were both made more true to their sex by having the offending opposite-sex attributes removed. Another suggestion is that the shedding of the foreskin was a symbolic imitation of the shedding of a snake's skin, an action that was widely thought to endow that reptile with immortality, since it reappeared so shining and bright after each shedding. The symbolic equation was straightforward enough: snake = phallus, therefore snakeskin = foreskin.

These and many other ingenious explanations have been put forward, but all seem to be inadequate when the phenomenon of sexual mutilation is viewed as a whole. It has occurred at some time or another in almost every corner of the globe, in literally hundreds of different cultures, and the precise form it has taken has varied considerably. It does not always involve simple foreskin or clitoris removal. In certain cases the parts removed are more extensive, or the mutilations are slits and cuts rather than amputations. In some tribes the female may be stripped of her labia as well as her clitoris, and in others the male may suffer the painful loss of the entire skin surface covering the lower belly, pelvis, scrotum and inner legs, or he may be subjected to the ordeal of having his penis split in two, down its whole length. The only overall common factor seems to be the act by human adults of perpetrating mechanical damage to the genitals of their juniors.

That this ancient form of adult aggression should have survived into present times in the form of male circumcision is something that might bear closer examination by the modern medical profession. Not since the anti-masturbatory assaults of the last century have young females been attacked in this way, presumably because, unlike the males, there was no hygienic justification left for the removal of any part of their genitals. It is fortunate that the situation was not reversed, for if the clitoris could have been proved to be unhygienic and a suitable medical excuse therefore found for its removal, the female would have suffered a considerable loss of sexual responsiveness. Recent careful tests have shown that the penis, by contrast, suffers little or no loss of sensitivity as a result of foreskin-removal, so that males who are mutilated in this way by the respectable modern equivalents of the ancient witch-doctors do not, at least, experience any reduction of sexual performance. These modern tests do, of course, make complete nonsense of the earlier, anti-masturbatory reason for surgically removing the foreskin. Mutilated or unmutilated, the adult male is still going to be able to obtain an unhindered sexual reward from his solitary indulgences in genital self-intimacy.

Summing up, then, it can be said that the reason why male circumcision has survived so widely, when virtually all other forms of archaic genital dismembering have been abandoned in 'civilized' communities, is that it is the only one which does not impair sexual activity and which, at the same time, has been able to acquire a respectable white-wash of medical rationalization.

Returning to masturbation itself, there only remains the question of whether, in the new-found self-stimulation freedom of the latter half of the twentieth century, there are any future hazards waiting in store for us. If we are all advised to 'masturbate to our heart's content' by popular magazine articles, has the pendulum of sexual opinion swung too far? Clearly the earlier rubbish about masturbation causing untold misery and sickness had to be thrown out with a vigorous propaganda campaign, and this has now successfully been done; but is there perhaps a danger that, in sweeping the ridiculous old ideas away, we may go too far in the opposite direction? Masturbation is, after all, a second-rate form of intimacy, like all the substitute social activities discussed in previous chapters. Anything done alone that is a mimic of something done with a companion must, of necessity, be inferior to the genuine act of body intimacy, and this rule must apply to masturbation as much as to any other form of self-intimacy. When there is nothing better available, then of course no justifiable argument can be brought against these substitute activities; but supposing something better is hoped for in the near future, is there not a danger of developing a fixation on the inferior substitute acts which later makes it more difficult to effect a transfer to the real thing?

Contemporary words of advice to a masturbating female stress that every woman should develop her own individual masturbation style, and that it is important to set aside several hours a week so that the new response pattern will become a stable one. She is informed that when she has educated her body in this way she will be able to guide the male, when making love, to positions that give her the maximum sensations. At least this approach is honest: the female works out and stabilizes her self-reward pattern and then it is up to the male partner to service her accordingly. This is recommended as a method of training the female body to become 'a superb instrument of love'. As a system for providing considerable sexual reward for a lonely or frustrated female it may be excellent, but as a system for enhancing love it perhaps leaves something to be desired. It overlooks completely the fact that human copulation is much more than an act of mutual sexual servicing. To approach a moment of intense, reciprocal body intimacy with a previously fixed pattern of reward-demand is to put the cart before the horse. It is no better than using the male's actions as substitutes for masturbation, rather than the other way around. Similarly, if a male has become too heavily fixated on a particular kind of manual masturbation, he may end up using the female vagina as a substitute for his hand, instead of the reverse. To approach copulation in this way is to reduce the partner to a small stimulation device, instead of a complete, intimate and loving person. Over-emphasis on the importance of advanced masturbatory techniques is therefore not perhaps as entirely innocent as the 'new liberalism' would have us believe.

This said, however, it cannot be stressed too strongly that such a warning must in no way be taken as an excuse for a return to the guilt-ridden restrictions of yesterday's forbidden self-intimacies. If the pendulum has perhaps swung a little too far, we are still in a much better position than our immediate ancestors, and we should be grateful for the sexual reformers of the twentieth century who have made this possible. In all probability the dangers of self-intimate fixations will not usually be too serious. If two people come to love one another sufficiently, the emotional intensity of their relationship stands a good chance of sweeping away the rigidity of their previous, solitary patterns of self-gratification, and allowing an increasingly free growth of the sexual interactions that occur between them. If their relationship is less intense and this does not happen, then they will at least be able to enjoy a mutual exchange of their stylized erotic stimulations, which is a good deal better than the Victorian situation, where the marriage partners felt themselves obliged to 'get the nasty business over' as quickly as possible before falling gratefully asleep.

9

RETURN TO INTIMACY

WE ARE BORN into an intimate relationship of close bodily contact with our mothers. As we grow, we strike out into the world and explore, returning from time to time to the protection and security of the maternal embrace. At last we break free and stand alone in the adult world. Soon we start to seek a new bond and return again to a condition of intimacy with a lover who becomes a mate. Once again we have a secure base from which to continue our explorations.

If, at any stage in this sequence, we are poorly served by our intimate relationships, we find it hard to deal with the pressures of life. We solve the problem by searching for substitutes for intimacy. We indulge in social activities that conveniently provide us with the missing body contacts, or we use a pet animal as a stand-in for a human partner. Inanimate objects are enlisted to play the vacant role of the intimate companion, and we are even driven to the extreme of becoming intimate with our own bodies, caressing and hugging ourselves as if we were two people.

These alternatives to true intimacy may, of course, be used as pleasant additions to our tactile lives, but for many they become sadly necessary replacements. The solution seems obvious enough. If there is such a strong demand for intimate contact on the part of the typical human adult, then he must relax his guard and open himself more easily to the friendly approaches of others. He must ignore the rules that say, 'Keep yourself to yourself, keep your distance, don't touch, don't let go, and never show your feelings.' Unfortunately, there are several powerful factors working against this simple solution. Most important of these is the unnaturally enlarged and overcrowded society in which he lives. He is surrounded by strangers and semi-strangers whom he cannot trust, and there are so many of them that he cannot possibly establish emotional bonds with more than a minute fraction of them. With the rest, he must restrict his intimacies to a minimum. Since they are so close to him physically, as he moves about in his day-to-day affairs, this requires an unnatural degree of restraint. If he becomes good at it, he is likely to become increasingly inhibited in *all* his intimacies, even those with his loved ones.

In this body-remote, anti-intimate condition the modern urbanite is in danger of becoming a bad parent. If he applies his contact restraint to his offspring during the first years of their life, then he may cause irreversible damage to their ability to form strong bonds of attachment later on. If, in seeking justification for his inhibited parental behaviour, he (or she) can find some official blessing for such restraint, then it will, of course, help to ease the parental conscience. Unhappily, such blessings have occasionally been forthcoming and have contributed harmfully to the growth of personal relationships within the family.

One example of this type of advice is so extreme that it deserves special mention. The Watsonian method of child-rearing, named after its perpetrator, an eminent American psychologist, was widely followed earlier in this century. In order to get the full flavour of his advice to parents, it is worth quoting him at some length. Here are some of the things he said:

> Mothers just don't know, when they kiss their children and pick them up and rock them, caress them and jiggle them upon their knee, that they are slowly building up a human being totally unable to cope with the world it must later live in . . . There is a sensible way of treating children. Treat them as though they were young adults . . . Never hug or kiss them, never let them sit on your lap. If you must, kiss them once on the forehead when they say goodnight . . . Can't a mother train herself to substitute a kindly word, a smile, in all of her dealings with the child, for the kiss and the hug, the pickup and the coddling? . . . If you haven't a nurse and cannot leave the child, put it out in the backyard a large part of the day. Build a fence around the yard so that you are sure no harm can come to it. Do this from the time it is born . . . If your heart is too tender and you must watch the child, make yourself a peephole so that you can see it without being seen, or use a periscope . . . Finally, learn not to talk in endearing and coddling terms.

Since this was described as treating a child like a young adult, the obvious implication is that the typical Watsonian adults never kiss or hug one another either, and spend their time viewing one another through metaphorical peepholes. This is, of course, precisely what we are all driven to do with the *strangers* who surround us in our daily lives, but to find such conduct seriously recommended as the correct procedure between parents and their babies is, to say the least, remarkable.

The Watsonian approach to child-rearing was based on the behaviourist view, to quote him again, that in man 'There are no instincts.

We build in at an early age everything that is later to appear . . . there is nothing from within to develop.' It therefore followed that to produce a well-disciplined adult it was necessary to start with a well-disciplined baby. If the process was delayed, then 'bad habits' might start to form which would be difficult to eradicate later.

This attitude, based on a totally false premise concerning the natural development of human behaviour in infancy and childhood, would merely be a grotesque historical curiosity were it not for the fact that it is still occasionally encountered at the present day. But because the doctrine lingers on, it requires closer examination. The main reason for its persistence is that it is, in a way, self-perpetuating. If a tiny baby is treated in this unnatural manner it becomes basically insecure. Its high demand for bodily intimacy is repeatedly frustrated and punished. Its crying goes unheeded. But it adapts, it learns – there is no choice. It becomes trained and it grows. The only snag is that it will find it hard ever to trust anyone again, in its entire life. Because its urge to love and be loved was blocked at such a primary stage, the mechanism of loving will be permanently damaged. Because its relationship with its parents was carried on like a business deal, all its later personal involvements will proceed along similar lines. It will not even enjoy the advantage of being able to behave like a cold automaton, because it will still feel the basic biological urge to love welling inside it, but will be unable to find a way of letting it out. Like a withered limb that could not be fully amputated, it will go on aching. If, for conventional reasons, such an individual then marries and produces offspring, the latter will stand a high chance of being treated in the same way, since true parental loving will now, in its turn, have become virtually impossible. This is borne out by experiments with monkeys. If an infant monkey is reared without loving intimacies with its mother, it later becomes a bad parent.

For many human parents the Watsonian regime appeared attractive, but far too extreme. They therefore employed a softened, modified version of it. They would be stern with their baby one moment, then give in the next. In some ways they applied rigid discipline, in others they coddled it. They left it to cry in its cot, but they gave it lots of expensive toys and cooed over it at other times. They forced it into early toilet training, but they kissed and cuddled it. The result, of course, was a totally confused baby which grew into what was called a 'spoilt child'. The fundamental error was then made of ascribing the 'spoiltness', not to the confusion, or to the early baby-stage disciplinary elements, but entirely to the moments of 'softness'. If only they had stuck to the rigid regime and not given in so often, the parents told themselves, then all would have been well. The growing child, now being awkward and demanding, was therefore told to 'behave itself', and discipline was strengthened. The result, at this stage and later, was tantrum and rebellion.

Such a child had seen what love was, in those early 'softer' moments, but, having been shown the entrance, had then had the gate repeatedly slammed in its face. It knew how to love, but it had not been loved enough, and in its later rebellions it repeatedly tested its parents, hoping to prove at last that they loved it no matter what it did – that they loved it for itself and not for its 'good behaviour'. All too often it got the wrong answer.

Even when it got the right answer, and the parents forgave its latest outrage, it still could not believe that all was well. The early imprints were too deeply engraved, the early, intermittent disciplines too unloving for a baby's mind. So it tested them again, going further and further in its desperate attempt to prove that, after all, they really did love it. Then the parents, faced with chaos, either finally applied strict discipline and confirmed the child's darkest fears, or they gave in over and over again, condoning increasingly anti-social acts out of a sense of dawning guilt – 'Where did we go wrong, how have we failed? We have given you everything.'

All this could have been avoided if only the baby had been treated as a baby in the first place, instead of a 'young adult'. During the first years of life, an infant requires total love, nothing less. It is not 'trying to get the better of you', but it does need the best of you. If the mother is unstressed, and has not herself been warped in infancy, she will have a natural urge to give her best, which is why, of course, the disciplinarian has to repeatedly warn mothers against giving in to those tender 'weaknesses' that 'tug at their heart-strings', to use a favourite Watsonian phrase. If the mother *is* under pressure, as a result of our modern way of life, it will not be so easy; but even so, without an artificially imposed regime, it is still not impossible to come close enough to the ideal to produce a happy and well-loved baby.

Far from growing into a 'spoilt child', such an infant will then be able to mature into an increasingly independent individual, remaining loving, but with no inhibitions about investigating the exciting world around it. The early months gave it the assurance that there is a truly safe and secure base from which to venture forth and explore. Again, experiments with monkeys bear this out. The infant of a loving monkey mother readily moves off to play and test the environment. The offspring of a non-loving mother is shy and nervous. This is the exact opposite of the Watsonian prediction, which expects that an 'excess' of early loving, in the intimate, bodily sense, will make for a soft, dependent creature in later years. The lie to this can even be seen by the time the human child has reached the third year of life. The infant that was lavished with love during its first two years already begins to show its paces, launching out into the world with great, if unsteady, vigour. If it falls flat on its face it is not more, but less, likely to cry. The infant that was less loved and more disciplined as a tiny baby is already less adventurous, less curious about what it sees, and less inclined to start making the first fumbling attempts at independent action.

In other words, once a totally loving relationship has been established in the first two years of life, the infant can readily move on to the next stage in its development. As it grows, however, its headlong rush to explore the world *will*, at this later phase, require some discipline from the parents. What was wrong at the baby stage now becomes right. The Watsonian distaste for the doting, over-protective parents of *older* children has some justification, but the irony is that where protection of this type occurs to excess, it is probably a reaction against the damage caused by earlier Watsonian baby-training. The child that was a fully loved baby is less likely to provoke such behaviour.

During later life the adult who, as a baby, formed a strong bond of attachment with its parents in the primary phase of total love will also be better equipped to make a strong sexual bond of attachment as a young adult and, from this new 'safe base', to continue to explore and lead an active, outgoing, social life. It is true that, in the stage before an adult bond of attachment has formed, he or she will be much more sexually exploratory as well. All exploring will have been accentuated, and the sexual sphere will be no exception. But if the individual's early life has been allowed to pass naturally from stage to stage, then the sexual explorations will soon lead to pair-formation and the growth of a powerful emotional bond, with a full return to the extensive body intimacies typical of the loving baby phase.

Young adults who establish new family units and enjoy uninhibited intimacies within them will be in a much better position to face the harsh, impersonal world outside. Being in a 'bond-ful', rather than a bond-starved, condition, they will be able to approach each type of social encounter on its own terms and not make inappropriate, bond-hungry demands in situations which, inevitably, will so often require emotional restraint.

One aspect of family life that cannot be overlooked is the need for privacy. It is necessary to have private space in order to enjoy intimate contacts to the full. Severe overcrowding in the home makes it difficult to develop any kind of personal relationship except a violent one. Bumping into one another is not the same as performing a loving embrace. Forced intimacy becomes anti-intimate in the true sense, so that, paradoxically, we need more space to give body contact greater meaning. Tight architectural planning that ignores this fact creates unavoidable emotional tension. For personal body intimacy cannot be a permanent condition, like the persistent impersonal crowding of the urban world outside the home. The human need for close bodily contact is spasmodic, intermittent, and only requires occasional expression. To cramp the home-space is to convert the loving touch into a suffocating body proximity. If this seems obvious enough, then it is hard to understand the lack of attention that has been given to private home-space by the planners of recent years.

In painting this picture of the 'intimate young adults', I may have given the impression that, if only they can acquire an adequate private home-space, have a loving infancy behind them, and have formed strong new bonds of attachment to one another, then all will be well. Sadly, this is not the case. The crowded modern world can still encroach on their relationship and inhibit their intimacies. There are two powerful social attitudes that may influence them. The first is the one that uses the word 'infantile' as an insult. Extensive body intimacies are criticized as regressive, soft or babyish. This is something that can easily deter a potentially loving young adult. The suggestion that to be too intimate constitutes a threat to his independent spirit, summed up in such sayings as 'the strongest man is the man who stands alone', begins to make an impact. Needless to say, there is no evidence that for an adult to indulge in body contacts typical of the infant stage of life necessarily means he will find his independence impaired at other times. If anything, the contrary is the case. The soothing and calming effects of gentle intimacies leave the individual freer and better equipped emotionally to deal with the more remote, impersonal moments of life. They do not soften him, as has so often been claimed; they strengthen him, as they do with the loved child who explores more readily.

The second social attitude that tends to inhibit intimacies is the one which says that bodily contact implies sexual interest. This error has been the cause of much of the intimacy restraint that has been needlessly applied in the past. There is nothing implicitly sexual about the intimacies between parent and child. Parental love and infantile love are not sexual love, nor need the love between two men, two women, or even between a particular man and a particular woman be sexual. Love is love – an emotional bond of attachment – and whether sexual feelings enter into it or not is a secondary matter. In recent times we have somehow come to overstress the sexual element in all such bonds. If a strong, primarily non-sexual bond exists, but with minor sexual feelings accompanying it, the latter are automatically seized upon and enlarged out of all proportion in our thinking. The result has been a massive inhibition of our non-sexual body intimacies, and this has applied to relationships with our parents and offspring (beware, Oedipus!), our siblings (beware, incest!), our close same-sex friends (beware, homosexuality!), our close opposite-sex friends (beware, adultery!), and our many casual friends (beware, promiscuity!). All of this is understandable, but totally unnecessary. What it indicates is that in our true sexual relationships we are, perhaps, not enjoying a sufficiently erotically exhausting degree of body intimacy. If our pair-bond sexual intimacies were intensive and extensive enough, then there should be none left over to invade the other types of bond relationships, and we could all relax and enjoy them more than we seem to dare to do at present. If we remain sexually inhibited or frustrated with our mates, then of course the situation is quite different.

The general restraint that is applied to non-sexual body contacts in modern life has led to some curious anomalies. For example, recent American studies have revealed that in certain instances women are driven to use random sex simply for the purpose of being held in someone's arms. When questioned closely, the women admitted that this was sometimes their sole purpose in offering themselves sexually to a man, there being no other way in which they could satisfy their craving for a close embrace. This illustrates with pathetic clarity the distinction between sexual and non-sexual intimacy. Here there is no question of body intimacy leading to sex, but of sex leading to body intimacy, and this complete reversal leaves no doubt about the separation between the two.

These, then, are some of the hazards facing the modern intimate adult. To complete this survey of intimate human behaviour, it remains to ask what signs of change there are in the attitudes of contemporary society.

At the infant level, thanks to much painstaking work by child psychologists, a greatly improved approach to the problems of child-rearing is being developed. A much better understanding now exists of the nature of parent/offspring attachments, and of the essential role that warm loving takes in the production of a healthy growing child. The rigid, ruthless disciplines of yesterday are on the wane. However, in our more overcrowded urban centres, the ugly phenomenon of the 'battered baby syndrome' remains with us to remind us that we still have a long way to go.

At the level of the older child, constant gradual reforms are taking place in educational methods, and a more sensitive appreciation is growing of the need for social as well as technical education. The demands for technological learning are, however, heavier than ever, and there is still a danger that the average schoolchild will be better trained to cope with facts than with people.

Amongst young adults, the problem of handling social encounters seems, happily, to be solving itself. It is doubtful whether there has ever before been a period of such openness and frankness in dealing with the intricacies of personal interaction. Much of the criticism of the conduct of young adults, on the part of the older generation, stems from a heavily disguised envy. It remains to be seen, however, how well the new-found freedom of expression, sexual honesty and disinhibited intimacies of present-day youth survive the passage of time and approaching parenthood. The increasingly impersonal stresses of later adult life may yet take their toll.

Amongst older adults there is clearly a growing concern about the survival of resolved personal life inside the ever-expanding urban communities. As public stress encroaches more and more on private living, a mounting alarm can be felt concerning the nature of the modern human condition. In personal relationships, the word 'alienation' is constantly heard, as the heavy suits of emotional armour, put on for social battle in the streets and offices, become increasingly difficult to remove at night.

In North America, the sounds of a new rebellion against this situation can now be heard. A new movement is afoot, and it provides an eloquent proof of the burning need that exists in our modern society for a revision of our ideas concerning body contact and intimacy. Known in general terms as 'Encounter Group Therapy', it has appeared only in the last decade, beginning largely in California and spreading rapidly to many centres in the United States and Canada. Referred to in American slang as 'Bod Biz' (for 'show business' read 'body business'), it goes under a number of official titles, such as 'Transpersonal Psychology', 'Multiple Psychotherapy' and 'Social Dynamics'.

The principal common factor is the bringing together of a group of adults for sessions lasting from roughly one day to one week, in which they indulge in a wide variety of personal and group interactions. Although some of these are largely verbal, many are non-verbal and concentrate instead on body contacts, ritual touchings, mutual massage, and games. The aim is to break down the façade of civilized adult conduct, and to remind people that they 'do not *have* bodies; they *are* bodies'.

The essential feature of these courses is that inhibited adults are encouraged to play like children again. The avant-garde scientific atmosphere licenses them to behave in an infantile manner without embarrassment or fear of ridicule. They rub, stroke and tap one another's bodies; they carry one another around in their arms and anoint one another with oil; they play childlike games and they expose themselves naked to one another, sometimes literally, but usually metaphorically.

This deliberate return to childhood is explicitly expressed in the following words, in connection with a four-day course entitled 'Become as You Were':

> The adjusted American achieves a dubious state of 'maturity' by burying many child parts under layers of shame and ridicule. Relearning how to be a child may enrich the man's experience of being masculine and the woman's experience of being feminine. Re-experiencing being child with mother may shed light on one's approaches to loving, love-making and love-seeking. Paradoxically, making contact with childish helplessness releases surges of power and contacting childish tears opens the channels for expression and joy.

Other similar courses called 'Becoming More Alive through Play' and 'Sensory Reawakening: Rebirth' also emphasize the need to return to the intimacies of childhood. In some cases the process is taken even further with the use of 'womb-pools' kept at precisely uterine temperature.

The organizers of these courses refer to them as 'therapy for normal people'. The visitors are not patients; they are group members. They go there because they are urgently seeking some way of finding a return to intimacy. If it is sad to think that modern, civilized adults should need official sanction to touch one another's bodies, then it is at least reassuring that they are sufficiently aware that something has gone wrong to actively do something about it. Many of the people who have been through such sessions repeatedly return for more, since they find themselves loosening up emotionally and unwinding in the course of the ritual body contacts. They report a sense of release and a growing feeling of warmth in connection with their personal interactions at home.

Is this a valuable new social movement, a passing fad, or a dangerous, new, drugless addiction?* With dozens of new centres opening up every month, expert opinions are varied. Some psychologists and psychiatrists vigorously support the encounter-group phenomenon, others do not. One argues that group members 'don't improve – they just get a maintenance dose of intimacy'. If this is true, then even so the

---

* The encounter group movements of the 1970s have since gone into decline, partly because of the successful encouragement of more extensive sexual intimacy within the private world of the paired couple, and partly because Aids has inhibited more widespread body intimacies.

courses may at least see certain individuals through a difficult phase in their social lives. This puts group attendance at the intimacy level of going dancing, or going to bed with a cold and being comforted there, but there is nothing wrong with that. It merely adds one more string to the bow of a person seeking a 'licensed to touch' context. Other criticisms, however, are more severe. 'The techniques that are supposed to foster real intimacy sometimes destroy it,' says one. A theologist, no doubt sensing a new form of serious competition, comments that all that people learn in encounter groups is 'new ways to be impersonal – a new bag of tricks, new ways to be hostile and yet appear friendly'.

It is certainly true that, listening to the leaders of the movement talking to the general public about their methods and their philosophy, there is sometimes an unmistakable air of smug condescension. They give the impression of having discovered the secret of the universe, which they are gracious enough to impart to other, lesser mortals. This point has been stressed as a serious criticism by some, but it is probably no more than a defence against anticipated ridicule. It is reminiscent of the tactics of the world of psychoanalysis in earlier days. Like encounter-group veterans, those who had been through analysis could not help smiling smugly down at those who had not. But analysis is past this stage now, and if encounter groups survive the novelty phase, the attitude will no doubt change, as the new cult matures to become an accepted pattern.

The more severe criticism that the group sessions actually do serious harm has yet to be proved. 'Instant intimacy', as it has been called, does, however, have its hazards for the returning devotee when he steps back, fully or partially 'reawakened', into his old environment. He has been changed, but his home companions have not, and there is a danger that he may make insufficient allowance for this difference. The problem is essentially one of competing relationships. If an individual visits an encounter group, has himself massaged and stroked by total strangers, plays intimate games with them, and indulges in a wide variety of body contacts, then he is doing more with them than he will have been doing with his true 'intimates' in his home setting. (If he is not, then he had no problem in the first place.) If – as will inevitably happen – he later describes his experiences in glowing detail, he is automatically going to arouse feelings of jealousy. Why was he prepared to act like that at the encounter centre, when he was so remote and untouching at home? The answer, of course, was the official, scientific sanction for such acts in the special atmosphere of the centre, but that is no comfort to his 'real life' intimates. Where couples attend intimacy sessions together, the problem is greatly reduced, but the 'back home' situation still requires careful handling.

Some have argued that the most distasteful aspect of the encounter groups is the way in which they are converting something which should be an unconscious part of everyday life into a self-conscious, highly organized, professional pursuit, with the act of intimacy in danger of becoming an end in itself, rather than as one of the basic means by which we can intuitively help ourselves to face the outside world.

Despite all these understandable fears and criticisms, it would be wrong to scorn this intriguing new trend. Essentially, its leaders have seen an increasing and damaging shift towards impersonality in our personal relationships and have done their best to reverse this process. If, as so often happens, by the 'law of reciprocal errors', they are swinging the pendulum rather wildly in the opposite direction, then this is a minor fault. If the movement spreads and grows to a point where it becomes a matter of common knowledge, then, even for the non-enthusiasts, it will exist as a constant reminder that something is wrong with the way in which we are using – or, rather, not using – our bodies. If it does no more than make us aware of this, it will be serving its purpose. Again, the comparison with psychoanalysis is relevant. Only a small proportion of the general population have ever been directly involved in analysis, and yet the basic idea that our deepest, darkest thoughts are not shameful or abnormal, but are probably shared by most others, has permeated healthily throughout our culture. In part, it is responsible for the more honest and frank approach to mutual personal problems in young adults today. If the encounter-group movement can provide the same indirect release for our inhibited feelings concerning intimate bodily contact, then it will ultimately have proved to have made a valuable social contribution.

The human animal is a social species, capable of loving and greatly in need of being loved. A simple tribal hunter by evolution, he finds himself now in a bewilderingly inflated communal world. Hemmed in on all sides, he defensively turns in on himself. In his emotional retreat, he starts to shut off even those who are nearest and dearest to him, until he finds himself alone in a dense crowd. Unable to reach out for emotional support, he becomes tense and strained and possibly, in the end, violent. Lost for comfort, he turns to harmless substitutes for love that ask no questions. But loving is a two-way process, and in the end the substitutes are not enough. In this condition, if he does not find true intimacy – even if it is only with one single person – he will suffer. Driven to armour himself against attack and betrayal, he may have arrived at a state in which all contact seems repellent, where to touch or to be touched means to hurt or be hurt. This, in a sense, has become one of the greatest ailments of our time, a major social disease of modern society that we would do well to cure before it is too late. If the danger remains unheeded, then – like poisonous chemicals in our food – it may increase from generation to generation until the damage has gone beyond repair.

In a way, our ingenious adaptability can be our social undoing. We are capable of living and surviving in such appallingly unnatural conditions that, instead of calling a halt and returning to a saner system, we adjust and struggle on. In our crowded urban world, we have battled on in this way, further and further from a state of loving, personal intimacy, until the cracks have begun to show. Then, sucking our metaphorical thumbs and mouthing sophisticated philosophies to convince ourselves that all is well, we try to sit it out. We laugh at educated adults who pay large sums to go and play childish games of touch and hug in scientific institutes, and we fail to see the signs. How much easier it would all be if we could accept the fact that tender loving is not a weakly thing, only for infants and young lovers, if we could release our feelings, and indulge ourselves in an occasional, and magical, return to intimacy.

CHAPTER REFERENCES

It is impossible to list all the many works that have been of assistance in writing *Intimate Behaviour*. I have therefore included only those which either have been important in providing information on a specific point, or are of particular interest for further reading. They are arranged below on a chapter-by-chapter and topic-by-topic basis. From the names and the dates given, it is possible to trace the full references in the bibliography that follows. The bibliography also contains the titles of several broader works, not listed below against specific topics, which have proved of value in relation to the general subject.

Most of the statements concerning body contacts are, however, based on my own personal observations. Where specific statements are made, such as that a particular action is, say, three times as common in females as in males, they are based on a sample of 10,000 randomly selected units of behaviour. An archive of human contact actions, based on this study, was compiled and used as the basis for future publications, such as *Manwatching* and *Bodywatching*.

1 THE ROOTS OF INTIMACY

Foetal behaviour: Munn, 1965; Tanner and Taylor, 1966.
Behaviour at birth: Prechtl, 1965; Smith, 1968.
Rocking: Ambrose, in Bowlby, 1969; Bowlby, 1969; Morris, 1967.
Heartbeat: Morris, 1967; Salk, 1966.
Swaddling: Smith, 1968; Spock, 1946.
Discipline: Watson, 1928.
Crying and smiling: Ambrose, 1960; Bowlby, 1969.
Transitional objects: Spock, 1963; Vosper, 1969.
Adolescence: Cohen, 1964; Freud, 1946.

2 INVITATIONS TO SEXUAL INTIMACY

Crotch: Morris, 1967.
Codpiece: Broby-Johansen, 1968; Fryer, 1963; Rabelais, 1653.
Human self-mimicry: Morris, 1967; Morris and Morris, 1966a; Wickler, 1967.

Prehistoric buttocks: Ucko, 1968.
Bustle: Broby-Johansen, 1968; Laver, 1963.
Breast variations: Ford and Beach, 1952; Levy, 1962.
Depilation: Gould and Pyle, 1896.
Chin: Hershkovitz, 1970.
Blush: Darwin, 1873.
Belladonna: Wedeck, 1962.
Pupil dilation: Coss, 1965; Hess, 1965.
Hair in Egypt: Murray, 1949.
Dancing: Bloch, 1958; Fryer, 1963; Licht, 1932.

3 SEXUAL INTIMACY

General: Kinsey *et al.*, 1948, 1953; Masters and Johnson, 1966;
  Morris, 1967, 1969.
Oral-genital contacts: Legman, 1969.
Sexual prudery: Fryer, 1963.
Primate copulation: Carpenter, 1934, 1942; Goodall, 1965; Hall and
  DeVore, 1965; Morris and Morris, 1966; Reynolds and Reynolds,
  1965; Simonds, 1965; Southwick, Beg and Siddiqui, 1965; Yerkes,
  1943.
Cross-cultural variations: Ford and Beach, 1952; Rachewiltz, 1964.

4 SOCIAL INTIMACY

Baby clapping: Ainsworth, 1964.
Hand-waving nationalities: Brun, 1969.
Men holding hands: Froissart, 1940.
Non-nutritional sucking: Bowlby, 1969; Wolff, 1969.
Bow and curtsy: Wildeblood and Brinson, 1965.
Religious kiss: Beadnell, 1942; Wildeblood and Brinson, 1965.
Handshake: Sorell, 1968; Wildeblood and Brinson, 1965.
Modern etiquette: Lyons, 1967; Page, 1961; Sara, 1963; Vanderbilt,
  1952.

5 SPECIALIZED INTIMACY

Microbes on man: Rosebury, 1969.
Physical illness: Morris, 1971.
Mental illness: Szasz, 1961.

Hairdressers: Williams, 1957.
Dancing: Bloch, 1958; Brend, 1936; Fryer, 1963; Lewinsohn, 1958;
Licht, 1932.
Midwives: Forbes, 1966; Fryer, 1963.
Groupie girls: Fabian and Byrne, 1969.

6 SUBSTITUTES FOR INTIMACY

Man/animal relationships: Morris, 1967, 1969; Morris and Morris,
1965, 1966a, 1966b.
Petishism: Szasz, 1969.
Animal experiments: Heim, 1971; Matthews, 1964; Russell and Burch,
1959.

7 OBJECT INTIMACY

Dummies and pacifiers: Bowlby, 1969; Spock, 1946.
Hand sculpture: Miller, 1942.
Dildoes: Bauer, 1926; Dearborn, 1961; Henriques, 1963; Masters and
Johnson, 1966.
Copulation machine: Lacey, 1967.

8 SELF-INTIMACY

Female leg-crossing: Birdwhistell, 1970.
Masturbation: Comfort, 1967; Dearborn, 1961; 'J', 1970; Kinsey *et
al.*, 1948, 1953; Lewinsohn, 1958; Malinowski, 1929; Masters and
Johnson, 1966; Morris, 1969.
Circumcision: Comfort, 1967; Lewinsohn, 1958; Mollon, 1965;
Morris and Morris, 1965; Rachewiltz, 1964; Smith, 1968; Spock,
1946; West, 1966.

9 RETURN TO INTIMACY

Child discipline: Watson, 1928.
Monkey rearing: Harlow, 1958.
Overcrowding: Morris, 1969; Russell and Russell, 1968.
Sex as comfort: Hollender *et al.*, 1969; Hollender, 1970.
Encounter-group therapy: Gunther, 1969; Howard, 1970.

BIBLIOGRAPHY

Ainsworth, M. D. 'Patterns of infantile attachment to the mother', in *Merrill-Palmer Quart.* 10 (1964), pp. 51–8

Ambrose, J. A., 'The smiling response in early human infancy' (Ph.D.thesis, London University, 1960)

Argyle, M. *Social Interaction* (Methuen, London, 1969)

Bauer, B. A. *Woman* (Cape, London, 1926)

Beadnell, C. M. *The Origin of the Kiss* (Watts, London, 1969)

Birdwhistell, R. L. *Kinesics and Context* (University of Pennsylvania Press, Philadelphia, 1970)

Bloch, I. *Sexual Life in England Past and Present* (Arco, London, 1958)

Bowlby, J. *Attachment and Loss* (Hogarth Press, London, 1969)

Brend, W. A. *Sacrifice to Attis* (Heinemann, London, 1936)

Broby-Johansen, R. *Body and Clothes* (Faber, London, 1968)

Brun, T. *The International Dictionary of Sign Language* (Wolfe, London, 1969)

Carpenter, C. R. 'A field study of the behavior and social relations of Howling Monkeys', in *Comp. Psychol. Monogr.* 10 (1934), pp. 1–168

Carpenter, C. R. 'Sexual behaviour of free ranging Rhesus Monkeys', in *J. Comp. Psychol.* 33 (1942), pp. 113–62

Cohen, Y. A., *The Transition from Childhood to Adolescence* (Aldine, New York, 1964)

Comfort, A. *The Anxiety Makers* (Nelson, London, 1967)

Coss, R. G. *Mood Provoking Visual Stimuli* (University of California, 1965)

Crawley, E., *Dress, Drinks and Drums* (Methuen, London, 1931)

Darwin, C. *The Expression of the Emotions in Man and Animals* (Murray, London, 1873)

Dearborn, L. W. 'Autoerotism', in *The Encyclopedia of Sexual Behavior* (Hawthorn, New York, 1961)

Fabian, J., and J. Byrne. *Groupie* (New English Library, London, 1969)

Fast, J. *Body Language* (Evans, New York, 1970)

Forbes, T. R. *The Midwife and the Witch* (Yale University Press, New Haven, 1966)

Ford, C. S., and F. A. Beach. *Patterns of Sexual Behaviour* (Eyre & Spottiswoode, London, 1952)

Frank, L. K. 'Tactile Communication', in Carpenter and McLuhan (eds), *Explorations in Communication* (Cape, London, 1970), pp. 4–11

Freud, A. *The Ego and Mechanisms of Defense* (International Universities Press, New York, 1946)

Froissart, J. *The Chroniles of England, France and Spain* (Everyman Library, London, 1940)

Fryer, P. *Mrs Grundy* (Dobson, London, 1963)

Goodall, J. 'Chimpanzees of the Gombe Stream Reserve', in DeVore (ed.), *Primate Behavior* (Holt, Rinehart and Winston, New York, 1965)

Gould, G. M., and W. L. Pyle. *Anomalies and Curiosities of Medicine* (Saunders, Philadelphia, 1896)

Gunther, B. *Sense Relaxation* (Macdonald, London, 1969)

Hall, K. R. L. 'Baboon social behaviour', in DeVore (ed.), *Primate Behavior* (Holt, Rinehart, Winston, 1965), pp. 53–110

Harlow, H. F. 'The nature of love', in *Amer. Psychol.* 13 (1958), pp. 673–85

Hass, H. *The Human Animal* (Putnam, New York, 1970)

Heim, A. *Intelligence and Personality* (Pelican, London, 1971)

Henriques, F. *Prostitution in Europe and the New World* (MacGibbon & Kee, London, 1963)

Hershkovitz, P. 'The decorative chin', in *Bull. Field Mus. Nat. Hist.* 41 (1970), pp. 6–10

Hess, E. H. 'Attitude and pupil size', in *Sci. Amer.* 212 (1965), pp. 46–54

Hollender, M. H. 'The need or wish to be held', in *Arch. Gen. Psychiat.* 22 (1970), pp. 445–53

Hollender, M. H., L. Luborsky and T. J. Scaramella. 'Body contact and sexual excitement', *Arch. Gen. Psychiat.* 20 (1969), pp. 188–91

Howard, J. *Please Touch* (McGraw-Hill, New York, 1970)

'J'. *The Sensuous Woman* (Lyle Stuart, New York, 1970)

Jourard, S. M. 'An exploratory study of body accessibility', in *Brit. J. soc. clin. Psychol.* 5 (1966), pp. 221–31

Kinsey, A. C., W. B. Pomeroy and C. E. Martin, *Sexual Behaviour in the Human Male* (Saunders, Philadelphia, 1948).

Kinsey, A. C., W. B. Pomeroy, C. E. Martin and P. H. Gebhard, *Sexual Behaviour in the Human Female* (Saunders, Philadelphia, 1953).

Lacey, B. 'An evening with Bruce Lacey' (Lecture-demonstration at the Institute of Contemporary Arts, London 1967)

Laver, J., *Costume* (Cassell, 1963)

Laver, J., *Modesty in Dress* (Heinemann, London, 1969)

Legman, G. *Rationale of the Dirty Joke* (Cape, London, 1969)

Levy, M. *The Moons of Paradise* (Barker, London, 1962)

Lewinsohn, R. *A History of Sexual Customs* (Longmans, Green, London, 1958)

Licht, H. *Sexual Life in Ancient Greece* (Routledge & Kegan Paul, London, 1932)

Lowen, A. *Physical Dynamics of Character Structure* (Grune & Stratton, New York, 1958)

Lyons, P. *Today's Etiquette* (Bancroft, London, 1967)

Malinowski, B. *The Sexual Life of Savages* (Routledge & Kegan Paul, London, 1932)

Masters, W. H., and V. E. Johnson, *Human Sexual Response* (Churchill, London, 1966).

Matthews, L. H. 'Animal Relationships', in *Med. Sci. and Law* (1964), pp. 4–14

Miller, D. C. (ed.) *Americans 1942* (Museum of Modern Art, New York, 1942)

Mollon, R. *The Nursery Book* (Pan, London, 1965)

Morris, D., *The Naked Ape* (Cape, London, 1967)

Morris, D., *The Human Zoo* (Cape, London, 1967)

Morris, D., 'The Biology of Illness' (1971, in press).

Morris, R. and D. Morris, *Men and Snakes* (Hutchinson, London, 1965).

Morris, R. and D. Morris, *Men and Apes* (Hutchinson, London, 1966a).

Morris, R. and D. Morris, *Men and Pandas* (Hutchinson, London, 1966b).

Munn, N. L. *The Evolution and Growth of Human Behavior* (Mifflin, Boston, 1965)

Murray, M. A. *The Splendour that was Egypt* (Sidgwick & Jackson, London, 1949)

Page, A. *Etiquette for Gentlemen* (Ward, Lock, London, 1961)

Prechtl, H. F. R. 'Problems of behavioral studies in the newborn infant', in Lehrman, Hinde and Shaw (eds), *Advances in the Study of Behavior* (Academic Press, New York, 1965)

Rabelais, F. *The Works of Mr Francis Rabelais* (Navarre Society, London, 1931)

Rachewiltz, B. de. *Black Eros* (Allen & Unwin, London, 1969)

Russell, W. M. S., and W. M. S. Russell, *Violence, Monkeys and Man* (Macmillan, London, 1968).

Russell, C., and R. L. Burch. *The Principles of Humane Experimental Technique* (Methuen, London, 1959).

Salk, L., 'Thoughts on the concept of imprinting and its place in early human development', in *Canad. Psychiat. Assoc. J.* 11 (1966), pp. 295–305.

Sara, D. *Good Manners and Hospitality* (Collier, New York, 1963)

Simon, W., and J. H. Gagnon. 'Pornography – Raging menace or paper tiger?', in Gagon and Simon (eds), *The Sexual Scene* (Aldine, New York, 1970)

Simonds, P. E. 'The bonnet macaque in South India', in DeVore (ed.), *Primate Behavior* (Holt, Rinehart and Winston, New York, 1965), pp. 175–96

Smith, A., *The Body* (Allen & Unwin, London, 1968)

Sorell, W. *The Story of the Human Hand* (Weidenfeld & Nicolson, London, 1968)

Southwick, C. H., M. A. Beg and M. R. Siddiqi. 'Rhesus monkeys in North India', in DeVore (ed.), *Primate Behavior* (Holt, Rinehart and Winston, New York, 1965), pp. 111–74

Spock, B. *Baby and Child Care* (Giant Cardinal, New York, 1946)

Spock, B. 'The striving for autonomy and regressive object relationships', in *Psychoan. Study Child* 18 (1963), pp. 361–4

Szasz, K. *Petishism* (Holt, Rinehart and Winston, New York, 1969)

Szasz, T. S. *The Myth of Mental Illness* (Hoeber-Harper, New York, 1961)

Tanner, J. M., and G. R. Taylor. *Growth* (Time-Life, New York, 1966)

Tomkins, S. S. *Affect, Imagery, Consciousness* (Springer, New York, 1962–3)

Ucko, P. J. *Anthropomorphic Figurines* (Szmidla, London, 1968)

Vanderbilt, A. *Complete Book of Etiquette* (Doubleday, New York, 1952)

Vosper, J. *Baby Book* (Ebury, London, 1969)

Watson, J. B. *Psychological Care of Infant and Child* (Norton, New York, 1928)

Wedeck, H. E. *Dictionary of Aphrodisiacs* (Parrish, London, 1966)

West, J. *Parent's Baby Book* (Peter Owen, London, 1962)

Wickler, W. 'Socio-sexual signals and their intra-specific imitation among primates', in Morris (ed.), *Primate Ethology*, (Weidenfeld & Nicolson, London, 1967), pp. 68–147

Wildeblood, J., and P. Brinson. *The Polite World* (Oxford University Press, London, 1965)

Williams, N. *Powder and Paint* (Longmans, Green, London, 1957)

Wolff, C. *A Psychology of Gesture* (Methuen, London, 1945)

Wolff, P. H. 'The natural history of crying and other vocalizations in early infancy', in Foss (ed.), *Determinants of Infant Behaviour*, vol. 4 (Methuen, London, 1969)

Yerkes, R. M. *Chimpanzees. A Laboratory Colony* (Yale University Press, New Haven, 1943).